D1518314

The Fabrication
of American Literature

MATERIAL TEXTS

Series Editors

Roger Chartier	Leah Price
Joseph Farrell	Peter Stallybrass
Anthony Grafton	Michael F. Suarez, S.J.

A complete list of books in the series
is available from the publisher.

The Fabrication
of American Literature

Fraudulence and Antebellum Print Culture

LARA LANGER COHEN

PENN

UNIVERSITY OF PENNSYLVANIA PRESS

PHILADELPHIA

Published by
University of Pennsylvania Press
Philadelphia, Pennsylvania 19104-4112
www.upenn.edu/pennpress

Printed in the United States of America on acid-free paper
10 9 8 7 6 5 4 3 2 1

Library of Congress Cataloging-in-Publication Data
Cohen, Lara Langer.
The fabrication of American literature : fraudulence and
antebellum print culture / Lara Langer Cohen.—1st ed.
p. cm.— (Material texts)
Includes bibliographical references and index.
ISBN 978-0-8122-4369-7 (hardcover : alk. paper)
1. American literature—1783-1850—History and
criticism.   2. Truthfulness and falsehood in literature.
3. Fraud in literature.   I. Title.   II. Series: Material texts.
PS208.C64   2012
810.9′003—dc23
2011030830

Contents

Introduction

American Literary Fraudulence

The Fabrication of American Literature investigates a paradox at the heart of American literary history: at the very moment when a national literature began to take shape, many observers worried that it amounted to nothing more than what Edgar Allan Poe described as "one vast perambulating humbug."[1] Scholarly accounts of nineteenth-century American literature tend to emphasize its authority, particularly its role in converting sociopolitical conflict into cultural coherence. But the period's readers and writers tell a different story—one of subterfuge, impostures, and plagiarism, in which they likened literature to inflated currency, land bubbles, and quack medicine. This book accordingly recovers the controversies over literary fraud that plagued the period in order to gain new understanding of how antebellum literature worked, or failed to do so. It examines American literature as a "fabrication" in two senses of the word—in the most benign sense, as a project under active construction and, more ominously, one that struck many as fundamentally false. While the notion of fabrication in the former sense has long undergirded the study of antebellum American literature, we have tended to overlook the latter sense, but I contend that the two prove to be historically inseparable from one another. "Formerly every Thing printed was believed, because it was in Print," Benjamin Franklin observed in 1765, but he sensed the beginnings of a change: "Now Things seem to be disbelieved for just the very same Reason."[2] *The Fabrication of American Literature* takes Franklin's complaint as a prescient glimpse of a new era of print culture in which fraudulence came to be indissociable from American literature, and even definitive of it.

Historians have long noted the ubiquity of hoaxes, confidence games, and other forms of "humbug" during these years. From Richard Adams

Locke's moon hoax to P. T. Barnum's Feejee Mermaid, from table-rappers to perpetual motion machines, deception, it seems, established itself as the national pastime in the nineteenth-century United States.[3] Critical accounts of the era's humbug, however, tend either to leave literature out or to call upon it as an impartial observer. Literature thus chronicles the cultural logic of fraud without being subject to it, as antebellum writers register the national fascination with deception in their characters (con artists, social climbers), plots (subterfuge, hypocrisy, entrapment), and forms (the detective story, the exposé).[4] When critics address the issue of *literary* fraud, they tend to treat it as a circumscribed genre consisting of hoaxes, forgeries, plagiarism, and similarly calculated acts of deception. But antebellum readers worried that fraud could not be so easily contained. The sheer frequency with which antebellum literary discourse slips into the language of deception stymies critics' attempts to isolate fraud as a narrative theme or literary anomaly, because both of these approaches assume that fraud could be reliably differentiated from literature itself.

In this respect, "fraud" is something of a misnomer, implying as it does a deliberate deception regarding what legal scholars call a "matter of fact." This book is less about fraud than it is about the more elusive condition of fraudulence. Frauds are specific crimes perpetrated by particular agents with intent to deceive. They are actionable because they cause discernible injury to identifiable victims. Fraudulence, by contrast, can be neither decisively located nor contained, and its effects, while palpable, are not necessarily measurable. Fraud is actual, or at least aspires to be so; fraudulence is perceptual, a matter of determination. *The Fabrication of American Literature* argues that the primary threat faced by literature in the antebellum United States was not fraud, such as impostures, forgeries, plagiarisms, and hoaxes, so much as fraudulence, or the hopelessness of distinguishing impostures, forgeries, plagiarisms, and hoaxes from literature proper. This difficulty stems both from a familiar problem of representation—literature cannot be said to represent or misrepresent "matters of fact"—and from a historically specific variation on this problem: in the antebellum years, Americans increasingly called upon literature to represent formations such as nationhood, democracy, and race that were not themselves "matters of fact." The expedients readers, writers, critics, and editors devised to fulfill these impossible tasks, the accusations of fraudulence that inevitably resulted, and the attempts some writers made to turn this fraudulence to account are the subject of this book.

The Failures of Cultural Work

To a certain extent, the suspicions that readers brought to bear on literature were continuous with a broader cultural obsession with deception that seemingly permeated all areas of nineteenth-century life. The era witnessed a flurry of exposés of contemporary quackery, ranging from targeted attacks on patent medicine, Freemasonry, or political conspiracies, for example, to omnibus warnings like David Meredith Reese's *Humbugs of New-York* (1838), which billed itself as a "Remonstrance Against Popular Delusion; Whether in Science, Philosophy, or Religion." (Even these categories cannot encompass all the humbugs that torment Reese, however, and his preface anticipates a second volume. Sadly, it never appeared.) When New England newspaper editor and author Thomas Green Fessenden first published his satirical poem "Terrible Tractoration" in London in 1803, it was a denouncement of a pseudo-medical device called a metallic tractor; when he republished it in 1836, however, he was obliged to expand it significantly to include "Phrenology, Abolition, Amalgamation, Temperance, Reformation, &c. &c."[5]

The sprawling range of these books tells us that literature was only one fraud among many during this period. Yet literary fraudulence should claim our notice for several reasons. First, literature becomes a particular focal point for discussions of fraudulence during these years—in part because, as I noted above, its deceptions appeared at once so endemic and so very difficult to pin down. This book's archive of warnings, exposés, and denunciations provides the broadest evidence for this claim, but the history of the term "puffing," or promoting something without regard to merit—the subject of Chapter 1—exemplifies on a smaller scale literature's tendency to magnetize ideas about fraud. In the late eighteenth- and early nineteenth-century United States, "puffing" primarily referred to political machinations and commercial ploys; a newspaper might be induced to puff a brand of shoe polish, for example, or a candidate for election. Around the 1830s, however, literature came to monopolize the term, and "puffing" almost exclusively signified the extravagant, inflated praise of a book.

Second, the credibility problems that beset antebellum literature change the picture of literary history in a way that, say, bogus skin cream does not. Our understanding of nearly any aspect of the period's literature transforms once we recognize that it labored under the shadow of readers' suspicions, particularly given that the antebellum years are typically associated with

American literature's triumphant emergence. The goal of this book is not simply to invert these celebrations into some sort of literary dystopia—indeed, it will argue that historically the two characterizations are closely related and need to be read in tandem with one another. However, it does emphasize that readers' skepticism toward American literature should considerably complicate our understanding of what this literature *does* at this moment. It is a national embarrassment as much as a point of pride, a hazard as much as an instrument of authority, a miscommunication technology as much as a communication technology. Moreover, because literature was the preeminent vehicle for this period's incipient mass culture, its workings—and glitches—have ramifications that extend beyond its own form to the experiences of knowledge and affiliation it mediated. This book accordingly aims to reread literature's place in the period's volatile social and political climate in light of its own fundamental volatility.

Finally, the suspicions that plagued American literature at the moment of its institutionalization require us to rethink one of most influential paradigms we use to understand the role of literature, that of "cultural work." Assessments of literature's cultural work have differed widely since Jane Tompkins popularized the phrase in her groundbreaking 1986 study, *Sensational Designs: The Cultural Work of American Fiction, 1790–1860*. Some critics have stressed its benevolent side, or its role in fostering democracy, personal and legal freedoms, and sexual equality, among other forms of social justice. Another strand of scholarship, however, approaches literature's cultural work as a disciplinary force, or as a means to manage "cultural anxiety," police dissent, and direct social relations and political commitments. Yet while these approaches evaluate the "cultural work" of print quite differently, they share a common confidence in its efficacy. Whether liberating or disciplinary, unifying or divisive, opening up political possibilities or foreclosing them, literature operates with authority. To put it more bluntly, these approaches assume that cultural work always *works*. But to understand literature as fully functional (whether for good or for ill) necessarily abstracts and arrests it, investing it with a stability that, in the antebellum years, at least, is far from assured. *Uncle Tom's Cabin*, that juggernaut of political reform, offers a case in point. Stowe's novel is probably the most frequently cited example of antebellum literature's "power to work in, and change, the world," in Tompkins's words.[6] But when we use it to measure literature's cultural work, it is worth remembering that a year after publishing *Uncle Tom's Cabin*, Stowe felt obliged to legitimate its claims by issuing *The Key to Uncle Tom's Cabin*, a book that undertakes the extraordinary task of providing evidence for a work of fiction. Stowe and her contemporaries may well have had "designs on the world," but this does not necessarily entail that their texts executed them effectually.[7] Indeed, this book assembles a large body of evidence of literary fallibility, from scathing magazine exposés to fretful readers' marginalia, which does not conform to such functionalist paradigms. It clamors for a more disorderly account of antebellum literature.

To produce such an account, I have juxtaposed the period's proliferating ideologies of literature with the material history of how literature was actually produced, circulated, read, and discussed in print, paying particular attention to ways in which the theory and practice of literature diverged from, jostled, or even undermined each other. My sense of the instability of antebellum print culture, as well as my interest in its unpredictable outcomes, owes a great deal to recent work in the field by Leon Jackson, Trish Loughran, and Meredith McGill, who have told the history of the book in the United States as a far richer and more complex story than it appeared before. Their books, as well as Adrian Johns's and Susan Stewart's studies of print in somewhat different contexts, highlight the multiple registers on which print functions as an object of intense, sometimes contradictory cultural fantasies whose efficacy often depends on the separation of print from its conditions of production. Against familiar notions of literary authority, then, the following chapters aim to resuscitate a forgotten literary discourse that circulated during the antebellum period, one whose obsession with fraudulence portrays literature not as eminently functional but as troublingly dysfunctional. Alongside the celebrated print explosion of the antebellum years, this book discovers an obstinate chorus of words like *fraud, imposture, puffing, sham, hoax, plagiarism, quackery, humbug,* and *counterfeit*—a shadow history of American literature we have since forgotten.

The Print Explosion and the Print Implosion

This book argues that if American literature was a far more dubious enterprise than we tend to imagine in retrospect, ironically, its failures had much to do with its success. This paradox instructively distinguishes the antebellum uproar over fraudulence from earlier controversies over the deceptiveness of novels, for instance. While eighteenth- and early nineteenth-century

British and American moral gatekeepers accused novels of encouraging false but beguiling notions of reality, the antebellum concerns over literary fraudulence measure the distance literature had traveled in the interim, as these later commentators worried that literature might be deceptive precisely to the extent that it was expected to be valid and, indeed, important to the nation's well-being. Generations of critics have noted that imaginative writing achieves an increased cultural status in the early nineteenth-century United States, and they have offered various explanations for its newfound consequence. Traditionally, most have followed a teleological narrative, in which American literature overcomes a series of obstacles (lack of precedent, inadequate subject matter, an overly practical national character, British scorn) in order to fulfill its inevitable promise. But three more material factors also emerge, whose workings—and malfunctions—I am more interested in pursuing here. The antebellum years saw, first, major developments in the production and distribution of print; second, the consolidation of a market culture that allowed printed goods to be viable commodities; and third, the elevation of printed *literature*, in particular, to a cultural institution. Below I briefly describe these factors in the establishment of American literature and how their contributions also became liabilities.

Innovations in Print Technology

A rapid succession of technological and economic innovations in the early nineteenth century transformed the early republican period's largely artisanal print shops into a major commercial industry.[8] Improvements to the flat-bed press in the 1810s and 1820s, the introduction of horsepower in the 1820s and steam power a few years later, and the invention of the cylinder press in the 1830s greatly sped up production rates, as did the development of the stereotyping and electrotyping processes in the 1810s and 1840s, respectively. Former hand processes like paper and board manufacturing, typesetting, and binding were swiftly mechanized. By 1830 a single machine could make paper on rolls (rather than sheet by sheet, as hand production required) and cut it to size.[9] The introduction in the 1820s of cased bindings, covers assembled separately and then sewn to the printed pages, was especially transformative. In the past, publishers had generally issued books in paper wrappers or pasteboard covers, which readers then had bound as they chose or could afford. Cased bindings allowed publishers to issue books in uniform editions with fixed prices. For sure sellers, publishers would produce books in multiple bindings, each tailored to different tastes and budgets; thus in 1856 a reader looking for Irving's *Sketch-Book* could buy an edition bound in cloth for $1.25, with illustrations and gilt decoration for $2.25, or in elegant morocco covers for $3.50.[10] Improved papermaking and binding techniques made possible two of the most spectacular feats of antebellum print technology: the ornate gift books, or literary annuals, which flourished around mid-century, and the "mammoth weeklies" of the 1840s. Published at the end of the year to be exchanged as holiday presents, gift books compiled sentimental poetry, short fiction, and essays, but the real appeal lay in their alluring exteriors: heavily embossed leather or watered silk bindings bedecked with elaborate ornaments, color illustrations, marbled endpapers, copious amounts of gilding, and even mother-of-pearl. The mammoth weeklies also capitalized on visual impact. Gigantic newspapers containing fiction (usually British reprints), some news, and usually incongruous illustrations, the mammoths competed to offer the largest editions; when the *Universal Yankee Nation* (motto: "The Largest Paper in All Creation") emerged as the victor, it reached nearly eleven feet tall.[11]

Clearly, the growth of the printing industries provided the material basis for antebellum literature's new cultural stature. What is less obvious is that the print explosion also tended to destabilize those foundations at an epistemic level. When scholars assume that going into print confers a sense of stability upon writing, we confuse print culture with the technology of print. As a technology, print fixes impressions, but print *culture*—the array of material forms, cultural discourses, economic systems, and lived practices that invest print with meaning—is just as likely to unsettle them, a distinction of which antebellum Americans were only too aware. As Adrian Johns has shown, the unmoored claims of the printed book elicited constant questions from its very beginnings: Was it a "true copy" or did it misrepresent the manuscript, intentionally or unintentionally? Did the author named really write it? Was it the kind of text its title purported it to be? Could its contents be trusted?[12] Moreover, the print culture of the early nineteenth-century United States possessed a peculiar volatility all its own: it was a "culture of reprinting," in Meredith McGill's words, in which "circulation outstripped authorial and editorial control."[13] Scholars in performance studies and new media studies often define their objects of study against the inert printed word, but print was more likely to invest antebellum texts with mobility than to fasten them in place.[14] In the whirl of reprinting, no text was fixed. Magazine editors regularly republished each other's articles, British and American "bookaneers" competed to issue first editions on each shore or undersell existing editions, and writers often found their words altered, cut, rearranged, or attributed to others, or had unfamiliar words attributed to them. Printed texts cited, commented upon, and reappropriated each other to an extent that compares with the most viral internet meme, and the print/performance binary means little during a period when poems were routinely set to music and issued as songsheets, and a sign of a novel's popularity was how quickly it was dramatized.[15] Longfellow's *Song of Hiawatha* (1855), for example, was almost instantly converted into music, several plays, endless parodies, an advertisement for patent medicine, captions for humorous engravings, the punch line to a joke, and a painted scene to decorate sleighs.[16] Perhaps always, but in the nineteenth century especially, the medium of print did not decisively inscribe meaning but rather ensured that its inscriptions remained continually available for adaptation.

The print explosion could create an inverse relation between print and legibility, as the two examples of its achievements cited above, the mammoth weekly and the gift book, also illustrate. When critics worried that mammoth weeklies were printed on paper so huge and set in type so small that they would ruin readers' eyesight, they may have missed the point, because it was never clear to what extent the mammoth weeklies were actually intended to be read. One could hardly hold the weeklies, much less read them, a trade-off that one, the *Boston Notion*, unperturbedly publicized on its masthead. A cheerful family scene, it situates the *Notion* among an array of other reading materials, including books, a standard-sized newspaper, and a scrapbook (figure 1). While these texts lie conveniently on a table, however, the *Notion* must be spread out on the floor. The family gathers around the giant newspaper, but no one actually reads it. Instead, the adults look admiringly at it from afar (the only plausible vantage from which to admire it), while the children play on it, climbing over and under the pages. As the *Notion*'s masthead readily acknowledges, the attraction of the mammoth weeklies lay less in their contents than in their spectacular form.

Gift books more starkly illustrate the dubious achievements of antebellum literary publishing, for next to their sumptuousness, their most characteristic feature was their spuriousness. Publishers routinely repackaged pages from old gift books in new bindings, took pages from unsold periodicals and rebound them as gift books, or erased the gilt date from

Figure 1: Masthead of the *Boston Notion* (detail). (Courtesy of the American Antiquarian Society)

the bindings of old annuals and restamped them with the current year, much as a counterfeiter would erase the dollar amount from a bill and replace it with a higher number. An 1840 letter from publisher and jobber J. A. Noble to Otis, Broaders, and Company, a powerful publisher and periodical agent, shows how the practice worked. Noble asks the company to order 500 copies of the previous year's edition of *The Token*, a long-running gift book edited by Samuel Goodrich, "With New Title page and fixed in every way to appear like an 1841 Annual. To be bound same style as last year except 1841 on the back instead of 1840 or the 1840 cut off entirely. . . . I give 90¢ for them in Neat Arabesque the Book to be as large at least as last year and to be called 'Token & affections Gift' for 1841 Edited by S. G. Goodrich." Noble is confident the scheme will succeed: "I bought 200 copies 1838 Token," he boasts, "got them bound & called 1840—New York [publisher's imprint]—& they sold well." Moreover, he has a plan to exploit the asymmetrical U.S. literary market: "What imprint would you put in—they must be either Boston N. Y. or Phila. Should you conclude to let me have them—every copy should be sold south of Virginia & West of the Alleghenies," regions far enough away from the northeastern publishing centers that unsuspecting readers might be duped by the bogus *Token*.[17] Gift-book bibliographer Ralph Thompson estimates that "about 35 American firms indulged in this questionable business, producing nearly 150 titles of the kind."[18] These numbers suggest that such "questionable business" was simply business as usual.[19]

The Development of a National Literary Market

The industrialization of print was an economic transition as much as a technological one. Mechanization led to a growing division of labor inside print shops and a deskilling of much work. These developments allowed owners to exploit cheaper labor (including that of women and children), decreasing manufacturing costs and increasing production quantities.[20] Once the finished product left the print shop (now often a factory), the steamship and the railroad carried it farther than ever before, while marketing innovations such as middlemen and trade sales likewise expanded and regularized distribution.[21] What had been local reading and writing communities thus became incorporated into a national literary market largely dominated by northeastern metropolises, although a plurality of print cultures persisted nonetheless.[22] In 1830, the total value of books produced and sold in the United States was $3.5 million, but just thirty years later it had more than tripled to $12.5 million.[23] The magazine trade, in particular, exploded, helped along by favorable postal regulations; Frank Luther Mott estimates that whereas fewer than one hundred magazines were published in the United States in 1825, by 1850 six times that many existed.[24] Such developments have led some historians to identify books as the prototypical industrial commodity, which paved the way for modern forms of both mass production and mass consumption.[25]

Like the new technologies of print production, however, the burgeoning literary marketplace at once underwrote American literature and undermined it. We are familiar with a version of this story that has become a staple of nineteenth-century literary history, in which writers struggle against the tyrannical market, pitting their creative energies against its stultifying power.[26] Certainly, some authors did see themselves at odds with commerce. But the predominance of this agonistic narrative tends to obscure the extent to which authorship and the market were mutually constitutive formations. Moreover, polarizing the two retrospectively invests each with a solidity it did not actually possess, overstating the conceptual coherence of authorship during these years while overlooking inherent tensions within the workings of literary capitalism itself.[27] A national literary market did not emerge *sui generis*, nor did it come to organize practices of reading and writing without friction. In his eye-opening study of antebellum literary economics, Leon Jackson describes what we call the development of a national literary market as a "disembedding" of previously "embedded" economic activities, which served "multiple social functions . . . of which the merely economic is only one."[28] On the one hand, the market facilitated the production and distribution of literature in the United States; on the other, its very structure raised new questions about how to evaluate the objects it circulated. Jackson explains that embedded economic activities "serve, typically, to create and sustain social bonds," but as "the economies through which authors worked became detached from the dense social worlds of which they were a part, . . . exchange became less personal and less trusting."[29] (Susan Stewart, tracking a parallel shift in eighteenth-century London, makes a similar observation: whereas earlier systems of literary transmission had been situated in contexts that defined text and audience—the face-to-face relations of oral performance; the highly codified settings of court, club, and coffeehouse; the contractual agreements of subscription publishing—the emergent "commodification of writing" separated texts "from their grounds of intelligibility and closure.")[30] Moreover, industrial book production exacerbated the uncertainties of market exchange by extending reading and publishing activities across a wider class terrain. Much of the mushrooming print output of these years consisted of so-called "cheap and nasty" literature, pamphlet novels and story papers reprinted from British editions or produced by a homegrown population of "penny-a-liners." Their presence in the market sharpened the generalized doubts Jackson and Stewart describe into very definite anxieties about social distinction. For many disgruntled observers, a mass-produced literature raised questions of what qualified as "literature" at all, an uncertainty that compelled the publishers Wiley and Putnam to distinguish their Library of Choice Reading series with the clarifying motto "Books Which Are Books."[31] And such skepticism traveled both ways across class divides, so that while the high-minded literati railed against "hack" literature's "ethics of humbug," so-called "hacks" like George Lippard accused the powerful literary elite of being the "Cream of Humbug, the Skim milk of American Book Charlatanism."[32]

These debates over aesthetic status are inseparable from the difficulties of assessing social status in a period of unprecedented class mobility, both upward and downward. But at the most basic level, they derive from the contradictions of the literary commodity itself, which brings capitalism's economic principles into collision with its ideological ones. Ideologically, the concept of literary value derives from a division of labor that distinguishes the creative from the manual and elevates the former above the latter. This distinction depends on two imaginative elisions: first, its notion of literary production must ignore the material processes that bring literature into being (paper-making, typesetting, printing, sewing, etc., as well as ambiguously literary activities like editing) in order to define literature solely as writing, and second, writing must be understood as a rarefied matter of inspiration rather than a laborious arrangement of words. Economically, however, the literary marketplace must put a price on the very values that the division of labor insists transcend it. Boston poet Thomas William Parsons's 1854 satire of the publishing industry vividly evokes the cognitive dissonance that results. Parsons contrasts what he (somewhat optimistically) sees as the dignity of literature in England with the treatment it receives on "this equalizing coast," where "this age of steam / Reduces poesy to weight and ream," converting the "tender shoots that bourgeon from the brain" into just so many wares. "How would'st thou shame to recognize thyself," he tells an English friend,

> In mammoth quartos, decked with wooden cuts,
> Meanly displayed 'mid candies, cake and nuts;
> Thumbed by coarse hands that paw before they choose,
> Whether a poem—or a pair of shoes![33]

To many observers, the antebellum literary commodity's double nature—its simultaneous claims to artistic value and exchange value—appeared as duplicity. Tellingly, booksellers were less likely to display their merchandise alongside "candies, cakes, and nuts" than alongside patent medicine. A visitor to Redding's Literary Depot in Boston, for instance, observed that its shelves "groan beneath the weight of wisdom and research" "sublimized into newspapers, books, magazine and pamphlets." Alongside *Graham's Magazine* and *Godey's Lady's Book*, however, Redding stocked "Pease's Hoarhound Candy, and the Unparalleled Dr. Sherman's Lozenges," whose "wonderful cures" are "stranger than fiction" (figure 2). Customers could find these "two . . . most valuable medicines of the age" "for sale at his counter in the cellar, in juxtaposition with literature," and the word "juxtaposition" seems precisely to the point.[34] Were *Graham's Magazine* and

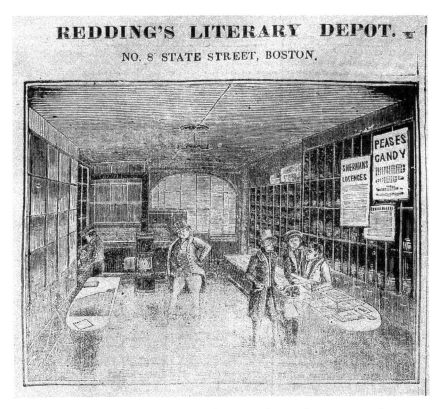

Figure 2: Redding's Literary Depot, featuring Sherman's Lozenges and Pease's Candy, from *Universal Yankee Nation* 1 (1 January 1842). (Courtesy of the American Antiquarian Society)

Pease's Hoarhound Candy like or unlike entities? Such combinations raised the question of whether literature resembled quack medicine in other ways as well.

American Literature Becomes a Cultural Institution

As the publishing industry expanded, the books and periodicals it produced became an increasingly prominent part of antebellum culture—not only materially, in their numbers and showy appearances, but also discursively, in the crystallization of a category called "American literature." This is not to say that literature did not exist in the United States before 1830, but that only in the early nineteenth century did imaginative writing develop into a recognizable entity (distinct from political writing, natural history, or theology, for example) with acknowledged cultural significance. An outpouring of writing *about* literature further helped usher it into existence as an object of knowledge. Literary criticism became an increasingly important fixture of magazines and newspapers (for reasons I explore in Chapter 1), but discussions of literature were not confined to book-review columns. Newspapers regularly reported on book auctions, bookstore openings, and publishers' celebrations. Articles touting the importance of literature, describing its ideal prospects, and worrying over its failures filled the pages of periodicals from women's magazines to labor newspapers. The growing literary nationalism movement made American literature, in particular, a favorite topic. Wiley and Putnam inaugurated their Library of American Books series in 1845, and the period saw an explosion of anthologies and reference works, most famously the indefatigable editor Rufus Griswold's *The Poets and Poetry of America* (1842), *Curiosities of American Literature* (1843), *The Prose Writers of America* (1847), and *The Female Poets of America* (1849), and, after many years in production, Evert and George Duyckinck's massive two-volume *Cyclopaedia of American Literature* (1855). At the same time, new marketing techniques helped keep literature squarely before the public eye. Publishers' advertisements—printed on handbills, placed in newspapers, and inserted in the backs of books—became a regular sight, replacing booksellers' staid lists of titles for sale with fulsome encomiums and tallies of the inevitably staggering number of copies already sold. At home, Americans stocked their shelves with figurines and candlesticks in the shapes of fictional characters, set their tables with china sets bearing literary motifs, carried handkerchiefs embroidered with memorable quotations, and hung portraits of authors and lithographs of favorite literary scenes on their walls.[35] Whereas eighteenth-century print aspired to transparency, as Michael Warner has shown, antebellum literary print cultivated attention—publicity, in other words, rather than Warner's virtuous publicness.[36]

Yet the cultural currency literature acquired in these years—its high visibility, the attractions it held for readers, its perceived influence on social relations—also had a tendency to backfire. One final example of literary dubiousness will illustrate the point. Enterprising businessmen used the popular literature of the day to hawk their decidedly nonliterary wares, so that even as the rise of advertising put literature on display, it also threatened to dissolve any difference between the respective rhetorical tactics of the two. Newspaper writer Fanny Fern viewed the bait-and-switch with mixed annoyance and admiration:

> I am fond of poetry; my eye catches a favorite extract from Longfellow, or [William Cullen] Bryant, or [James Gates] Percival, or [George P.] Morris; I read it over with renewed pleasure, blessing the author in my heart the while. I am decoyed into the building to which it serves as a fairy vestibule. Where do I find myself?
>
> By Parnassus! in a carpet warehouse—in a sausage-shop—in a druggist's—shoemaker's—tailor's—or hatter's establishment.
>
> Who shall circumscribe American ingenuity where dollars and cents are concerned?
>
> Answer me, great Barnum![37]

So attention-grabbing that it could be deployed as an advertising lure, antebellum literature attained the status of spectacle—and spectacle, as Barnum understood, was the defining characteristic of outright humbug. His encyclopedic *Humbugs of the World* explained that "'humbug' consists in putting on glittering appearances—outside show—novel expedients, by which to suddenly arrest public attention, and attract the public eye and ear."[38] Yet antebellum literature's "outside show" also invited scrutiny, as Fern's disclosive article indicates. The resultant exposés, complaints, screeds, and satires offer a historical elaboration of Foucault's aphorism, "Visibility is a trap."[39] While the growing visibility of antebellum literature signaled its unprecedented power, its conspicuousness also became a weakness. Like other kinds of power, literary power works best when least observed, but antebellum literature's place in the public eye brought its representational practices into focus. The attention it garnered as a result often sent representation, in its most neutral sense of depiction, into representation in its most negative sense of falsehood. This book recovers these moments of overexposure and overextension in order to reexamine the functionalist assumptions of print culture and literary studies. Its project, in short, is to reconstruct the basic strangeness of antebellum literature.

At the same time that the problem of fraudulence bedeviled antebellum literature, however, I also want to propose that it offered its own kind of rhetorical solution. Antebellum literature's credibility problems, I have been arguing, arose out of the definitional crisis it faced in the midst of its technological, cultural, and economic transformation. But the discourse of fraudulence—a discourse that is, after all, profoundly unsuited to the subject of literature—offers a fantasy of clear-cut assessment for a value that could never be satisfactorily assessed. Moreover, fraudulence holds out the possibility of authenticity, a binary opposition that replaces undeterminable claims of literary worth with the promise of clear-cut distinction. And finally, *identifying* fraudulence creates an impression of anomaly; in other words, it transforms pervasive fraudulence into particularized fraud. If fraud can be detected, there must be a legitimate system at work. The obsession with fraudulence generated by the print explosion makes one wonder whether Walter Benjamin's famous thesis about mechanical reproduction—that it jeopardizes "the authority of the object" that manual reproduction upheld—may get things backward. "The presence of the original is prerequisite to the concept of authenticity," Benjamin writes, and "the whole sphere of authenticity is outside technical—and, of course, not only technical—reproducibility."[40] Yet antebellum literary culture's insistent attempts to locate authenticity and distinguish it from fraudulence suggest that authenticity may not be a casualty of modernity—"that which withers in the age of mechanical reproduction"—so much as an invention of it. In other words, originality is a second-order phenomenon, which requires the idea of the copy to exist. It is the conceivability of the derivative that is the prerequisite for imagining, and privileging, the authentic. Thus while I began by positing that the success of American literature contributed to its failures, I want to end by giving this dialectic another turn to suggest that those failures may also have enabled its ultimate success. At times it seems miraculous that American literature survived the barrage of suspicion and assaults recounted in this book. But paradoxically, it might well have survived because of them. Pervasive as the controversies over fraudulence were, by transfiguring thornier questions of literary value, they helped establish that entity we now confidently call American literature.

Fraudulence from the Core to the Periphery

The chapters that follow track the shifting fortunes of American literature over the course of the antebellum print explosion, which began with the technological and market innovations of the 1830s and ground to a halt as the nation approached the Civil War. The first part of this study reexamines the cultural institutionalization of American literature in the 1830s and 1840s in order to show how antebellum efforts to produce an authentically American literary culture instead created one beset by accusations of fraudulence. My focus on literature's reputation for fraudulence, rather than specific acts of fraud, means that although at times I highlight particular authors, one aim of this section is to intervene in theoretical frameworks in which individual "subversion," "transgression," or "resistance" offer the only means of disrupting cultural hegemony. On the one hand, these models assign aggrandized agency to authors; while they underscore the reach of hegemony (after all, the authors they privilege must have something to challenge), they posit a kind of exemption from these strictures on behalf of select authors. On the other hand, they totalize hegemony, which while dominant, is rarely monolithic. Yet in these models, hegemony hits its limits only in response to external challenges such as the deliberately oppositional acts named above. Attention to such acts of resistance is immensely valuable, of course. But this book argues that the material instantiation of hegemony—here, in print—sometimes poses problems of its own.

Put differently, in addition to its archival and analytical projects, this book has designs on a methodological intervention. It aspires to a materialist approach that would fuse two senses of the word: historical materialism and the study of material texts. Despite their shared commitment to the primacy of material objects and practices, these approaches have historically had little to say to each other. As a result, book history has acquired a reputation as a depoliticized field that focuses on material texts and the processes that produce them in isolation from the broader economic and social systems of which they form a part. There are certainly important exceptions to this rule, but it is generally true that the field has tended to privilege fine-grained detail over systemic analysis. At the same time, Marxist historical materialism often pays equally scant attention to the actual materiality of its material basis. Thus although Marxism posits materialism as an alternative to idealism, its often frictionless sense of the material can itself tend toward the idealist. Marx's discussion of money offers a case in point. For Marx, money functions as the "universal equivalent form" of commodities. By contrast, in the antebellum United States, the decentralized printing of banknotes, massive inflation, and rampant counterfeiting significantly compromised money's efficacy as a medium of exchange, as we will see in Chapter 1.[41] As I suggested above, however, these tendencies toward idealism are most pronounced in discussions of ideology, especially in the foundational statements of Louis Althusser (ironically, the most truculent critic of Marxist idealism). "Ideology has a material existence," Althusser asserts in "Ideology and Ideological State Apparatuses (Notes Towards an Investigation)"; it "always exists in an apparatus, and its practice, or practices."[42] But despite Althusser's insistence on materialized "apparatuses" ("a small mass in a small church, a funeral, a minor match at a sports' club, a school day, a political party meeting, etc."), materiality proves strangely transparent in his account.[43] In other words, although ideology must take material form, those material forms never modify ideology; they just obligingly transmit it. Although few critics would argue that ideology is a sure thing, they tend to assume that its breakdowns occur through their own analytical interventions. By contrast, I propose that when material forms mediate ideologies, they do not always do so as intended. Thus while I trace the development of certain ideologies of literature, I am especially interested in how these ideologies overheat, recoil, or founder when they take form in print.

The first chapter of *The Fabrication of American Literature* is set among the largely northeastern, urban, white, and middle- to upper-class writers, editors, and critics who dominated the national literary market. From there, the book follows the story of fraudulence as it moves from this literary core to the subordinated groups on its economic, regional, racialized, and gendered periphery. I use the terms "core" and "periphery" in a structural rather than essential sense. I borrow them from Immanuel Wallerstein's world-systems analysis, where Wallerstein uses them to describe an integrated system of capitalism in which elements "seemingly outside the system are in fact inside it."[44] Wallerstein's world-systems analysis is not, of course, congruent with the study of antebellum literature. But the notion of an interdependent core and periphery aptly characterizes the relations between mainstream and marginalized literary cultures during these years, for even as women, people of color, and rural populations gained new footholds in literary culture, their incorporation ultimately helped consolidate the mainstream's own authority as it came under attack for being rotten at the core.

The production of a literary periphery served the literary core in two apparently contradictory ways: by embodying authenticity and by embodying fraudulence. Lacking cultural clout, literary productions from the margins could be seen as more natural (and thus more appropriately national), and the literati eagerly hailed them as embodying the authenticity they themselves were perceived as lacking. Indeed, the allure of the margins proved so strong that the antebellum years saw a profusion of fake peripheral productions manufactured in metropolitan publishing centers, including the minstrel performances, ersatz backwoodsmen's tales, and false slave narratives I discuss in Chapters 2 and 3. At the same time, if writers in the mainstream commented on one characteristic of peripheral writings more frequently than their authenticity, it was their fraudulence. Thus while the productions of backwoodsmen, slaves, and women assumed new cultural currency as repositories of genuine literary expression, they also became indelibly associated with imposture, tall tales, and artifice. It is not difficult to detect in these characterizations a displacement of the fraudulence that dogged the literati's own efforts. But it is important to emphasize that this was less a matter of expunging fraudulence than moving it somewhere else. Troubling at the center of literary culture, fraudulence proved salutary at a safe distance because its presence there instituted a principle of difference that produced a normative authenticity at the center. In this way, the expanding literary marketplace transformed fraudulence from a national dilemma into a sorting mechanism that helped define racial, regional, and gender identities. Yet fraudulence was not reliably subjugating, either, and the second half of the book also explores how a number of figures turned their dubious reputations to account, solving the problem of fraudulence by making a virtue of it.

Chapter 1, "'One Vast Perambulating Humbug': Literary Nationalism and the Rise of the Puffing System," revisits the literary nationalist movement of the 1830s and 1840s in order to read it against its troublesome historical counterpart: the system of critical "puffery" that many readers accused of propping up a sham American literature. Literary nationalism promoted American literature on the basis of its unprecedented natural qualities, which supporters contrasted favorably with the stifling conventions of European tradition. But skeptics argued that the preponderance of support given American literature inflated it far beyond its natural proportions. The second half of the chapter expands from specifically literary nationalist puffery to the full scope of the puffing system, whose impressive repertoire of underhanded promotional tactics dominated literary criticism during the period. Even when puffery did not serve explicitly literary nationalist aims, I argue, it was nonetheless seen to pose a threat to national

identity, because it contravened the nationalist shibboleth that literary criticism would embody the distinctly democratic approach to literature in the
United States. Guiding the reader through this profusion of puffery is Edgar
Allan Poe, who at once excoriated the system in his reviews, parodied it in
his fiction, and was perhaps inevitably incorporated into it. In the last part
of the chapter, I propose that he also allegorized it in the numerous figures
of balloons that fill his work, most notably in the seldom-read tale "The
Unparalleled Adventure of One Hans Pfaall." In contrast to the abstract
public sphere theorized by Jürgen Habermas, I argue, these balloons image
a more particular, even peculiar, kind of public sphere, one filled not with
rational-critical discourse but with hot air.

Chapter 2, "Backwoods and Blackface: The Strange Careers of Davy
Crockett and Jim Crow," acts as the hinge between the suspect literary
nationalism discussed in the first chapter and the construction of a literary
periphery in later chapters. Building on the ironies of Jacksonian democracy outlined in the Introduction and Chapter 1, this chapter establishes the
double casting that governed the mainstream's investment in the marginalized, whom the literati recruited simultaneously to authenticity and to
fraudulence. It examines how two figures defined by their alterity, frontier
legend Davy Crockett and minstrel character Jim Crow, became surprisingly enmeshed both in each other and in the supposedly distant cultural
mainstream. I use the historical links between the two figures to interrogate
the secret to their success—not only their popularity among the working
classes, already the subject of considerable study, but also their considerable
appeal among the literary elite, who lit upon these two outlandishly fabricated creations as evidence of a genuine native literary spirit. In Jim Crow
and Davy Crockett, the literati discovered (or, more accurately, devised) a
revitalizing national vernacular, one that would rehabilitate the intractable
problem of fraud by recasting it in the regionalized, racialized forms of
backwoods tall tales and black posturing. Unpacking the fabrication of subaltern fabricating, the mainstreaming of marginality, and the authentication
of falsehood, this chapter shows the operations of antebellum fraudulence
at their most tortuous. In a rather dizzying train of cultural logic, it argues
that Crockett and Crow's fake alterity promoted the idea that alterity was
prone to fakeness; remarkably, this fakeness could also provide the authentic American literature that literary nationalism failed to produce.

Extending Chapter 2's discussion of the intersecting antebellum constructions of race and fraudulence, Chapter 3, "'Slavery Never Can Be

Represented': James Williams and the Racial Politics of Imposture," examines the slave narrative's neglected relative, the pseudo-slave narrative. This chapter investigates the very different ways in which fraud played out across the color line by juxtaposing examples of the genre from white authors Richard Hildreth and Mattie Griffith with the only known (or believed) false slave narrative by an African American author, *The Narrative of James Williams* (1838). The first slave narrative published under the auspices of the American Anti-Slavery Society, *The Narrative of James Williams* was discredited soon after its publication in a scandal that assumed national proportions. The abolitionist movement's suspicion of African Americans' truthfulness and the influence of these suspicions on the writing of fugitive slaves are well known, but the controversy over Williams gave an unexpected twist to this story: abolitionists actually balked at suggestions that Williams had fabricated his narrative, refusing to attribute to him creative capacities that they considered inconceivable in an African American writer.

Chapter 4, "Mediums of Exchange: Fanny Fern's Unoriginality" further pursues the volatility of fraudulence by turning to a writer who converted fraudulence's stigma into a wildly popular product. Focusing on the pseudonymous best-selling author Fanny Fern, whose newspaper columns and fiction made her a celebrity in the 1850s and 1860s, this chapter investigates the language of artifice and imitation that supervised the influx of women into the mid-century literary marketplace. Yet I argue that Fern, who trafficked in convention and dropped her given name in favor of her pseudonym, embraced such associations so forcefully as to splinter the disciplinary logic they initially sustained. Rather than defining female identity in the literary marketplace, Fern's enthusiastic artifice left readers wondering, not only "Who is Fanny Fern?" as one newspaper put it, but even "What is Fanny Fern?" The transition from "who" to "what" suggests that fraudulence worked to reify its perceived subjects, and the previous chapters indicate that it enjoyed considerable success. But Fern's collaboration in her fraudulence demonstrates that its reifying effects could not be guaranteed—or more accurately, that reification might have pleasures and possibilities of its own.

Finally, the Conclusion, "The Confidence Man on a Large Scale," turns to perhaps the most famous account of antebellum fraud, Herman Melville's commercially disastrous final novel, *The Confidence-Man*. This may seem a strange place to end, given that I have tried hard to distinguish this book's subject from the kinds of crimes perpetrated by "confidence men," a phrase that originated eight years before the publication of Melville's novel as the moniker given a New York swindler. But despite the title's promise of particularity, the greatest obstacle to reading the book lies in determining what differentiates the confidence man from the other people he encounters. Melville's contemporaries might not have been surprised. When the city police arrested the swindler, commentators expressed little satisfaction, protesting that New Yorkers had been tricked once more: the real criminal was not the Confidence Man but what one newspaper called "The Confidence Man on a Large Scale," the everyday machinations of business and politics.[45] Counterintuitively, then, *The Confidence-Man* formally registers the broadest argument of this book, that antebellum fraudulence cannot be embodied in individual acts and persons. More specifically, Melville continually threads meditations on the nature of literature through his swindling plot, to the point that the two endeavors prove difficult to distinguish. Yet even as *The Confidence-Man* in some ways epitomizes the pervasive fraudulence of the antebellum years, its own reception also marks the end of this era, for as dismal as it was, it was in no way disruptive. In 1837, an objectionable book like *The Confidence-Man* would have been pronounced a fraud. In 1857, it was simply ignored.[46] To some extent, this shift reflects the saturation of literary capitalism, which increasingly organized a questionable business into more neatly defined niches of high and low, romantic and realist, commercial and artistic. Perhaps, too, it testifies to the success of the efforts to manage fraudulence described in Chapters 2 through 4. Or we might see it as evidence of the possibility I raised earlier: that the panic over fraudulence itself helped eradicate the problem by giving the impression that modern critics have indeed taken away from *The Confidence-Man*—that fraudulence is an anomaly that can be satisfactorily detected.

Chapter 1

"One Vast Perambulating Humbug": Literary Nationalism and the Rise of the Puffing System

> I have no fear that the poetry of democratic peoples will be found timid or that it will stick too close to the earth. I am much more afraid that it will spend its whole time getting lost in the clouds and may finish up by describing an entirely fictitious country.
>
> —Alexis de Tocqueville, *Democracy in America*

In March 1837, the booksellers of New York City held a lavish dinner to celebrate the accomplishments of American literature. Seemingly every major literary figure attended the event, including authors William Cullen Bryant, Fitz-Greene Halleck, Washington Irving, and James Kirke Paulding; magazine editors Lewis Gaylord Clark, Evert Duyckinck, and N. P. Willis; and publishers Fletcher Harper and George Palmer Putnam, as well as a host of political, legal, academic, religious, and cultural luminaries. The dinner made headlines in all the major city papers. After some opening remarks and musical numbers, each guest offered a toast—to the magazines, to the printing press, to the "republic of letters," and so on. When Charles King, editor-publisher of the *New-York American* and future president of Columbia University, had his turn, however, he raised his glass to "the Author of the modern discoveries in the Moon," Richard Adams Locke, who had cooked up the *New York Sun*'s infamous "moon hoax" two years before. (British astronomer Sir John Herschel, Locke reported at the time, had developed a telescope so powerful that it allowed him to observe life on the moon, where unicorns, bipedal beavers, and winged men lived in harmony.) "Mr. R. A. Locke being here loudly called for, rose and parried the compliment in a humorous manner, which drew forth great applause," the *New-York American* reported.[1] How did the triumphs of American literature come to keep such close company with a notorious newspaper stunt? At least one guest at the dinner found the association entirely appropriate. Several years later, from the editor's desk of *Graham's Magazine*, Edgar Allan Poe summed up his opinion of American efforts to manufacture a native literature in terms that shed light on Locke's relation to the literati. "As a literary people," Poe declared, "we are one vast perambulating humbug."[2]

This chapter investigates the problem hinted at in the booksellers' toasts and witheringly named in Poe's remark: just as American literature became cause for celebration, many antebellum readers found it difficult to distinguish from a fraud. To resurrect the controversies over literary humbug, I revisit a subject that once scaffolded the study of American literature and now tends to embarrass it: the literary nationalist movement that swept the United States in the 1830s and 1840s. Rather than taking literary nationalists' strident declarations of independence at their word, however, I turn to the considerable backlash they generated, particularly the controversies over nationalist "puffery" that earned antebellum literature comparisons to inflated paper currency and western land bubbles. The second half of the chapter explores the growth of puffery beyond simple chauvinism. Even instances of puffery that never mentioned the nation were nonetheless seen to violate one of the central tenets of nationalist culture, the idea of American literature as a democratic enterprise—an idea that became all the more vital as party politics and electioneering scandals made the democracy of the state appear increasingly dubious. I argue that the puffing system at once tested readers' beliefs in a literary democracy and, paradoxically, helped prop up its image in print. Consequently, recovering the history of puffing also allows us to find new meaning in the shape literary democracy has assumed in years since, the print public sphere. Poe appears as a recurring figure throughout this chapter, as both the puffing system's most vehement critic and, at times, an avid participant. The conclusion brings him to center stage, however, in order to show that while Poe has a great deal to say about puffery in many contexts, it is his seemingly unrelated tales of ballooning, especially "The Unparalleled Adventure of One Hans Pfaall," that offer his fullest treatment of literary fraudulence and the era's most telling depiction of the puffed-up public sphere.

Imaginary Communities: The Trials of Literary Nationalism

In returning to the unfashionable subject of literary nationalism, my challenge is to show that its study does not necessarily work in favor of nationalist literary histories but rather in tandem with current scholarly interest in thinking outside the purview of the nation-state. Scholars' interest in literary nationalism arguably peaked in the early years of the Cold War, but after enjoying many years as the mandatory framework for American literature, the nation as an organizing concept has fallen out of favor as critics have put increasing pressure on the exceptionalist and teleological narratives constructed around it. In the past decade, especially, scholars have brought to light a much richer and more complex "American" literary history than earlier works imagined by tracing vectors of literary circulation, influence, commentary, and competition that crossed borders, oceans, and languages. Even within U.S. borders, they have pointed out, local and regional cultures continued to generate alternative modes of belonging. This "spatial turn" in American literary studies has posed a much needed challenge to assumptions that nationalism was either inevitable or commendable. Indeed, it has challenged the nation's usefulness as an interpretive category at all. Wai Chee Dimock, for example, contends that the "manmade fiction" of the nation lacks the integrity of a more "grounded entity" like the planet.[3] Amy Kaplan goes further, warning that to read through the lens of the nation is not only futile but dangerous because it replicates the logic of American exceptionalism, which views the United States as "the apotheosis of the nation-form."[4]

Yet simply shifting our attention from the national to the transnational (or any other spatial configuration), without asking how the national came to obstruct these paradigms in the first place, risks leaving it intact. If anything, rediscovering these alternative paradigms makes the question of the national all the more urgent, for they reveal the strident Americanism of the 1830s and 1840s in all its improbability. Even as our familiar national frameworks give way to more dynamic, transnational understandings of American literature, we nonetheless need to account for the persistent historical presence of national*ism*—for the discursive practices that erected those frameworks in the first place, however outmoded we now consider them.

Furthermore, skepticism about the nation-form does not belong to contemporary academics alone. Even as nationalism, literary and otherwise, dominated the antebellum scene, many observers, as we will see, simply found themselves unable to believe in American literature. Their history offers an arresting counterpoint to Benedict Anderson's influential argument that nations construct themselves as "imagined communities" through print. According to Anderson, "Communities are to be distinguished, not by their falsity/genuineness, but by the style in which they are imagined," and a nation comes into being when "in the minds of each [of its members] lives the image of their communion."[5] For Anderson, the origin of these imaginings lies in print-capitalism, or the widening circulation of print enabled by an emerging market economy, "which made it possible for rapidly growing numbers of people to think about themselves, and to relate themselves to others, in profoundly new ways."[6] Anderson's two primary examples of print-capitalism are the newspaper and the novel, and his deft readings of the latter constitute the primary body of evidence in *Imagined Communities*.[7] Anderson summons an impressively diverse array of examples, but in each case, he shows how literature proves crucially *conducive* to national feeling, as "fiction seeps quietly and continuously into reality, creating that remarkable confidence of community in anonymity which is the hallmark of modern nations."[8]

Anderson's emphasis on the role that print, especially literature, plays in the emergence of nations has made *Imagined Communities* as vital to literary studies as it is to political theory. Recent work by Trish Loughran and Lloyd Pratt, however, has worked to uncouple print and nation in the antebellum United States and show that the relation between the two created as much friction as community. In *The Republic in Print: Print Culture in the Age of U.S. Nation Building, 1770–1870*, Loughran dismantles familiar narratives in which the nation arises out of print by arguing not only that the circulation of print in the early republic was profoundly uneven and disconnected, but that "consensus and consolidation could have succeeded *only* under such scattered conditions." When print networks finally did integrate the disparate parts of the nation in the mid-nineteenth century, the result "did not in fact lead to a golden age of U.S. nationalism but instead ushered in the era of high sectionalism" as "these new material conditions ultimately exposed the geographical incoherence over which the fiction of union had originally been written."[9] Where Loughran examines the mismatched spatial scales of the virtual and actual nation, Pratt's *Archives of American Time: Literature and Modernity in the Nineteenth Century* tracks the implications of their equally irregular temporal scales. To do so, he distinguishes between "figures of print," which index a "tidy account of how modern print culture homogenized time to secure the emergence of American identity," and actual literature, whose conventions and genres stubbornly encoded a plurality of times that "did as much (or more) to disorder American identity as it did to reassemble it on an expanding scale."[10] This chapter builds on Loughran's and Pratt's arguments by investigating how the disjunction of nation and print—in particular, the literary nationalism that constituted one of print's chief products—reflected back on American literature's own reputation and on that of the nation itself. It argues that, far from "seep[ing] quietly and continuously . . . into reality," Anderson's fictions of nationhood may backfire, as the imagined community of the new nation continually threatened to reveal itself as an imaginary community instead. No nation *actually* can be "distinguished . . . by its falsity/genuineness," in Anderson's words, but the United States was distinguished by a profound *experience* of falsified nationhood.[11]

Literary nationalism ran into problems elsewhere, as well; indeed, its best-known scandals transpired in eighteenth-century Britain, which saw a remarkable spate of invented literary traditions that included James Macpherson's "Ossian" poems, Thomas Chatterton's invention of the fifteenth-century poet Thomas Rowley, and William Henry Ireland's "recovered" Shakespeare plays.[12] But these forgeries were antiquarian in mode, while in the United States, literature's credibility problems were bound up in a nationalist project of artistic innovation, rather than recovery. Sporadic rallying cries by authors, editors, and critics on behalf of "home literature" had begun to appear by the late eighteenth century. However, these gave little indication of the pitch literary nationalism would reach in the mid-1830s when, propelled by developing economic and transportation networks, the examples of European nationalist movements, and an expansionist ideology, such previously isolated pleas on behalf of American writing coalesced into a well-organized campaign.[13] The literary nationalists insisted that the absence of an established tradition did not guarantee failure, but on the contrary offered great scope. The nation's youth seemed to promise unprecedented possibilities for authentic literary expression untrammeled by convention, leading Ralph Waldo Emerson to delineate "the task offered to the intellect of this country" by announcing, "The perpetual admonition of nature to us, is, 'The world is new, untried. Do not believe the past. I give you the universe a virgin today.'"[14] Proponents argued that literary nationalism would have a salutary effect not only on

literature but also on the nation itself, which "can never acquire a profound, permanent character until she owns a home literature."[15] As the
primary mouthpiece of the nationalist movement known as Young
America, the *Democratic Review*, explained, "It is only by its literature that
one nation can utter itself and make itself known to the rest of the world."[16]
Therefore, American authors must not just "be filled with the spirit of their
nation," according to Orestes Brownson; they must, in fact, *be* the nation:
"the impersonations of its wishes, hopes, fears, and sentiments."[17]

Yet despite the literary nationalists' claims to channel a surge of popular
sentiment, the movement did not enjoy universal support. As Perry Miller's
classic study *The Raven and the Whale* recounts, the New York-based literary nationalists had to contend with their rivals, the Whiggish, cosmopolitan circle around the *Knickerbocker*, who rejected what they considered
Democratic Young America's crude marriage of literature and politics.
When critics today recall the resistance to literary nationalism, we tend to
do so in the terms set by Miller's vivid, often hilarious history of several
decades worth of sniping between the literary cliques: you were either for
it or against it in principle. But literary nationalism also faced further opposition, which objected less to the ideal of literary nationalism than the dis-
crepancy between ideal and reality.

Many observers balked at what they perceived as a gross disjunction
between the boisterous ideology of literary nationalism and the anemic
reality of a national literature. If Brownson saw literary "impersonation" as
the means for American authors to consolidate national identity in print,
to these detractors such "impersonation" sounded suspiciously like fraud.
Accordingly, literary nationalism faced a host of accusations asserting that
its strenuous efforts to act naturally had manufactured a sham American
literature. "We are farthest from wishing to see what many so ardently pray
for—namely a *National* literature," James Russell Lowell declared. "But we
do long for a *natural* literature."[18] His satirical poem *A Fable for Critics*
skewered the reigning confusion between the two, blaming critics for boost-
erism and a lack of discrimination:

> With you every year a whole crop is begotten,
> They're as much of a staple as corn is, or cotton;
> Why, there's scarcely a huddle of log-huts and shanties
> That has not brought forth its own Miltons and Dantes;
> I myself know ten Byrons, one Coleridge, three Shelleys,

Two Raphaels, six Titians (I think), one Apelles,
Leonardos and Rubenses plenty as lichens,
One (but that one is plenty) American Dickens,
A whole flock of Lambs, any number of Tennysons.[19]

Lowell's list of critical darlings lampoons one of the most telling paradoxes of literary nationalists' obsession with originality: the highest compliment it paid to American writers was to give them the names of European masters. Thus James Fenimore Cooper became the "American Scott," Lydia Sigourney the "American Hemans," and eternal laughingstock Cornelius Mathews the self-appointed "American Dickens." Even Young America, literary nationalism's umbrella movement, borrowed its name from the revolutionary examples of Young Ireland, Young Germany, and Young Italy. Lowell's pastoral setting, full of "log-huts and shanties" in which authors and artists grow like "crops" and "lichens," becomes ironized as he juxtaposes it with the artifice of this manufactured literary culture. Nationalism here appears quite literally unnatural, an impossible profusion of American genius.

Elsewhere Lowell more fully explained his complaint against critics: he feared their bluffs had sadly deluded readers. "A great babble is kept up concerning a national literature," he wrote in *Graham's Magazine*, "and the country, having delivered itself of the ugly likeness of a paint-bedaubed, filthy savage, smilingly dandles the rag baby upon her maternal knee, as if it were veritable flesh and blood, and would grow timely to bone and sinew."[20] As Meredith McGill observes of this bizarre, densely packed image, Lowell's "disgust at American literary production registers most powerfully as a proliferation of figures for crudity and inauthenticity."[21] But more than that, its jumble of fake Native Americans and misplaced maternal affection registers as a misrecognition of figures of inauthenticity *for* figures of authenticity. The image of the "rag baby" in the shape of a "filthy savage" is probably a topical jab at the rage for romanticized stories of Native Americans fueled by James Fenimore Cooper's Leatherstocking novels. But the reference also transforms so-called "natural man" into that consummately artificial man, a doll—even as, thanks to the press's "great babble," the nation embraces this obvious counterfeit as its genuine brainchild.

Others took Lowell's concerns one step further, depicting American literature as not just unnatural but horribly supernatural. In her essay "American Literature: Its Position in the Present Times, and Prospects for the

Future," Margaret Fuller warned that concerted attempts to produce a
national literature "must end in abortions like the monster of Frankenstein,
things with forms and the instincts of forms, but soulless and therefore
revolting."[22] An article in the *Literary World* agreed that nationalist criticism
had created a monster. Contrary to accusations that the country has "no
scope for mystery," the writer archly protests, "America is in possession of
a first-rate phantom."

> Sometimes our good phantom looms up as the Coming Man, who
> is to sing peace, progress, and the spirit of the age in novel strains
> of dulcet harmony, before unheard from the very beginning of the
> world; then it assumes the vast and shadowy likeness of a Thing, and
> is known as American nationality; and then, for a time, reverting
> to human habiliments, we have Phantom in an elegant anniversary
> address, as a sort of spiritual Napoleon, in cocked hat and tights,
> who is to rush through the provinces of literary achievement with
> something of the speed and audacity of the energetic Corsican
> corporal.[23]

The anonymous author of an article in the *American Review* declined even
to dignify his subject with the definite name of "American literature," pre-
ferring the more spectral title "Literary Phenomena." He sneers,

> An office for the sale of reputations might be opened, or a mutual
> insurance with a graduated set of prices. An American Hemans
> might be made cheap, and guaranteed for a month, though not more
> than a dozen policies to be out on this head at a time; an American
> Tennyson is worth a higher premium; the price of a Dickens would
> vary in the market as a "Martin Chuzzlewit" or a "Christmas Carol"
> happened to be his last English production; an American Coleridge
> probably cheap as the demand is considerable. We have known sev-
> eral. An American Scott should be paid for by at least a dozen cham-
> pagne suppers.[24]

The irony of the writer's suggestion that the traffic in American authors
presents a lucrative field for investment lies in the essential immateriality
of the product: their reputations are both desirable and liable to fail,
financing both a sales office and an insurance company. In fact, the writer

maintains that even the apparent lifespan of literary reputations is illusory: "A newspaper reputation can be made in a day, and by picking and ordinary care may be made to last like the gravedigger's tanner, 'some eight year or nine year,' . . . by special conjuror six months longer, till it falls to pieces, 'a nearly liquid mass of loathsome, detestable putrescence'" (405). In a remarkable instance of the intertextuality characteristic of so much antebellum print culture, this final quotation compares the state of American literature to one of its recent inventions: Poe's tale "The Facts in the Case of M. Valdemar," which had been published in the *American Review* ten months earlier. (In fact, one might argue that the magazine's resurrection of the tale in this article actually exemplifies the extraordinary measures used to extend literary lives that it condemns.) "The Facts in the Case of M. Valdemar" relates the narrator's attempt to mesmerize Valdemar on his deathbed in order to place him in a state of suspended animation. The patient exhibits all the physical signs of death but still breathes and even, when addressed, tries to speak. Months pass, until one day the narrator attempts to awaken Valdemar, at which point he cries out, "*I say to you that I am dead!*" and melts into the disgusting puddle cited in "Literary Phenomena." Significantly, the voice does not emerge voluntarily from Valdemar but is called forth by the interventions of the narrator, who "earnestly struggled" to "re-compose" his subject.[25] When the author of "Literary Phenomena" borrows the scene to picture American literature as past death and nearly bodiless, but horrifyingly articulate nonetheless, he capitalizes on this potential pun on printing to assert that it is "sustain[ed]" by that "special conjurer," the press.[26] In its appropriation of Poe's story, "Literary Phenomena" accuses literary nationalist enthusiasts of artificially animating a body of literature that is better off dead.

Moreover, if the reference to Poe's tale sharpens the writer's critique, the tale's dubious genre adds insult to injury. For not only does the allusion compare American literature to a hideous talking corpse; it simultaneously compares American literature to a hoax, and a successful one at that. On its initial publication, "The Facts in the Case of M. Valdemar" created considerable consternation along the East Coast: the *Popular Record of Modern Science* reprinted it as a news report, and the *New York Tribune* struggled to assure the "sorely puzzled" that it was "of course a romance."[27] The reception history of "The Facts in the Case of M. Valdemar" piles additional charges on American literature, which in this light appears not only grotesque but also consummately fraudulent. The article's allusion, in other words, registers the disappearance of the kinds of printed "facts" advertised in Poe's title, associating American literature with trickery instead.

Thus when Alexis de Tocqueville regretfully observed that American writers "inflate their imaginations and swell them out beyond bounds, so that they achieve gigantism, missing real grandeur" and "abandoning truth and reality, create monsters," he merely repeated a common complaint among his hosts. They also shared Tocqueville's sense that the false claims of American literature had very real consequences for national identity. "I have no fear that the poetry of democratic peoples will be found timid or that it will stick too close to the earth," Tocqueville continued; "I am much more afraid that it will spend its whole time getting lost in the clouds and may finish up by describing an entirely fictitious country."[28]

An Expanding Nation: Puffery, Currency Inflation, and Land Bubbles

For readers in the United States, Tocqueville's images of gross inflation and dangerous buoyancy would have all but named the quintessential mechanism behind literature's empty "gigantism": the vigorous antebellum puffing system. Of all the mechanisms that overextended American literature, the puffing system demands particular attention for several reasons. The first is simply a matter of its pervasiveness. Although critics since the nineteenth century have tended to relegate puffery to embarrassed footnotes or humorous anecdotes, it was less the exception than the rule of antebellum literary culture. Second, puffery was so fundamental that it generated a rich figurative language to describe American literature, which traded on its resemblance to inflated currency and land bubbles—timely metaphors that not only indict literature for its fraudulence but link that fraudulence to the overexertions of nation-building. Finally, examining puffery transfigures the dominant model for print culture by revealing the devices that swelled the public sphere of letters. Thus, while the controversies over the puffing system provide a counterhistory of what we have come to know as the print public sphere, they also suggest that the very notion of a print public sphere may itself be an artifact of the puffing system's machinations.

Under the puffing system, reviewers and editors promoted, or "puffed," certain works without regard to merit. The term "puffery" dates back to eighteenth-century Britain, but its practice in the antebellum United States

Blow ye the trumpet in Zion

Mutual Puffing.

Figure 3: Two puffing magazine editors, from "Mutual Puffing," *Old American Comic Almanac* (1841). (Courtesy of the American Antiquarian Society)

was widely agreed to surpass that of its inventors. By the late 1830s it had become, as the *Baltimore Monument* wryly observed, "an established profession," so much so that it furnished a visual joke for the 1839 edition of the *Old American Comic Almanac*, which pictured two bloated editors puffing each other up with bellows (figure 3).[29] As puffery developed into the literary critical norm, it came to encompass a wide array of ingenious arrangements to promote the fortunes of various literary cliques, including paid reviews, self-reviews, and exchanges of favors. I discuss these efforts later in the chapter, but I want to begin with the broadest and perhaps most notorious example of the form, the "unfortunate propensity," as one critic put it, "to admire indiscriminately, and with little qualification, *everything American*."[30] Nationalist puffing remained "our general editorial course" well into the 1840s, at least according to its detractors.[31] In the years, since, however, it has largely faded from critical memory. When more recent literary critics have acknowledged this history of nationalist puffery at all, they have tended to explain it away as a short-lived and ultimately inconsequential response to the casual disdain of English reviewers made famous by Sydney Smith's much quoted slight: "Who reads an American book?" But Smith seems to have posed his question in response to extant puffery. He continues, "When these questions are fairly and favourably answered, their laudatory epithets may be allowed: But, till that can be done, we would seriously advise them to keep clear of superlatives."[32] Although British taunts may have accelerated the American puffing system, it cannot be attributed to them. Puffery, as its critics recognized, was perhaps the only natural outgrowth of literary nationalism.

These critics offered dire predictions of nationalist puffery's destructive effects on American literature, often in terms that themselves notably overstate the development of American literature at that moment. "There is no abuse of the press so detrimental to the progress of the national intellect, as the present system of puffing," a typical article on the subject warned; it "spreads, as a taint of mildew, over our whole literature," another complained.[33] The "Literary Reviews," an article titled "American Criticism on American Literature" concluded severely, "are obnoxious to the charge of giving currency to false doctrine in Literature, and of misleading those who rely on their published opinions."[34] Even Poe, who placed considerably less faith in literary nationalism than many of his colleagues, warned that the "indiscriminate laudation of American books" is "a system which, more than any other one thing in the world, had tended to the depression of that 'American Literature' whose elevation it was designed to effect."[35] In an appreciative review of Lambert Wilmer's 1841 satire of the literary scene, *The Quacks of Helicon*, Poe elaborated further: "Should the opinions promulgated by our press at large be taken, in their wonderful aggregate, as an evidence of what American literature absolutely is, (and it may be said that, in general, they are really so taken,) we shall find ourselves the most enviable set of people upon the face of the earth. Our fine writers are legion. Our very atmosphere is redolent of genius; and we, the nation, are a huge, well-contented chameleon, grown pursy by inhaling it."[36] In Poe's monstrous imagery, literary nationalism endangers not only literature but also the nation itself. Far from defining "we, the nation," literary nationalism places its identity in doubt, swelling it with ersatz "genius" until it becomes "a huge, well-contented chameleon" with no fixed character of its own.

Other writers similarly seized on the metaphor of puffing to portray American literature as grotesquely inflated to false proportions, literally larger than life. An 1847 verse satire of the contemporary literary scene by the pseudonymous "Lavante," *The Poets and Poetry of America* (which ridicules the Rufus Griswold anthology of the same name), offers an ironic tribute to the era's overblown cultural and technological progress:

> What age can boast improvements like our own,
> When men to gods, and idiots bards have grown?
> No want of rhyme, though oft as light as chaff,
> Vain as a bustle or a cenotaph;
> Dreams, clouds, or gas-light, all are made
> At cheapest rate by *Espy* or a blade!
> Oh wondrous age! whose glories far excel
> All which romancers dream or fictions tell!
> When monster banks can raise a monstrous panic,
> And infants gain their growth by means galvanic![37]

The passage derides the pretensions of American poetry by juxtaposing its ready manufacture with its bogus character, comparing it first to a series of objects whose magnificent forms belie their meager content (as bustles delineate false curves and cenotaphs mark empty tombs), and then to spurious versions of natural phenomena. Any American hack can fabricate "dreams" as gas lamps make light and as James Pollard Espy, the meteorologist whose investigations into storms made him a popular lecturer in the early 1840s, made clouds in an early version of a cloud chamber—artificially, and for a price.[38] Next we see American literature analogized to another "monster," this time the so-called "Monster" Second National Bank of the United States, which Jacksonians accused of causing the massive currency inflation that led to the Panic of 1837. *The Poets and Poetry of America* offers one last memorable trope for American literature in the form of a child whose development is sped "by means galvanic," a reference to the contemporaneous craze for wearing galvanic batteries on the body to spur growth. Like fashionable prostheses, inflated currency, and quack medicine, the "Poets and Poetry of America" exceed "all which romancers dream or fictions tell," making American literature's greatest imaginative feat the story of its own existence.

As a term, puffing gained particular traction because it linked American literature with two other conspicuous examples of national overreaching: inflated currency, as in Lavante's poem, and land bubbles. The Jacksonian era has become known as the market revolution, but as Charles Sellers demonstrates, this term's concision belies the actual development of capitalism in the United States, which was contentious, messy, and fraught with doubt.[39] Nineteenth-century Americans did increasingly translate goods into money; historian Edward Pessen calculates that the value of notes in circulation swelled fiftyfold between 1821 and 1837.[40] But it is important to specify that this number represents the *face* value, which inevitably required its own evaluation. Before the National Bank Act of 1863, currency was not issued by the federal government but by over a thousand individual banks, led throughout the 1820s by the Second National Bank of the United States (which was in fact private, but held the government's deposits). Expanding transportation and communication networks, western land speculation, and laissez-faire ideology encouraged the banks to issue currency and extend credit in ever growing quantities, creating dangerous levels of inflation and, in the case of the Second National Bank, consolidating enormous influence over the economy. When in 1832, Andrew Jackson broke the power of the Second National Bank by vetoing the renewal of the bank's charter and transferring the government's deposits to a number of state banks, he assumed that dissolving the Bank would restrain the ballooning credit economy. But state-chartered and private banks also proved susceptible to the charms of soft money, and their solvency was often fleeting. Throughout the 1830s and well into the 1840s, the economy swung between periods of inflation and deflation, as banks issued currency in quantities that far exceeded specie reserves and then, unable to redeem notes, suspended payment. Not surprisingly, enterprising counterfeiters were quick to take advantage of the system; several historians put the number of counterfeit bills in circulation as high as forty percent, and contemporaneous accounts were even more dire.[41] But as Stephen Mihm points out in his illuminating history of nineteenth-century counterfeiting, counterfeiters did not break economic laws so much as capitalize on an economy already riven by ambiguity, "teeming with notes neither totally real nor completely counterfeit: genuine bills of banks that had suspended specie payments or had gone into receivership; notes of defunct banks that had been altered to imitate still-thriving concerns; genuine notes of solid banks that had been 'raised' from a lower denomination to a higher one, notes that purported to be the issues of legitimate banks but looked nothing like the real thing; notes of banks that sounded genuine, but did not exist; and real notes of 'wildcat' banks with little or nothing in the way of assets backing their promises to pay."[42] At any given moment, Americans literally did not know what their money was worth. Such financial chaos both led to and was in turn aggravated by the panics and depressions that frequently shook the antebellum economy, most disastrously in 1837 and 1857. The unreliability of antebellum currency affected all commodities, but as a metaphor it stuck especially fast to literature, whose paper-thin representations rivaled its own.[43]

Ironically, one of the most striking uses of paper money as a trope for literary fraudulence comes from a text central to narratives of American cultural authenticity, Ralph Waldo Emerson's "Nature" (1836). Emerson opens "Nature" with a familiar call to break the cultural dominance of other times and other places, demanding, "Why should not we also enjoy an original relation to the universe?"[44] Like the literary nationalists, Emerson insists that such originality should come naturally to Americans: the "floods of life" around us, he explains, "invite us, by the powers they supply, to action proportioned to nature" (7). Emerson does not locate this nature as precisely as he would the following year in "The American Scholar," where he urges "the sluggard intellect of this continent" to discard "the sere remains of foreign harvests" and cultivate its own intellectual growth.[45] Nonetheless, when he exclaims, "How does Nature deify us with a few and cheap elements!" his examples pit "Nature" and "us" against Europe and the classical world. Crucially, the essay's invocation of a geo-determinist logic that Emerson condenses as "new lands, new men, new thoughts" suggests that there is no nature so natural as the New World's nature (7). The American poet's role, then, is to illuminate nature so that others may fully apprehend it, or to use language to draw out the "occult relation between man and the vegetable" (10).[46] But not far into the essay, the poet's idealized sympathy with nature suddenly veers into a nightmarish vision of its corruption: "When simplicity of character and the sovereignty of ideas is broken up by the prevalence of secondary desires,—the desire of riches, of pleasure, of power, and of praise,—and duplicity and falsehood take place of simplicity and truth, the power over nature as an interpreter of the will is in a degree lost; new imagery ceases to be created, and old words are perverted to stand for things which are not; a paper currency is employed, when there is no bullion in the vaults. In due time the fraud is manifest, and words lose all power to stimulate the understanding or the affections" (20). The entrance of these all too ordinary "secondary desires" suddenly overwhelms Emerson's vision of the American poet, transforming his ideal linguistic specie into linguistic speciousness. Emerson's currency metaphor, a product of the massive inflation that would lead to crisis a year later, evokes the complete collapse of representation. A "paper currency is employed" not to stand in for a gold standard of value, but only "when there is no bullion in the vaults"—a worryingly recursive bit of rhetoric for the poet, whose currency by definition lies in paper. This essay, which begins so boldly, shows unbidden the project of a natural poetics founder-ing into a fraudulence from which it never fully recovers.

When Emerson goes on in "Nature" to invoke the poet's "imperial muse," who "subordinates[s] nature for the purposes of expression" (31), he unwittingly offers the reader a fuller picture of antebellum Americans' appetite for "paper currency" of all kinds. Expansionism, perhaps the chief form nationalism took in the 1830s and 1840s, became one of the primary engines of financial inflation as sales of public lands fueled a rash of western land bubbles that swelled the credit economy to the bursting point. Land sellers drew up elaborate municipal plans and advertised them to potential investors in the northeast, who eagerly poured their money into these "paper towns." In Cairo, Illinois, the notorious capital of frontier specula-tion (where a suburb called "Future City" still exists today), the Cairo City and Canal Company issued its prospectus along with a tempting array of documentation, all equally disingenuous. This included the proposed city's articles of agreement with the Illinois Central Rail Road (for a line that was not built until 1855), a map showing planned improvements (although it neglected to state that they had not yet taken place), testimonies to the healthfulness of the location (which was infested with mosquitos), and a deed of trust with the New York Life Insurance and Trust Company. The volume also conveniently tipped in a bond certificate, along with coupons to redeem interest, and a stock certificate, for bolder speculators. Yet Cairo's "mine of golden hope" was built "on the faith of monstrous repre-sentations," as a horrified Charles Dickens observed on his 1842 visit to the United States. In person he saw: "A dismal swamp, on which the half-built houses rot away: cleared here and there for the space of a few yards, and teeming then with rank, unwholesome vegetation, in whose baleful shade the wretched wanderers who are tempted hither, droop, and die, and lay their bones; . . . a hotbed of disease, an ugly sepulchre, a grave uncheered by any gleam of promise: a place without one single quality in earth, or air, or water, to commend it: such is this dismal Cairo."[47] Two years later, Dickens would memorialize Cairo as "Eden," "the flourishing city" in which a naïve Martin Chuzzlewit invests all of his savings, only to skirt death on its pestilent banks. The accompanying illustrations contrast "The Thriving City of Eden as It Appeared on Paper" (figure 4) with "The Thriving City of Eden as it Appeared in Fact" (figure 5). As the second illustration underscores, of Eden's few decayed cabins, the "most tottering, abject, and forlorn among them, was called, with great propriety, the Bank and National Credit Office. It had some feeble props about it, but was settling deep down in the mud, past all recovery."[48] Dickens's joke about the "great propriety" of the decrepit "National Credit Office" suggests that while Cairo appears a world away from the country's more prosperous metropolises, it is not exceptional but representative. As Martin's traveling companion Mark Tapley puts it, Cairo is "a reg'lar little United States in itself."[49]

With land bubbles as with currency inflation, and often in the same breath, a chorus of contemporary observers eagerly conflated (and deflated) the nation's literary and financial situations. When George Lippard, in his short-lived 1843 serial "The Spermaceti Papers," mocked the literati's zeal to invent "Something higher than the Rocky Mountains—deeper than the Atlantic—broader than the Pacific!" he set it in not in Philadelphia, where the writers and editors he skewered actually lived, but in Cairo, "a great field for literary enterprise." There his knot of puffers, blowhards, and hacks, masquerading as a long "list of 'Distinguished American Contributors,'" set up their "editorial sanctum"—not coincidentally, with a view of "the deserted ***** Bank."[50] Likewise, when poet and journalist Lambert Wilmer devoted his satire *The Quacks of Helicon* to exposing "the system of universal puffery," he did so by analogizing it to both currency inflation and land bubbles.[51] "Bold imposture rules," Wilmer contends,

When pseudo-critics and their authors try
Who best can utter or enact the lie,
And seem and say what is not, to mislead
By bold mendacity of word and deed;

The thriving City of Eden, as it appeared on paper.

Figure 4: "The Thriving City of Eden as It Appeared on Paper," from Charles Dickens, *Martin Chuzzlewit* (1844). (Courtesy of the Newberry Library)

The thriving City of Eden, as it appeared in fact.

Figure 5: "The Thriving City of Eden as It Appeared in Fact," from Charles Dickens, *Martin Chuzzlewit* (1844). (Courtesy of the Newberry Library)

When fools, like merchants just about to break,
Unite their stock and interests at stake
In corporations, chartered to commit
Base frauds on all the currency of wit;
While every member of the firm is bless'd
With all the aid and vouchings of the rest,
Resolv'd the common credit to uphold,
And substitute their rags and brass for gold. (9)

"Pseudo-critics and their authors," like bankers and land agents, conspire to keep the "common credit" afloat by flooding the market with worthless scrip—whether currency or literature. In mock resignation, Wilmer concludes,

'Twould seem no less than destiny's decree
That we the victims of all frauds should be:
Our literature and currency are both
Curs'd with the evil of an overgrowth;

.   .   .   .

By banks and bards we slavishly submit
To be o'er-ruled, o'er-ridden and o'er writ. (34)

The comparison with "banks" proves the "bards'" title a sham. Far from serving as the voice of the people, American literature here outstrips its "o'er-ruled, o'er-ridden and o'er writ" subjects. So what subtends, or distends, this nation of puffed-up authors? Initially, Wilmer pictures the residents of the "temple" of American literature as "dark, hideous forms of novelist and bard," recalling Fuller's "soulless forms" and the *Literary World*'s national phantoms. But a closer examination reveals that their distorted proportions result from natural causes. He finds:

Each form compos'd of vapor or of wind.
And, as inflated bladders, when compress'd,
Send forth a windy murmur from their windy breast,
So these, responsive with vindictive groans,
May shed mephitic fumes and filthy tones;
And, were my nasal faculties less stout,
'Tis more than likely they might stink me out. (8)

As Wilmer learns at his peril, the afflatus of American literature proves not only inflated but flatulent, harboring a noxious threat to those who would dare to burst its bubble.[52]

Yet if currency inflation and land bubbles proved useful tropes to illustrate the problem of American literary fraudulence, they might also have supplied a kind of rhetorical solution. Theoretically, both currency and land index a baseline of value: specie reserves, in the former case, and use value, in the latter. But even under the best circumstances, literary value cannot be referred to such a baseline—and certainly this moment, when the value of literature in the United States was very much in doubt, was not the best of circumstances. While comparisons to inflated currency and land bubbles clearly condemn American literature for its fraudulence and causally tie that fraudulence to the labors of nation-building, they simultaneously offer a fantasy of valuation for a value that could never be satisfactorily assessed. Indeed, these analogies, which rhetorically pose a solution to the very problem they diagnose, raise the possibility that as angry as they often were, critiques of puffery as a whole might have served a similar function. There is something tautological, even wishful, about the dire warnings against puffery's impact on American literature, given how little "American literature" existed in the foreign reprint-dominated 1830s and 1840s. That is, the panic over puffery projected a "whole literature," to return to the words of one of the critics above, under attack where only the most fitful and contested attempts existed, just as warnings against "false doctrine in literature" suggested there might be a true doctrine to uphold against it. Such unexpected rewards of disapproval leave us with the counterintuitive notion that nationalist puffery and its critics may ultimately have served similar ends, for critics' eagerness to defend American literature from puffery's destructive effects itself fosters the idea that there was an American literature whose integrity could be defended.

Democratic Representations

Up to this point, I have concentrated on explicit cases of literary nationalist puffery, which extolled books on the basis of their American authorship. Yet while expressly nationalist puffery arguably constituted the most notorious example of the form, these cases actually only provide part of the picture, for both puffery and the problems it posed for literary nationalism extended well beyond the direct promotion of "home literature" to less obvious attempts at manufacturing literary reputations. Since the Philadelphia publisher Mathew Carey founded and assumed editorship of the *American Museum* in 1787, the book trades and literary reviews had been intertwined, and relations between the two remained cooperative, to say the least, until well into the middle of the nineteenth century. Harper and Brothers ran both their own publishing house and *Harper's Monthly Magazine*, for instance, while George Palmer Putnam did the same for *Putnam's Magazine*, dual roles that allowed the publishers to direct readers' tastes to their own catalogs. In these cases, puffery promoted books for reasons more private than nationalist, such as financial gain, cultural capital, or literary reputation.

One might expect that the ubiquity of puffery would have diffused the pressure on literary nationalism, which emerges, after all, as just one inflationary mechanism among many. But even when puffery did not overtly dilate upon the nation, it was still seen to threaten the integrity of American literature. The problem lay as much in the form of the puffing system—the manipulation of literary criticism—as in the specific content of its overblown claims, because the practice of disinterested criticism was itself so crucial to the literary identity claimed for the nation. According to many observers, literary criticism suited the national temperament as many feared imaginative writing did not. As William Alfred Jones, a member of the Young America clique, explained, "Criticism should flourish in this country, if no other form of prose writing meet with favor, for Americans are confessedly an acute and shrewd race. These faculties applied to the judgment of books and authors, by educated men, ought to be made the most of in the absence of original power and creative genius."[53] Unlike imaginative writing, literary criticism appealed to antebellum Americans' reputation for hard-nosed rationality, or what Neil Harris has termed their "operational aesthetic," "a delight in observing process and examining for literal truth."[54] Literary criticism's pursuit of "literal truth" possessed all the more appeal because, as we have seen, its object of inquiry was widely considered to be rather less than true. Thus James Russell Lowell's revulsion at the prospect of the nation cuddling its grotesque literary nationalist "rag baby" quickly led him to the conclusion that "before we have an American literature, we must have an American criticism."[55]

Most important, however, editors and critics assured readers that literary criticism could manifest an American identity that imaginative writing struggled to define. All along, proponents of literary nationalism had wrestled with a perplexing question: given that a national literature was in order, what made a literature national? "Home literature" must not only come from "home writers," literary nationalists maintained; it must also treat "home themes." Cornelius Mathews, perhaps the most strident partisan of literary nationalism, helpfully ticked off a list of native resources: "descriptions of our scenery," "the illustration of passing events," "the preservation of what history has rescued from the past," and "the exhibition of the manners of the people."[56] But others looked askance at what they saw as a myopic obsession with Native Americans, Revolutionary War heroes, and, above all, the glories of Niagara Falls. In his novel *Kavanagh*, even the normally decorous Longfellow twitted literary nationalism in the person of a blustering Mr. Hathaway, plainly based on Mathews, who intends to found a magazine (called *The Niagara*, of course) that will foster an American literature "commensurate with Niagara, and the Alleghenies, and the Great Lakes!"[57] With "home themes" a target of easy ridicule, many advocated a different approach to writing nationally. "The vital principle of an American national literature must be democracy," the *United States Magazine and Democratic Review* announced in its first issue in 1837: "We have a principle—an informing soul—of our own, our democracy, though we allow it to languish uncultivated; this must be the animating spirit of our literature, if, indeed, we would have a national American literature."[58] The *Boston Quarterly Review* agreed that a national literature "must be informed with the national soul," and the "national soul of America is democracy." "This Idea is the only element of life that American literature can possess," the magazine insisted; "Ours must be a democratic literature."[59] By 1842, it was no longer a matter of infusing literature with the spirit of democracy. This time the *United States Magazine and Democratic Review* could simply proclaim, "The spirit of Literature and the spirit of Democracy are one."[60]

Some writers interpreted the injunction to produce a democratic literature thematically and encouraged authors to include a greater range of plots, settings, and characters in their works. Others interpreted it economically and advocated for publishers to issue domestic books at prices that would supplant the "cheap and nasty" foreign reprints most easily available to working-class readers. But to those who made claims on behalf of American literature's democratic character, the burgeoning genre of criticism offered especially promising evidence of national literary freedom, rational judgment, and self-determination. Its operational aesthetic proved especially attractive because, as Harris explains, it exploited "a peculiarly patriotic position in Jacksonian America." The confidence it placed in individual powers of judgment complemented a "concern with popular verdicts and diffused competence," allowing P. T. Barnum, Harris's primary exemplar of the operational aesthetic, to frame even his most dubious exhibits at the American Museum as exercises in democratic citizenship. When pressed to say whether they were real or fakes, Barnum replied that such decisions were precisely the point: visitors had the "right to form their own opinions."[61] The same rhetoric of principled rationality likewise allowed literary critics to portray their work as "not an art but a service," in Nina Baym's words.[62] Across the Atlantic, literary criticism might be beholden to ossified conventions or the fiat of an elite group of tastemakers, but in the United States critics served as public servants. As one writer put it, "They are regarded with respect, as men above the reach or the persuasion of contemptible motives; and with the law of courteous impartiality guiding their pens, they perform, with honest impulses, their duty to the literary efforts of their countrymen."[63] The *United States Magazine and Democratic Review* agreed with this picture of the critic's disinterested independence: "It is his office—a most ungrateful task—to strip off the disguises of imposture, to reduce the bloated swaggerer to his original proportions, and utterly to discard all those patches of art and disguises of custom, that would make the world believe genius existed, when not indeed a particle of it was to be found."[64] Such an enlightened sense of civic responsibility made literary criticism the ideal manifestation of the nation's democratic institutions.

If the antebellum critics' faith in the democratic structure of the world of letters sounds familiar, it may be because it anticipates a much better known theory of the relationship between literary criticism and the political realm: Jürgen Habermas's model of the print public sphere, most famously outlined in his 1962 study *The Structural Transformation of the Public Sphere*. Although Habermas bases his theory on eighteenth-century European examples, Americanists have avidly imported his model over the past two decades.[65] Moreover, because Habermas often writes in multiple registers simultaneously—mapping out the origins of the public sphere as both a linear narrative history and a structural account of its conditions of possibility, and as a phenomenon of both political and "literary" writing—Americanists have applied his model of the print public sphere to the eighteenth-century revolutionary period (which fits Habermas's overall periodization and emphasis on print culture's separation from the state), as well as the early nineteenth century (which fits his account of the rise of a commercial press and his emphasis on the constitutive role of literary criticism). David Henkin, for instance, argues that while "it is tempting . . . to follow Habermas and many twentieth-century critics of modernization in treating the public life of the nineteenth-century metropolis as a symptom of the disintegration of the Enlightenment public sphere," the urban print culture of the period "actually extended the central features of Enlightenment publicity" to "a far more inclusive and democratic public."[66] Applications of Habermas's public sphere to the nineteenth century have gained further traction because they often, as here, accord with long-standing portrayals of the antebellum print explosion as an expression of "literary democracy," to quote the title of Larzer Ziff's well-known study, in which the proliferation of print bespeaks the dispersal of political authority—depictions that echo antebellum critics' own claims.[67]

I agree with Henkin and others that Habermas's model sheds a good deal of light on early nineteenth-century print culture, but I would argue that it does so most of all when we read for the friction between Habermas's multiple registers, rather than attempting to assimilate them to one another. Although this approach makes it harder to view the print public sphere as a genuinely democratic formation, it offers a glimpse of how this image might have been created in the first place. For Habermas, when an emerging "public sphere in the world of letters" detached the notion of a political "public" from state authority, it inaugurated a more democratic formation of "civil society" defined by "people's public use of their reason."[68] Although Habermas devotes considerable attention to political discourse, like many antebellum Americans, he assigns special importance to the role of literature, and especially literary criticism, in establishing the public sphere. Thus the public sphere's transformation reaches its high point when the print culture of "pure news" gives way to the establishment of "literary journalism" specializing in "rational-critical public debate" (28, 182). Habermas explains, "A press that had evolved out of the public's use of its reason and that had merely been an extension of its debate remained thoroughly an institution of this very public: effective in the mode of a transmitter and amplifier, no longer a mere vehicle for the transportation of information but not yet a medium for culture as an object of consumption" (183).

Yet Habermas's description of the operations of the print public sphere contains a strange hiccup. "The privatized individuals coming together to form a public," he writes, "reflected critically and in public on what they had read, thus contributing to the process of enlightenment which they together promoted" (51). In this account of the "process of enlightenment," Habermas offers not one but two explanations for its development: on the one hand, it is the result of collaborative public reflection; but on the other, it is an extant idea that requires a concerted "promotion" to establish itself. In other words, although Habermas insists that enlightenment is a process, a phenomenon brought into being by a particular social configuration, in the same sentence he raises the possibility that it may actually be a deliberately crafted product. However inadvertently, Habermas's account of the origins of print "enlightenment" fleetingly locates them in a circular, self-perpetuating myth. My point here is not to debunk Habermas's account by calling attention to its contradictions, but to suggest that such local tautologies actually make his account all the more valuable to Americanists by providing a fuller picture of the print public sphere as it actually existed in the early nineteenth-century United States.

Antebellum literary critics, as we have seen, encouraged an image of their work that closely resembles Habermas's public sphere. But it is no coincidence that their shared taste for the operational aesthetic places literary critics in the company of P. T. Barnum, for even as literary criticism established itself as an important cultural institution, a flurry of newspaper jeremiads, magazine exposés, jokes, satirical poetry, and fictional accounts denounced it as a humbug. William Alfred Jones may well have believed that literary criticism should be a perfect match for American sensibilities, but he found his contemporary critics "wanting in true literary feeling, in honest enthusiasm, or as honest indignation, in independence, in knowledge," unhappily concluding, "we should not wonder at the vile subterfuges and miserable apologies for criticism, that pass under its name."[69] Even the *United States Magazine and Democratic Review* writer whom we earlier saw so enamored of the critic's capacity to "strip off the disguises of imposture" and "reduce the swaggerer to his original proportions" admitted, "And now, here, in these glorious United States of ours, how fares the art of criticism? But weakly! . . . Take the body of writers and readers in the country (one that lives on periodical literature), and see how little true, honest, and sincere criticism there is."[70] Likewise, while a writer for the *New-York Mirror* piously observed, "In the republick of letters, as in all other republicks, it must be the voice of the majority which will eventually prevail," the writer was also forced to admit, "In this age of humbug, there is no system of imposture more successful than that practiced by the reviews and critical journals of the day."[71] The glimpses of the puffing system visible from these complaints suggest that where Harris sees the operational aesthetic's "examin[ation] for literal truth" anchoring cultural practices from P. T. Barnum to the Transcendentalists, savvy authors and critics recognized that the operational aesthetic need not be a practice. It could simply be an aesthetic.

Far from "reducing" American literature to its "original proportions," criticism seemed to constitute the primary mechanism for inflating it. Consequently, at least one writer drew the same damning comparison that had plagued literary nationalism, declaring, "Reviews are the paper money of literature. . . . Like paper-money, they never give you the exact value of the article they represent; for reviewers are brokers in literature, and their trade is artifice."[72] These observers protested that the print public sphere's outward show of disinterested debate was puffed up through the quite private contrivances of editors and reviewers. Once again, Poe was on the front lines of this attack (although once again, he was guilty of the same practices that he excoriated in others).[73] In his review of Wilmer's *The Quacks of Helicon*, he attacked the "*coteries* which, at the bidding of leading booksellers, manufacture, as required from time to time, a pseudo-public opinion by wholesale," with a venom that barely tolerated punctuation.

> The prevalence of the spirit of puffery is a subject far less for merriment than for disgust. . . . Is there any man of good feeling and of ordinary understanding—is there one single individual among all our readers—who does not feel a thrill of bitter indignation, apart from any sentiment of mirth, as he calls to mind instance after instance of the purest, of the most unadulterated quackery in letters, which has risen to a high post in the apparent popular estimation, and which still maintains it, by the sole means of a blustering arrogance, or of a busy wriggling conceit, or of the most barefaced plagiarism, or even through the simple immensity of its assumptions—assumptions not only unopposed by the press at large, but absolutely supported in proportion to the vociferous clamor with which they are made—in exact accordance with their utter baselessness and untenability?[74]

The picture that emerges here is something like an inverted Habermasian print public sphere: where Habermas credits rational-critical literary journalism with precise calibrations of literary value, reliably singling out works of merit and dismissing less deserving productions, Poe insists that literary journalism functions according to the opposite principle, "absolutely support[ing]" works "in exact accordance with their utter baselessness and untenability."

Given the influence of antebellum puffery, on the one hand, and how thoroughly it has dropped out of literary historical memory, on the other, I want to take some time to anatomize its primary strategies here. In the most common arrangement, literary criticism availed itself of the rituals of gift exchange that Leon Jackson has demonstrated to be so fundamental to antebellum publishing.[75] Back-scratching "mutual admiration societies" heaped praise on each other as a matter of course, and obliging magazine editors felt no compunctions about printing the ready-made notices that publishers sent out with review copies.[76] The *Southern Literary Journal* explained the system in a three-part series of articles:

> "My friend," says the editor, "whom I have so plentifully bespattered, surely will not, if there is such a thing as gratitude in the world, forget his kind eulogist. I may reasonably expect, engaged as I am in a similar vocation, to get part, at least, of my praise back again, and it may, perchance, be repaid with interest." Thus, the press, which should be employed to enlighten the public mind, is prostituted to a miserable puffing system, and we have nothing but puffs, re-puffs, and sur-re-puffs, issued from our presses from one end of the continent to the other. They constitute, in fact, a large share of what is styled at the present day, American literature, and, if published by themselves, would certainly fill folios.[77]

Of course, not every would-be author or publisher could expect to be on intimate terms with every editor, but what friendship could not accomplish, complimentary copies might, as Jackson and William Charvat have documented.[78] Failing that, there was always the possibility of cash payoffs. Poe took aim at this practice in his 1844 satire of magazine publishing, "The Literary Life of Thingum Bob," in which the poet-narrator, author of a poem that runs "To pen an Ode upon the 'Oil-of-Bob' / Is all sorts of a

job," boasts that "the extent of my renown will be best estimated by reference to the editorial opinions of the day."[79] The "critical notices" he
reprints do indeed all fawn over his "diamond-like effusion," but they contain "the hieroglyphical marks, 'Sep. 15–1t,' appended to each of the critiques"—signifying that they have been paid to run on that date for one
time (1137, 1136). (Tellingly, Thingum Bob's subject, "Oil-of-Bob," is patent
medicine.) As absurd as the story is, Poe hardly seems to have exaggerated.
Rufus Griswold, whom Charvat singles out as the era's most energetic
critic-for-hire, performed such jobs on a regular basis. Charvat quotes a
letter from the Philadelphia publisher T. B. Peterson to Griswold: "I would
like you to get a good notice of [Peterson's twenty-five-cent edition of Anne
Brontë's *Agnes Gray*] in the Tribune and any other papers in New York you
can, *all of them if possible*, and you can send your Bill to me for your
trouble."[80] Moreover, Griswold enjoyed "powerful connections with some
thirteen publishing houses, twelve magazines, and eight newspapers,"
arrangements which made his opinions, if not his name, ubiquitous.[81]

A critic's job, in other words, did not necessarily entail criticism, an
irony Herman Melville drives home in his 1852 novel *Pierre; or, The Ambiguities*. In a chapter titled "Young America in Literature" (which later Melville slyly rephrases as "juvenile American literature"), the teenage Pierre
attains literary celebrity after gracing magazine pages with such pieces as
"The Tropical Summer: A Sonnet," "The Weather: A Thought," "Life: An
Impromptu," and "The Pippin: A Paragraph." The critics

> bestowed upon him those generous commendations, which, with
> one instantaneous glance, they had immediately perceived was his
> due. They spoke in high terms of his surprising command of lan-
> guage; they begged to express their wonder at his euphonious con-
> struction of sentences; they regarded with reverence the pervading
> symmetry of his general style. But transcending even this profound
> insight into the deep merits of Pierre, they looked infinitely beyond,
> and confessed their complete inability to restrain their unqualified
> admiration for the highly judicious smoothness and genteelness of
> the sentiments and fancies expressed.[82]

When "an elderly friend of a literary turn" ventures, "this is very high
praise, I grant, and you are a surprisingly young author to receive it; but I
do not see any criticisms as yet":

"Criticisms," cried Pierre, in amazement; "why sir, they are all criticisms! I am the idol of the critics!"

"Ah," sighed the elderly friend, as if suddenly reminded that that
was true after all—"Ah!" (246)

With the proceeds of his celebrated poems, Pierre buys cigars,

> so that the puffs which indirectly brought him his dollars were again
> returned, but as perfumed puffs; perfumed with the sweet leaf of
> Havana. So that this highly-celebrated and world-renowned
> Pierre—the great author—whose likeness the world had never seen
> (for had he not repeatedly refused the world his likeness?), this
> famous poet, and philosopher, author of "The Tropical Summer: a
> Sonnet"; against whose very life several desperadoes were darkly
> plotting (for had not the biographers sworn they would have it?),
> there he would sit smoking, and smoking, mild and self-festooned
> as a vapory mountain. (263)

Melville's manic punning takes the puffing system's manipulations of writing at their word, while his choice of words to play on drives the point
home: all relate to the media apparatus of celebrity. Thus figurative magazine puffs recur as literal cigar puffs (though both are equally "vapory"),
while the jokes on "likeness" and "lives" collapse representations (portrai-
ture, biography) with the realities they represent. What makes Melville's
parody both outrageous and accurate is its fulfillment of antebellum literary
culture's virtual reality: in a system that pivots on the power of words,
particularly printed ones, Melville imagines a world in which print has outstripped its subject, a world the verbal makes in its own image, rather than
the other way around.

While "mutual admiration societies" promoted books through
exchanges of favors and money, in another branch of the puffing system,
authors simply assumed the roles of critics themselves. Well into the late
nineteenth century, most editorials and criticism in American periodicals
were unsigned, a convention that preserved a republican pose of disinterest.
Moreover, critics often turned the impression of impersonality into outright plurality through a habitual use of the pronoun "we," which "has
a most imposing and delusive sound," Washington Irving observed in a

Knickerbocker article on contemporary criticism. (His own article, by contrast, appeared under the instantly recognizable pseudonym Geoffrey Crayon—a name that, not coincidentally, affiliates itself with embodied manuscript writing over the disembodied ruses of print.) Irving explains, "The reader pictures to himself a conclave of learned men, deliberating gravely and scrupulously on the merits of the book in question; and when they have united in a conscientious verdict, publishing it for the benefit of the world: whereas the criticism is generally the crude and hasty production of an individual." Self-effacement thus offered excellent opportunities for self-aggrandizement, as Irving recognized: "Such the mystic operation of anonymous writing; such the potential effect of the pronoun *we*, that [the critic's] crude decisions, fulminated through the press, become circulated far and wide, control the opinions of the world, and give or destroy reputation."[83]

While anonymity proliferated individual opinions in the guise of a critical consensus, it conferred the additional benefit of allowing authors to review their own works with impunity. Although it is impossible to estimate the extent to which authors took advantage of the expedient of self-reviewing, bibliographic scholarship has turned up a number of impostures that provide some insight into the practice. Fittingly, one of the best-documented histories of self-reviewing belongs to the self-proclaimed poet of democracy, Walt Whitman, who inserted anonymous reviews of *Leaves of Grass* in the *United States Review*, the *American Phrenological Journal*, and the *Brooklyn Daily Times*, which rapturously declared, "An American bard at last!"[84] But Whitman was hardly alone. In an unsigned 1847 article in the *United States Magazine and Democratic Review*, Cornelius Mathews, the inexhaustible champion of home literature, analyzes its importance and enumerates its representatives across time—Shakespeare, Milton, Addison, Montesquieu, Scott—before announcing, "The American writer who seems most deeply to have felt the want of, and who has most ably and earnestly, as well as earliest, insisted upon, nationality in our literature, is Mr. Cornelius Mathews." He goes on to quote himself at length.[85] Perhaps it is inevitable, then, that soon after becoming a poet, Poe's Thingum Bob takes up a career as a critic, and that his first act is to pen a review of his own "Oil-of-Bob," "occupying thirty-six pages" (1141). An 1834 poem entitled "Puffing, a Fable" memorably embodies the practice in a hen who acquires a "barn-yard reputation" by cackling each time she lays an egg, provoking her irritated fellow fowls to ask, "why need you publish all your joys?"

She, meanwhile scratching with one leg,
Soon gracefully up-drew it;
And poised upon a single peg,
Cried: "Oh! 'tis time you knew it;
'Tis the fashion now to lay an egg,
And then, sir, to REVIEW IT."[86]

In an ingenious variation on self-reviewing, the Philadelphia playwright, novelist, and critic James McHenry reputedly specialized in falsifying public demand for his works. In a long rejoinder to McHenry's slights to its own stable of authors in the *American Quarterly Review*, the *Knickerbocker* accused him of a pattern of "deceiving the public":

> Did he not once determine to take the general applause by storm, and on the publication of one of his unhappy novels, repeatedly stop the press, and cause the *second, third*, and *fourth* editions to be inserted in the title-page of the *same* impression? Was not the *third* edition for sale at the book-stores before the *first* was bound? . . . It is only by such modes of grasping at ephemeral praise, through trickery, coupled with advance eulogies and surmises in newspapers . . . that this critic has ever been honored, even with ridicule . . . . Thus, the argument spoken of as contained in his last Review— namely, that we have no great, long poem,—no big book of Ameri- can metre, and that there is now a want of it—is only to herald a manuscript volume of his, in some nineteen books.[87]

McHenry's disingenuous title pages, which reset a single line of type in what was otherwise the same print run, fabricate agency on behalf of the reading public by inventing an appetite for his work that necessitates a fourth edition. Furthermore, McHenry's disingenuous critical interventions use anonymity to disguise his own undue agency in determining the book's reception. Under other circumstances, the critic explains, "we might let such literary empirics make themselves as ridiculous as they please. But when, *because anonymous*, their bad taste infects even a limited number of readers, their influence becomes offensive."[88] While cultural and literary historians of the nineteenth century tend to emphasize the anxieties associ- ated with urban anonymity, perhaps the most troubling aspect of the Amer- ican literary crowd was the possibility that it was not anonymous at all.[89]

One "apologue" of puffing thus recounts the story of three rogues who swindle a Brahmin determined to sacrifice a sheep by persuading him to buy "an ugly dog, lame and blind," instead. The conspirators pull off the ruse by pretending to be objective strangers; each passes by and affirms that the dog is a sheep. Finally, the Brahmin, convinced that he must be delusional, buys the dog. In this fable, "calculated chiefly to benefit those who are simple enough to be gulled by a morsel of criticism," anonymity is itself a fraud.[90]

Here, too, Thingum Bob's career proves instructive, for Poe's tale juxtaposes the magazine world's pretensions to republican disinterest with its actual dependence on personal favors and abuse. When Thingum Bob becomes a magazine editor himself, he pseudonymously sends his first production to another magazine, which pronounces it "twattle" (1143). Not to be deterred,

> I reheaded the paper "Hey-Diddle-Diddle," by Thingum BOB, Esq., Author of the Ode on "The Oil-of-Bob," and Editor of the "Snapping Turtle." With this amendment, I re-enclosed it to the "Goosetherumfoodle," and, while I awaited a reply, published daily, in the "Turtle," six columns of what may be termed philosophical and analytical investigation of the literary merits of the "Goosetherumfoodle," as well as of the personal character of the editor of the "Goosetherumfoodle." At the end of a week the "Goosetherumfoodle" discovered that it had, by some odd mistake, "confounded a stupid article, headed 'Hey-Diddle-Diddle,' and composed by some unknown ignoramus, with a gem of resplendent lustre similarly entitled, the work of Thingum Bob, Esq, the celebrated author of 'The Oil-of-Bob.'" (1143–1144)

When Thingum Bob assumes what Michael Warner terms the "normally impersonal" stance of the public sphere, in which his writing would speak for him, he produces only "twattle."[91] When he throws off republican impersonality to trade on his proven cultural capital as "Author" and "Editor," however, his twattle becomes a "gem." In turn, Thingum Bob recounts, "From that day I took a liking to the 'Goosetherumfoodle,' and the result was I soon saw into the very depths of its literary merits, and did not fail to expatiate upon them, in the 'Turtle,' whenever a fitting opportunity occurred." Moreover, in "very peculiar coincidence," an identical "total revolution of opinion" transpires with each of his remaining rivals (1144).

Thingum Bob is so absurdly self-deluding that the tale seems poised to deliver his comeuppance. But instead, it ends with his reward: Thingum Bob becomes a literary celebrity whose fame "extends to the utmost ends of the earth" (1145). Far from being an object of ridicule, he proves to be a perfectly conventional participant in literary culture, as indeed his name— slang for anything or anybody—has suggested all along. When Thingum Bob begins by informing the reader that he considered titling his autobiography "Memoranda to Serve for the Literary History of America," it seems to be a delusion of grandeur; by the end, it seems all too accurate (1126). In the end, the most startling thing about "The Literary Life of Thingum Bob" is that it is not one of Poe's tales of eccentricity and madness, but a fable of antebellum print culture's normative fraudulence.

Poe's Balloons

"Must expose the wires," Poe scribbled in the notes for his unfinished study *The Living Writers of America*, and much of his fiction, like his critical writings, conducts a sustained attack on the stagecraft of print culture.[92] His attempts to expose the flimsy foundations of literary prestige are most obvious in satires like "The Literary Life of Thingum Bob, Esq.," "How to Write a Blackwood Article," "Lionizing," "X-ing a Paragrab," and "Loss of Breath." But Poe's fascination with puffing also gives a new relevance to one of his other literary enthusiasms, balloons. A relatively recent technology in the early nineteenth century, ballooning captured the public imagination, and Poe both caters to and parodies its popularity in tales like "The Unparalleled Adventure of One Hans Pfaall," "The Balloon-Hoax," "The Angel of the Odd," and "Mellonta Tauta," all of which prominently feature balloons. However, Poe's abiding obsession with inflated literary reputations raises the possibility that balloons may have appealed to him as much for their metaphorical possibilities as for their literal topicality. In an 1845 lecture on "The Poets and Poetry of America," he devoted considerable time to demonstrating that several popular poets "were afloat 'on bladders in a sea of glory'"—a metaphor the *New-York Mirror* received with enthusiasm, noting, "The pricking of these bladders, by the way, and the letting out of Miss [Catharine] Sedgwick's breath, and Professor [Samuel F. B.]

Morse's, and Mr. [Robert] Southey's, was most artistically well done."[93] I end this chapter by proposing that Poe's balloons, particularly the one built of newspapers at the center of his early tale "The Unparalleled Adventure of One Hans Pfaall," offer an especially vivid depiction of the print public sphere, while lending that phrase a relevance that Habermas never imagined. Over the course of "Hans Pfaall," the tale's ballooning plot comes to encompass many of the features of antebellum literary culture that have organized this chapter: print, American nationality, democracy, and fraudulence. These elements, which more often than not take the form of jokes, allusions, or digressions, admittedly do not add up to a very clear picture of puffery or, indeed, the adventures of Hans Pfaall. But the very looseness of their connections may tell us as much as the connections themselves, suggesting something of literature's own sliding chain of signification in these years, when it was so often called upon to represent something else.

Unexplained references to print culture constantly disrupt not only "The Unparalleled Adventure of One Hans Pfaall" but all of Poe's balloon tales, diverting their satirical charge. For example, "Mellonta Tauta," a burlesque of the 1840s from the point of view of the future, takes place on a balloon named the "Skylark," seemingly a reference to Shelley's famous poem. It may also mock Poe's old adversary Longfellow's injunction to American writers to abandon imitations of such foreign works for native themes, "Let us have no more sky-larks and nightingales," which was nearly as famous for a time.[94] Certainly Poe ties the balloon to American culture, since he abruptly ends the tale with the report of recent antiquarian discoveries that throw new light on the cultural accomplishments of Manhattan's "aboriginal inhabitants," "the Knickerbocker tribe of savages." "They were by no means uncivilized," the pedantic narrator writes to her friend, "but cultivated various arts and even sciences after a fashion of their own."[95] Balloons quite neatly figured one of the best-known "arts" that New York, foremost among major antebellum publishing centers, cultivated: puffing.

Balloons' metaphorical relation to puffing helps explain the odd cast of characters of "The Balloon-Hoax": both of the balloonists whose diaries the tale purports to excerpt are real people, but while one is Monck Mason, the inventor, the other is, seemingly inexplicably, the popular English author and magazine editor William Harrison Ainsworth. Ainsworth, however, was an exemplary product of the British puffing system. His novels were published by the English "Prince of Puffing," Henry Colbourn, and his partner (and later rival) Richard Bentley, who was nearly as notorious.

Both publishers counted on their authors' cooperation in their promotional strategies, but Ainsworth distinguished himself by becoming "the most energetic and persistent puffer among Bentley's authors," in the estimation of Bentley's biographer.[96] Poe had reviewed Ainsworth's novel *Guy Fawkes* for *Graham's Magazine* three years earlier; at the time he spent as much of the review deflating the puffs of an earlier novel by Ainsworth as he did evaluating *Guy Fawkes*.[97] The puffing system also seems to link the otherwise arbitrary events of "The Angel of the Odd," one of Poe's most baffling comic tales. The narrator, fed up with his current reading matter (which includes Joel Barlow's epic nationalist poem *The Columbiad* and Rufus Griswold's *Curiosities of American Literature*), takes up a newspaper. There he comes across a paragraph describing how a man playing the game of "puff the dart" accidentally drew his breath in, rather than pushing it out, and died as a result. "Upon seeing this I fell into a great rage, without exactly knowing why. 'This thing,' I exclaimed, 'is a contemptible falsehood—a poor hoax. . . . These fellows, knowing the extravagant gullibility of the age, set their wits to work in the imagination of impossibilities. . . . For my own part, I intend to believe nothing henceforward has any thing of the "singular" about it' " (1101–1102). Poe lifted the "puff the dart" anecdote from a Philadelphia newspaper, but he situates it in a new context (exasperation with available literature), while supplying an unexpected response (insistence that the episode is a hoax concocted by the press).[98] The narrator's newfound resolution not to believe what he reads, however, has terrible consequences: the "Angel of the Odd" immediately appears, "puff[ing] leisurely" (1109) on a pipe, and demands that the narrator renounce his skepticism. When the narrator does not, the Angel of the Odd proceeds to torment him for the rest of the story, and finally kills him—by dropping him out of a balloon.

Poe's most sustained treatment of ballooning, the magazine hoax that became known as "The Unparalleled Adventure of One Hans Pfaall," may seem like an unlikely candidate for a satire of the contemporary American literary scene.[99] The story recounts the dreamer Hans Pfaall's trip to the moon in a hot-air balloon, which he records in a journal he later sends back home, via the balloon, to be delivered by an elderly moon-man. Critics frequently read "Hans Pfaall," along with Poe's other hoaxes, as a jab at contemporary pseudoscience, and most of the story is thoroughly packed with implausible yet exhaustive explanations of the balloon's construction, Hans Pfaall's experiments with air pressure, his astronomical observations, and so on. Moreover, whatever action does not unfold in the sky takes place in Rotterdam, not the United States. But the tale's Dutch setting quickly founders under the weight of Poe's American allusions—Pfaall's inclusion of pemmican (a Native American mixture of dried meat and fat) among his provisions, for example, or the balloon's musical rendition of "Betty Martin," a popular American song in the 1830s and the source of the expression "All my eye and Betty Martin," or humbug.[100] Indeed, the seemingly problematic Dutch setting itself might direct readers toward an American location as easily as away from it. In the 1830s, "Dutch" designated New Yorkers as well as actual citizens of the Netherlands; this is the decade in which the city's (arguably the nation's) first major literary journal is launched under the name of the *Knickerbocker*, a reference to the Dutch colonists who settled in the former New Netherland.[101] The city of Rotterdam, in fact, may be particularly suited to host Poe's satire because it furnished the punchline to a contemporary joke about the magazine. According to the *Boston Evening Transcript*, the *Knickerbocker*'s famously fastidious editor, Lewis Gaylord Clark, "wrote the name of a famous Dutch city thus: Rotterd__m."[102]

It seems less likely that "Hans Pfaall" specifically addresses Clark's clique, however, than that Poe references it as shorthand for a more widespread set of critical practices. Poe wrote "Hans Pfaall" on the heels of "Tales from the Folio Club," a projected collection "intended as a burlesque upon criticism generally," and the elements of the story suggest that he did not break with his former themes completely.[103] Poe frames the story in outlandishly flowery prose that signals a literary target in addition to its apparent scientific one: "The day was warm—unusually so for the season—there was hardly a breath of air stirring; and the multitude were in no bad humor at being now and then besprinkled with friendly showers of momentary duration, that fell from the large white masses of cloud profusely distributed about the blue vault of the firmament" (387). And when the crowd of Dutch townspeople spot the balloon, they greet it with a shout whose sound "could be compared to nothing but the roaring of Niagara" (387), a seemingly incongruous reference that absurdly invokes the literary nationalists' favorite example of American grandeur. Likewise, when Pfaall initially imagines the surface of the moon as covered with "hoary and time-honored forests, and craggy precipices, and waterfalls tumbling with a loud noise into abysses without a bottom" (412), this topography bears little resemblance to the rolling Dutch countryside familiar to him. But it precisely describes the idealized vision of the American landscape that exerted such a powerful hold on contemporary literary discourse.

It comes as little surprise, then, that the vehicle Pfaall anticipates will convey him to this landscape is print itself—or more specifically, its inflation, for in "an egregious insult to the good sense of the burghers of Rotterdam" Pfaall's balloon is "manufactured entirely of dirty newspapers" (388). (Perhaps gesturing again to the peculiarly American relevance of such a notion, Poe inquires, "who, let me ask, ever heard of a balloon manufactured entirely of dirty newspapers? No man in Holland certainly.") The shape of the balloon leaves little question about the consequences of such fabrication, it "being little or nothing better than a huge fool's-cap turned upside down" (388). This fool's-cap shape images an analogy between print culture and humbug (and broadly hints at the tale's function as a hoax), but it also inscribes yet another literary pun—on "foolscap," or writing paper. The pun relies on precedent for its success: the revelation that the balloon is made of newspapers introduces the trope of paper that unpacks the "fool's cap" reference. Poe thus runs through the logic of etymological derivation backward and forward, suggesting "foolscap" from "fool's-cap" and then, through the pressure of context, making foolscap declare that it produces fool's-caps in print. Anticipating Lambert Wilmer by several years, he informs us that a "tasteless, but not odorless" (394) gas lifts this literal balloon of print, and the phrase's absurd unscientific method (who categorizes gas by taste?) alerts the reader to a different meaning of "tasteless" at work here—an aesthetic one. Later, Pfaall finds his flight in danger when he realizes that falling asleep will prevent him from attending to the air compression pump every hour, as necessary. After some thought, however, he devises a solution, "which, simple as it may seem, was hailed by me, at the moment of discovery, as an invention fully equal to that of the telescope, the steam-engine, or the art of printing itself" (415). In Poe's relentless, often awkward conjunctions of buoyancy and print, literature repeatedly replaces science as the tale's dubious principle of inflation.

Just as what Poe would later call "the most unadulterated quackery in letters," with no merit of its own, "rise[s] to a high post in the apparent popular estimation," Hans Pfaall seems singularly unqualified to achieve lift-off.[104] His wife, he recalls, "always looked upon me as an idle body—a mere make-weight—good for nothing but building castles in the air,—and was rather glad to get rid of me" (395). But Poe's convoluted wordplay folds a succession of contradictions into each other, so that ballast, far from hindering buoyancy, becomes inextricable from it; Pfaall appears not only as weight that floats but weight that floats by virtue of imaginatively defying gravity, or building castles in the air. Poe's disparaging figures of weight and weightlessness recall the double indictment implied in puffery, which condemns literature on charges of both grossness and lightness. "Puffing," that is, both levitates work that could not rise on its own and encourages artistic emptiness—an apparent contradiction that led James Russell Lowell to observe of American writers, "I am thinking not their own self-inflation will keep them from sinking; for there's this contradiction about the whole bevy,—though without the least weight, they are awfully heavy."[105] But just as Pfaall believes that the "crude ideas which, arising in ill-regulated minds, have all the appearance, may . . . often in effect possess all the force, the reality, and other inherent properties, of instinct or intuition" (392), American literary culture arises simply because it succeeds in making appearance—its vigorous promotion in print—trump reality.

Significantly, Poe identifies the print balloon of "Hans Pfaall" as a democratic phenomenon—or, more specifically, a phenomenon of democratic discourse. Pfaall undertakes his lunar journey when his business mending bellows collapses, a disaster he attributes to a surge of democratic fervor in Rotterdam. The causal logic here, as elsewhere in the tale, is loose at best, but the proliferation of print that results apparently prompts the townspeople to replace their bellows with newspapers: "We soon began to feel the effects of liberty and long speeches, and radicalism, and all that sort of thing. People who were formerly the best customers in the world, had now not a moment of time to think of us at all. They had as much as they could do to read about the revolutions, and keep up with the march of intellect and the spirit of the age. If a fire wanted fanning, it could readily be fanned with a newspaper" (391). The joke here, however, is that the newspapers of this revolutionary print culture do not "fan" metaphorical revolutionary "fires," as the first part of the passage would lead us to believe, but literal ones. Given the interchangeability Poe produces between bellows and a newspapers (bringing to mind the cartoon of "Mutual Puffing," in which the editors puff each other up with bellows), it only seems natural that these newspapers, filled with "revolutions, . . . the march of intellect and the spirit of the age," ultimately become Pfaall's balloon.

As this sequence of substitutions (bellows to newspapers to balloons) suggests, if "Hans Pfaall" materializes the puffing system in the central

image of the print balloon, puffery's primary strategies of replication, collu-
sion, and impersonation equally make their way into the pages of the tale.
Indeed, the puffing system's strategies of substitution operate so powerfully
in "Hans Pfaall" that it is easy to forget that Hans Pfaall himself never
appears in it. Instead of returning to earth in person, he sends a representative from the moon, who in turn delivers a letter from Pfaall containing the
account that comprises the bulk of the story. Poe's narration, like the workings of the puffing system, at once conceals the real Hans Pfaall and prolif-
erates a series of stand-ins: first, the lunar messenger, and second, the
written word. The balloon itself compounds the story's iterations. Built of
words, like the letter, its fool's-cap shape also echoes one association of
Pfaall's name, the Latin *follis*, or fool.[106] From here the repetitions pile up:
the messenger wears the fool's corresponding costume, a motley coat and
tight breeches, except that, to heighten the confusion, the customary bells
of the jester's hat do not appear on his own cap but on the "fool's-cap"
balloon. Finally, the other sense of "foolscap" returns us to the balloon's
paper structure and the letter it carries. And once the townspeople catch
sight of the balloon, they mirror its puffery back, as "every one to a man
replaced his pipe carefully in the corner of his mouth, and maintaining an
eye steadily upon the phenomenon, puffed, paused, waddled about, and
grunted significantly—then waddled back, grunted, paused, and finally—
puffed again" (388). The dizzying proliferation of figures that makes the
tale so difficult to follow is to the point: the practice of puffing outpaces
any of its individual manifestations. Thus while the language and practices
of literary nationalism subtend the narrative of "Hans Pfaall," antebellum
print culture's systemic logic of proliferation and impersonation makes its
way into the text as a problem of reading.

Ultimately, Poe puts his own tale to work to undercut the claims of print,
ending with the suggestion that Pfaall never reached the moon at all—which
is only to be expected, perhaps, from an aeronaut whose name inauspiciously
reads as "fall." (In this version of the story, the moon resembles a more
distant cousin of paper towns like Cairo, Illinois, which amaze audiences on
paper but lack any real existence.) Following the balloon's return visit with
Pfaall's account of his travels, a number of "rumors and speculations" begin
to circulate "decrying the whole business as nothing better than a hoax"
(427). These include the known hostilities of "certain wags in Rotterdam" to
the burgomasters and astronomers to whom Pfaall addresses his message;
the recent disappearance of a man from a neighboring city who closely

resembles the lunar messenger; the Dutch (rather than lunar) origins of the newspapers that form the return balloon; and a late sighting of Pfaall, supposedly still on the moon (427). This belated version of the story's events plainly casts the rest of the narration in doubt, opening a gap between printed appearance and reality in the text itself (which, in its own function as a hoax, also opens this gap off the page). In a final paragraph included in the tale's original 1835 publication in the *Southern Literary Messenger*, Poe underscores this gap by addressing skeptics of Pfaall's account directly: "I wonder, for my part, you do not perceive at once that the letter—the document—is intrinsically—is astronomically true—and that it carries upon its very face the evidence of its own authenticity" (427–428). But as this defense admits in its hyperbole, its halting punctuation, and its disquieting echo of the dubious "truth" of the story's own "astronomical" "documents," its assurances come too late: the information Poe provides under the cover of contempt has already shown that the supposed self-evidence of "letters" is itself a hoax. In the end, perhaps the story's most significant commentary on American literary fraudulence lies in the perverse way that, by preempting its own detection, it unhinges the hoax as a form. As Poe dismantles his tale's ability to function as a successful hoax, "Han Pfaall" suggests that, finally, fraudulence cannot be satisfactorily localized and thematized in a discrete event. Indeed, by the time Poe included the story in *Tales of the Grotesque and Arabesque* four years later, he had given up on its possibilities as a hoax entirely, instead interpolating it within the matrix of fantasy and satire implied in the volume's title and borne out in its other contents. Meanwhile, several months after its publication, "Hans Pfaall" furnished the inspiration (at least, so Poe believed) for another, far more successful hoax: Richard Adams Locke's "moon hoax," whose celebration at the American booksellers' dinner opens this chapter. Ironically, the warm welcome Locke's hoax received at the booksellers' dinner replicates the afterlife Poe's own hoax enjoyed as one of his now celebrated *Tales*, for in very different contexts, both render hoaxes and classic American literature indistinguishable.

This chapter has offered a counterhistory of literary nationalism by juxtaposing it with the history of the puffing system, whose mechanisms of artificial inflation, I have argued, constitute literary nationalism's unwanted alter ego. Even though critics have largely abandoned literary nationalism as a subject, we have tended to preserve one of its key myths intact: the image of the antebellum print explosion as a democratic public sphere. Yet Poe's balloons of print, like the other bloated figures that swell this chapter—Wilmer's "inflated bladders" of authorship, western land bubbles, inflated currency, the "huge, well-contented chameleon" of nationality, and of course, puffery itself—at once echo this most familiar trope for antebellum print culture and dramatically reimagine it. Together, they suggest that the balloon offers a more apt figure for antebellum print culture than its morphological cousin, the public sphere. Despite their similar shapes, the differences between the two spheres could hardly be greater. Rational discourse fills the public sphere, but the balloon is filled only with hot air; while the public sphere extends the polity, the balloon distends it; and where the public sphere is defined by its open inclusiveness, filling the balloon brings it ever closer to bursting. The literati's growing fears about the unsoundness of American literature, the measures they devised to keep the print public sphere aloft, and the unpredictable outcomes of those measures, are the subject of the rest of this book.

Chapter 2

Backwoods and Blackface: The Strange Careers of Davy Crockett and Jim Crow

> The term "far off West" seems, from general usage, to apply
> only to that section of our country which lies between the
> Allegheny and Rocky mountains. . . . Here Fancy, in her
> playful flights, may call into being empires which have no
> existence; and though perhaps sober reason would now
> chide her fairy creations, yet the time will come, when they
> will only be looked upon with the conviction of truth.
>
> —*The Life and Adventures of Colonel*
> *David Crockett, of West Tennessee*

> The Ethiopian melodies well deserve to be called, as they
> are in fact, the national airs of America. They follow the
> American race in all its migrations, colonizations, and
> conquests.
>
> —Bayard Taylor, *Eldorado, or,*
> *Adventures in the Path of Empire*

In the April 1836 issue of the *Southern Literary Messenger*, Edgar Allan Poe
launched into a furious indictment of "the present state of American criticism," which should by now sound quite familiar. Incensed by the "indiscriminate puffing of good, bad, and indifferent" that had become the
critical norm, he charged: "So far from being ashamed of the many dis-
graceful literary failures to which our own inordinate vanities and misap-
plied patriotism have lately given birth, and so far from deeply lamenting

that these daily puerilities are of home manufacture, we adhere pertinaciously to our original blindly conceived idea, and thus often find ourselves involved in the gross paradox of liking a stupid book the better, because, sure enough, its stupidity is American."[1] For Poe, the best evidence of this tendency lay in the critical adulation heaped upon Theodore S. Fay's novel *Norman Leslie*, which had been ushered on to the literary scene with great fanfare by the *New-York Mirror*, where Fay was co-editor, the year before. At the time, Poe had skewered the book's improbable plot, pretentious style, and grammatical infelicities, and now he could not resist returning to the subject. The end of the *Southern Literary Messenger*'s April 1836 "Critical Notices" contained the following squib: "Mr. Fay wishes us to believe that the sale of a book is the proper test of its merit. To save time and trouble we *will* believe it, and are prepared to acknowledge, as a consequence of the theory, that the novel of Norman Leslie is not at all comparable to the Memoirs of Davy Crockett, or the popular lyric of Jim Crow."[2] Poe's comparison is meant to be unflattering, and its sting lies in the obviously dubious "merit" of either Crockett's or Crow's literary contributions, coupled with their superior sales. Yet his riposte also captures a broader trend that began in the late 1830s, in which writers at the center of American literary culture, frustrated by its subjection to "every thing puffed, puffing, and puffable," increasingly turned toward its perceived margins in search of national authenticity.[3]

In fact, many of Poe's contemporaries made the same comparison with considerably more earnestness. For several decades following, Americans regularly lauded Davy Crockett as the best representative of the national character, and "the Jim Crows, the Zip Coons, and the Dandy Jims" of the minstrel stage as "our ONLY TRULY NATIONAL POETS," as one article put it.[4] Poe's comment is illustrative of this reorientation toward the cultural periphery not only because it extols the literary value of figures like Davy Crockett and Jim Crow (albeit ironically), but because it invokes them in the same breath. A rich body of scholarship, including influential books by Carroll Smith-Rosenberg, Alexander Saxton, and Eric Lott, has illuminated the roles that minstrelsy and the figure of Crockett played in the construction of national identity.[5] But whereas these studies treat blackface and backwoods performances individually, here I am most interested in how regularly antebellum readers thought of them together. The literary careers of the white frontiersman and the black slave, I argue, prove strange not least because they look so very much alike. Indeed, this chapter's examination of the songsheets, almanacs, plays, and fictitious autobiographies associated with each one finds Jim Crow and other blackface characters cropping up in Crockett's tall tales, and Crockett making frequent appearances on the minstrel stage. Taking the two figures together, as so many antebellum readers found them, helps us understand how writers in the largely northeastern metropolitan publishing industries fashioned nationalism out of the very groups they relegated to the nation's cultural margins. Crockett and Crow served other purposes as well, of course; scholars have shown that blackface minstrelsy was at least as crucial to the formation of the white working class as to the bourgeoisie, for instance. But the literati's embrace of these characters bears examination because it indexes a broader phenomenon, in which the literary core introduced in Chapter 1—the largely white, urban, middle-class men that dominated publishing in the United States—increasingly made capital out of its literary periphery. Exploring this history allows us to conceptualize the problem that frames the rest of this book: how the questions of fraudulence and authenticity that emerged as quandaries of nationalism came to shape new racial, regional, and gender identities.

I use "literary periphery" to describe not only literature associated with groups that were subordinated socially, but also literature defined as fraudulent, and one of my aims is to trace how these two meanings came into alignment. Thus in this chapter I propose that the transmutation of Davy Crockett and Jim Crow's regional and racial difference into national belonging cannot be understood without reference to their fraudulence—or more specifically, without asking how their fraudulence became converted into authenticity. For surely the most salient feature Crockett and Crow share is their thorough fakery. Both figures thematize fraudulence, so that minstrelsy laughs at the trickery and pretensions of Jim Crow and his blackface counterparts, while the Crockett literary industry makes wild tall tales the frontiersman's stock in trade. But on a formal level, each genre is also underwritten by imposture: Jim Crow's shams were acted out by white men themselves shamming as black, while Davy Crockett and the host of semiliterate "backwoods" characters he inspired were largely manufactured out of northeastern publishing centers. Critics, wincing at the politics of minstrelsy and frontier narratives, often read the extravagant fakery of these characters as the contortions of false consciousness. But I maintain that their fraudulence is not just proof of their ideological functions; it is itself fundamental to those functions. In a culture preoccupied with the problem of fraudulence, Crockett and Crow achieved the remarkable feat of parlaying a fake authenticity into an authentic fakeness.

Some readers may object that to study Davy Crockett and Jim Crow in tandem papers over the difference between the genres in which these figures took shape: the printed forms of the autobiography and the almanac, on the one hand, and the minstrel stage's musical, dance, and theatrical performances, on the other. In recent years, especially, the distinction between print and performance has sharpened, as the growth of performance studies as a field has provocatively challenged writing's longstanding disciplinary tyranny, and with it the assumption that inscriptions are prescriptions. As the title to Diana Taylor's influential study, *The Archive and the Repertoire*, makes clear, these interventions often rely on a dichotomy between print and performance, which contrasts print's fixity with performance's iterative, gestural, and situated acts. While interpretations of texts may change, Taylor argues, the texts themselves do not: "*Antigone* might be performed in multiple ways, whereas the unchanging text assures a stable signifier."[6] Yet an "unchanging text" was the rarest of things in the heterogeneous media culture of the antebellum United States. By contrast, the incessant republication, revision, citation, and adaptation of printed matter looks like nothing so much as a series of reenactments, or what Taylor calls a "scenario," whose "portable framework bears the weight of accumulative repeats."[7] Indeed, attempts to categorize Jim Crow or Davy Crockett as either printed or performed soon run into trouble: Jim Crow's stage success, for instance, prompted no fewer than three celebrity "autobiographies," while the enormous popularity of Davy Crockett's autobiographies and almanacs soon led to their translation into numerous songs. Rather than set print and performance against each other, it would be more useful, as Elizabeth Maddock Dillon has argued, to bring the insights of performance studies to inform our historical understanding of print. "The rubric of performance," she writes, "render[s] the book less a coherent, reproducible item" than "a set of enacted relations (staged between writer and publisher, between author and readership, between bookseller and consumer, between critic and reading public) that define a book as something far different from a lapidary text."[8] Dillon's contention that performance offers a better framework than traditional literary studies for early American print culture is especially relevant when it comes to the blackface and backwoods culture industries, which tended to take ephemeral and thus especially mobile forms—songsheets, almanacs, broadsides, pamphlets, and so on. Referencing and reworking each other, these artifacts compose a motile archive whose numerous versions of Jim Crow and Davy Crockett often staged one figure as a reenactment of the other, as well.

How to Write a Backwoods Article

Stories about the historical David Crockett, a soldier in the Creek War who reinvented himself as a backwoods "roarer" to bolster his chances for election to Congress, appeared frequently in U.S. newspapers in the late 1820s and early 1830s. Thanks to their popularity, Crockett also became the subject of no fewer than four autobiographies, none of which he probably wrote.[9] But it was the Davy Crockett almanacs that spread across the Northeast and into the Midwest from the mid-1830s to the mid-1850s that made their eponymous hero a national icon. Crudely printed and illustrated, the Crockett almanacs combined the usual almanac fare of astronomical calculations, weather predictions, and farming tips with "Adventures, Exploits, Sprees and Scrapes in the West, and Life and Manners in the Backwoods": outrageous stories, narrated in an equally outrageous backwoods dialect, of hunting wild animals, courting "terrificashus gals," and fighting Yankees, pukes (Missourians), suckers (Illinoisans), Native Americans, African Americans, bears, alligators, and catamounts.[10]

Despite the paper-and-ink evidence of their form, the almanacs strive to put as much distance as possible between the plain-speaking frontier world with which they align themselves and the specious metropolitan culture of print. "Of books the divil a one have I read," Crockett boasts, and writing is as alien to him as reading: "Although my I *dears* run through me like an hour glass that never wants turned, *rayly* when I try to write my elbow keeps coming round like a swingle-tree, and it is easier for me to tree a varmint, or swallow a nigger, than to write."[11] I want to bracket Crockett's eating habits temporarily in order to focus on how the material form of the almanac bears out his claims. In keeping with Crockett's predicament, the text of the almanacs works hard to disavow its own textuality. The almanacs' ersatz backwoods dialect is written as if spoken, while their comically phonetic orthography at once asserts the writers' semiliteracy and extends it to the audience by defying sight reading, requiring readers to sound out the words in order to decipher them. The introduction to the 1839 almanac represents its resistance to print culture quite literally:

Among the papers yet to print are the drollest yarns about wild
scrapes, terrible fights with the wild varmints of the west, both two
legged and four legged, and some with no legs at all, that ever was
heerd tell of. They are raal terrificashus. So much so that you must
reed em through a pare of spektakles or they will make your eyes
ake. It like to have broke the press down to print them, they are sich
hard karakters. A little dog that swollered one of the leaves of the
proof sheet was taken with the kollery morbuss, and is tung hung
out haff a yard till he died in the cutest agguny. You had best to
hoop your ribs before you reed em or you will shake your bowels
out a laffing.[12]

As "terrificashus" as any "wild varmints of the west," the almanacs become
lethal in printed form, physically threatening printing presses, readers, and
their dogs alike. At times their words cannot be conveyed on the page at
all. Crockett's sailor friend Ben Harding tells such good stories, Crockett
affirms, that "as I spose the reader would like to hear some of 'em, I think
I shall put 'em in print." This proves impossible, however, for "he had a
voice that was so ruff, I can't rite it doun, but I will have a cut made to
picktur it out."[13] The accompanying illustration pictures Harding with a
flood of jagged shards pouring from his mouth, words too "ruff" to render
in print (figure 6).

After Crockett's death at the Alamo, Harding supposedly assumes the
editorship of the almanacs, but even in this capacity, he remains deter-
minedly outside the world of print culture. An 1841 engraving picturing
Harding at almanac headquarters turns the sedate editorial offices of his
more professional colleagues on their heads (figure 7). Although propped
up at a conventional secretary, Harding clutches a quill pen in his fist as if
stabbing a knife into the desk; on the wall, a picture of a bear with the word
"BARE" written under it confirms Harding's tenuous grasp of the written
word. Harding is pleased to report that the wildly popular almanac "won't
stick to the bookseller's shelves no time at all," but he emphasizes that he
himself remains unknown in "New York," "Bostown," and "Fillydelphy."
"When I goes limping up Broadway and Washington Street or Chessnut
Street," the major publishing thoroughfares of each city, "fokes dont know
as i am a literary karaktur. Prehaps one wreizon of that is that the printurs
diddent send around the aulmynack to awl the noosepaypur fokes last yeer,
and so it hasent got about that i am the chap what makes 'em."[14] The

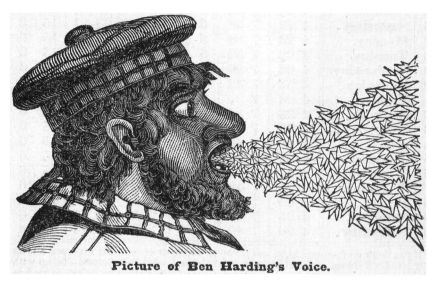

Picture of Ben Harding's Voice.

Figure 6: Ben Harding's voice, from "Adventures with a Tar," *The Crockett Almanac, 1839, Containing Adventures, Exploits, Sprees & Scrapes in the West, & Life and Manners in the Backwoods.* (Courtesy American Antiquarian Society)

almanacs' putative authors sidestep the official literary sphere and its mechanisms of publicity—indeed, they don't even register there—even as they attain a nation-wide readership. In this respect, the almanacs triumph over northeastern metropolitan print culture by beating it at its own game. Or just by beating it: story after story drives home the almanacs' oppositional power by subjecting Yankees and city slickers to acts of spectacular violence, as they are kicked, trashed, treed, shot, and insulted by Crockett or defeated by the western landscape itself—chased by bees, bitten by alligators, choked by bears.

Such flagrant unruliness has made the subversive content of the almanacs a basic premise of Crockett criticism. In his pioneering study of American folklore, for example, Richard M. Dorson contends that Crockett and his ilk "shocked the genteel sensibilities of eastern aristocracy with their ruffian antics and rowdy Jacksonian fervor," and subsequent studies of Crockett have tended to accept his assessment as axiomatic.[15] Yet for all the almanacs' jokes at the expense of variously priggish and conniving Yankees,

Figure 7: Editorial headquarters of *The Crockett Almanac*, from
"Introduction," *The Crockett Almanac, 1841, Containing Adventures,*
Exploits, Sprees & Scrapes in the West, & Life and Manners in the Backwoods.
(Courtesy American Antiquarian Society)

this narrative of Crockett's transgressive power fails to hold up historically.
References to Crockett abound in the polite literature of the time, suggesting that the almanacs found an enthusiastic reading audience among the
very members of the urban, eastern bourgeoisie that Dorson claims they so
affronted. To cite just two early examples from the magazine world, an 1837
issue of the *Yale Literary Magazine* approvingly quotes one of Crockett's
aphorisms, while an 1839 article in Horace Greeley's literary and news
weekly, the *New-Yorker*, recommends that Americans eschew the fashions
of London and Paris, which "will not suit Jonathan, and Jim Crow . . .
not to speak of . . . Davy Crockett . . . and many others who particularly

represent" the United States.[16] I will return to the conjunction of Jim Crow and Davy Crockett shortly, but here I simply want to emphasize their grouping with the generic American "Jonathan" as those who "particularly represent" the nation. Even Ralph Waldo Emerson championed Crockett for his role in ensuring that "the impending reduction of the transatlantic excess of influence on the American education is a matter of easy and frequent computation." Thanks to the "genuine growths" of "Kentucky stump-oratory, the exploits of Boone and David Crockett, the journals of western pioneers, agriculturalists, and socialists, and the letters of Jack Downing," Emerson predicted, "Our eyes will be turned westward, and a new and stronger tone in literature will be the result."[17] Emerson's list of western literary models contains an odd anomaly: Major Jack Downing, the fictional confidant of Andrew Jackson created by Seba Smith, was a Yankee caricature, a resident of Downingsville, Maine, not the West. But the miscategorization of Downing is illuminating because it enacts the very transformation that Emerson demands: the westernization of eastern culture.

In fact, the Crockett almanacs were hardly the "genuine growths" of the West, either. The earliest editions of the almanac (1835–1841) bore a Nashville, Tennessee, imprint, but as John Seelye has discovered, this was almost certainly a ruse. Seelye reveals that the Nashville almanacs were likely the work of Boston illustrator-editor-publisher Charles Ellms, noting that they reuse woodcuts from two of Ellms's publications, *The People's Almanac* (which Ellms began issuing in 1834) and *The Pirate's Own Book* (1837).[18] (One Nashville Crockett story even not-so-subtly puffs *The Pirate's Own Book*: Ben Harding tells Crockett that he's had some "cussed droll adventures," but "the slickest yarns I ever heered of is telled in the Pirate's Own Book. They've got it to sell at the Bookshops, and it is chock full of such stories about pirates as made my hair stand up when I heerd it read.")[19] In 1839, Philadelphia publisher Turner and Fisher and New York publisher Elton and Company each issued a Crockett almanac under their own names, and over the next decade Crockett almanacs—some reprints of each other, some unique—regularly appeared in the very literary centers where Ben Harding claims obscurity: Boston, Philadelphia, New York, and Baltimore. Occasional issues even cropped up in Detroit and Albany. Despite Emerson's effusions about the reinvigorating presence of the frontier, the Crockett almanacs were actually the inventions of northeastern literary professionals, written for a largely urban market. Nor was the Crockett literary industry exceptional in this respect; while the tall tale has a long history in southwestern oral culture, the readers and writers of the "backwoods" literature that became the rage in the 1830s and 1840s usually had little connection to its rural settings.[20] For example, although Augustus Baldwin Longstreet first published *Georgia Scenes* out of the offices of the *Augusta States Rights Sentinel* in 1835, it was the book's reprinting five years later by Harper and Brothers in New York that made it an enormous success. Likewise, Johnson Jones Hooper's tales of Captain Simon Suggs gained fame in William T. Porter's New York magazine, *Spirit of the Times*, which specialized in southwestern humor, and prominent Philadelphia publishers Carey and Hart issued the tales in book form in 1845. Moreover, both Hooper and Longstreet enjoyed pedigrees very different from the scruffy characters who made them famous. Longstreet was a Yale graduate, Georgia state legislator, judge, minister, and later president of Emory College (now University). Hooper's aristocratic North Carolina family fell on hard times during his childhood, but he became a lawyer and, like Longstreet, a newspaper editor, and later he was elected clerk for the state legislature. The tallest tales peddled by the Crockett almanacs and other works of southwestern humor, in other words, may have been the tales of their own cultural origins.

The production and reception history of the Crockett almanacs and other "backwoods" classics remind us that subversive actions on the page do not necessarily translate into subversive actions off of it. In fact, in one of the few studies of the almanacs, Carroll Smith-Rosenberg argues that their fetishization of the rough-and-tumble frontiersman constitutes "one of the earliest and most paradigmatic myths of the origins of the American bourgeoisie." Smith-Rosenberg points out that the almanacs "flourished during the very years when the bourgeoisie was struggling to legitimize itself as the country's dominant class and to establish itself as socially, as well as economically, distinct from and superior to the new working class."[21] With his disorderliness, perpetual adolescence, and violence towards his own father and the establishment more generally, Crockett provided the almanacs' audience of middle-class young men with a fantasy of rebellion against the dominant social order, but one conducted in a humorous idiom safely removed from actual critique. As Smith-Rosenberg explains,

The Crockett myth, by asserting that youthful autonomy toppled the old order, denied both the economic and political factors that gave

birth to the bourgeoisie and the economic and political realities of
the social order the bourgeoisie established to perpetuate its hegemony. By glorifying anti-structure and youth, the Crockett myth succeeds in obscuring the reality of social class. It substitutes nationalism
for economic and historical reality. At its very moment of birth, that
is, the American bourgeoisie sought to distort and obscure its
nature—to drain from its name all economic significance.[22]

Smith-Rosenberg's analysis of the Crockett almanacs makes two interre-
lated claims about the class politics of United States nationalism. First, she
contends that the ostensibly classless structure of nationalism helps to
establish bourgeois hegemony by burying class difference beneath national
affiliation. Second, she argues the antebellum bourgeoisie went further, not
only denying class difference but, through texts like the Crockett almanacs,
actually assuming an anti-establishment posture that figured nationalism as
a challenge to the social order rather than an instrument of it. Smith-
Rosenberg acutely dissects the ironies of Jacksonian class politics, helping
explain how an era marked by intensely populist discourse could simultaneously see the consolidation of economic, political, and cultural power.
Her analysis helps explain how what Antonio Gramsci dreamed of as the
national-popular emerged in the United States in an illusory version we
might call the national-populist. Where Gramsci's concept of the national-
popular repudiates a restrictive, "bookish" national formation and replaces
it with "a strong popular or national political movement from below,"
national-populism repudiates this national formation only to replace it with
a top-down movement that affects a vernacular form.[23]

   The vernacular signature of the Crockett almanacs, of course, was their
regionalism. Even as Crockett, in his backwoods posture, defiantly rejects
hegemonic forms of nationalism, he also paradoxically resolves some of
the most persistent challenges that literary nationalism faced. Whereas the
patriotic naturalists sought to catalog the landscape in their work, and the
Young Americans called for the literary expression of an American character, Crockett simply incorporates the continent and its contents in his pro-
digious body:

He can run faster, dive deeper, stay under longer, and come out
drier than any other chap this side the big swamp; and can grin the
bark off a tree—look a panther to death—take a steam boat on

his back—stand three streaks of lightning without dodging. . . . He
frightens the old folks, astonishes the natives—and beats the Dutch
all to smash! He makes nothing of sleeping under a blanket of snow,
and no more minds being frozen than a rotten apple. He lives,
moves, rides, walks, runs, swims, fights, hunts, courts, marries, and
has children, on a great scale! . . . He *liquors* on a glass of "thunder
and lightning" that's hotter than Tophet, and bites like a rattlesnake;
or for *bitters*, sucks away at a noggin of aqua fortis, sweetened with
brimstone, stirred with a lightning rod, and skimmed by a hurri-
cane! He walks like an ox, runs like a horse, swims like an eel, yells
like an Indian, fights like a devil, spouts an earthquake, makes love
like a mad bull, and can whip his weight in wild cats, or swallow a
nigger without choking, if you'll butter his head and pin his ears
back![24]

Crockett's outrageous claims at once mark out the backwoods as a world
apart and offer it up as a nationalist fantasy. Here Gramsci, who saw Italian
regional literature as a symptom of the failure to attain a genuine national-
popular, is again helpful. He writes, "The 'regional' people was seen 'pater-
nalistically' from the outside, with the disenchanted cosmopolitan spirit of
tourists in search of strong and original raw sensations."[25] As the quotation
marks around "regional" remind us, regional literature itself constructs this
division of inside and outside; after all, no people is any more "regional"
than any other. Yet Gramsci's description also captures how regional literature transmutes the regional into the national by inviting the reader's identification, his or her vicarious experience of the "strong and original raw
sensations" that the tired conceits of polite literary culture cannot provide.
Thus for all its hyperbolic difference, Crockett's trademark boast suits antebellum nationalism remarkably well. He at once fuses "nature's nation"
and makes it his own, as he spans the landscape (swamps, forests, rivers),
chastens those resistant to Young America ("old folks," "the Dutch," "Indians," "niggers"), and remains impervious to natural and man-made dangers alike.

The historical David Crockett, by contrast, famously fell victim to the
hazards of nationalism. It became all the more urgent, then, for the almanacs to preserve Crockett's body on paper after its real-world counterpart
became a casualty of expansionist ambitions in Texas. Long after Crockett's
death at the Alamo in 1836, the almanacs continued to publish stories in

his voice. The 1837 almanac plausibly explained that Crockett had left a cache of "reading and pictures enough to make several Almanacs," and the "heirs of Col. Crockett" and later Crockett's friend Ben Harding dutifully stepped into the editorial role to publish them. But eventually the conceit was dropped, and Crockett reappeared on the editorial page and as the primary storyteller. Several almanacs offered pretexts for Crockett's return, reporting that he had been captured, not killed, at the Alamo, and reprinting his letters from a Mexican prison.[26] Others, however, brought him back to life without explanation. While the historical Crockett exemplified the exigencies of expansion, the almanacs' Crockett prevails to realize the national imaginary in print. Indeed, the wounds Crockett receives only confirm his national incarnation; they form a pattern, he tells his readers, so "I might have been hung out for an American flag."[27]

Furthermore, for all their declared antipathies toward northeastern print culture, the Crockett almanacs sustain a fantasy of literature's material and political efficacy as vivid as any literary nationalist could desire. At the center of this fantasy lies the almanacs' representation of their own enviable circulation. As Ben Harding boasts in the introduction to one issue, the almanac "won't stick to the booksellers shelves no time at all" but "goes into all parts like a Jim Crow that is traveling all over the Union," a description that crosses lines of race and genre to compare the success of the almanacs to the ultimate benchmark of nationwide popularity, the traveling minstrel show.[28] Harding's analogy will resonate in multiple registers throughout this chapter. For now, though, it is sufficient to note how it slips the almanac not only out of the literary marketplace's promotional machinations but even its physical distribution networks, giving it an autonomous life of its own in the embodied figure of Jim Crow. The backstory of Harding's own editorship, a chance meeting with Crockett while afloat the Mississippi, serves to confirm this report of the almanacs' immense diffusion. Despite their very different spheres, the sailor Harding recognizes the backwoodsman Crockett immediately because he has already read and admired his literary output, exclaiming, "tell me for God's sake, old fogy, are you the feller that makes them allmynacks about cruising after panthers and snakes and swimming over the Mississippi?"[29] And of course the almanacs materially corroborated claims of their extensive circulation in their spurious Nashville imprint, which encouraged a northeastern audience to believe that the almanacs had traveled across the country, rather than down the street. Finally, at the same time that the almanacs gratify a

fantasy of a print public sphere that effectively transports deserving productions "all over the Union," they also paint a picture of literary democracy
far more convincing than those supplied by the more respectable writers
and critics described in Chapter 1. Where the literati struggled to show that
print culture could model democracy, the Crockett almanacs presented this
as an accomplished fact. With Ben Harding and Davy Crockett in control
of the means of literary production, what further evidence of literature's
accessibility to the people could be desired? The Crockett almanacs—
indeed, the entire Crockett literary industry—realized the fondest dreams
of a national literature in a regional anti-literature.

One impressive measure of the nationalization of regionalism, as well
as Crockett's central role in this feat, can be found in John Russell Bartlett's
hefty *Dictionary of Americanisms: A Glossary of Words and Phrases, Usually
Regarded as Peculiar to the United States.* Bartlett initially published his dictionary in 1848 and continued to issue revised and enlarged editions over
the following thirty years. His project does the literary nationalists' attempts
to establish a genuinely national literature one better; it attempts to establish a genuinely national *language,* a "class of words purely American in
their origin and use." As Bartlett explains in the introduction, the dictionary will enumerate "all the words, whatever their origin, which are used in
familiar conversation, and but seldom employed in composition—all the
perversions of language, and abuses of words into which people, in certain
sections of the country, have fallen, and some of those remarkable and
ludicrous forms of speech which have been adopted in the Western
States."[30] For a project with such declaredly national aspirations, Bartlett's
dictionary telescopes unexpectedly. What makes an "Americanism" turns
out not to be its national character but its regional one, a word's evocation
of "certain sections of the country"—New England, the South, and, as the
entries show, especially the West.

If Bartlett's genuinely national language is not indeed national, in a
familiar twist we also learn that neither is it genuine. One might expect
such a dictionary of words "used in familiar conversation, and but seldom
employed in composition" to have been assembled from oral evidence, especially given that the title page notes Bartlett's post as Corresponding Secretary of the American Ethnological Society. Bartlett admits, "The value of this
glossary would have been greatly enhanced, if, as is usual in the compilation
of similar works, I had been able to avail myself of the assistance of persons
residing in various parts of the country. No collection of words, professing

to contain the colloquial language of the entire country, can approach any degree of completeness or correctness, without the aid of many heads and hands." Of "the Western and Southern provincialisms," he acknowledges that only "one born and brought up where they are spoken, who has heard and used them when a boy, and grown up in their midst, can portray them in their true sense." But, Bartlett regrets, "The aid of such persons it was impossible to procure" (vii). How, then, has he compiled the dictionary? The raw material originates, he explains, from literature: from "extracts from American authors, whose writings relate to that class of people among which these words are chiefly found. These books contain descriptions of country life, scenes in the backwoods, popular tales, &c., in which the colloquial or familiar language of particular states predominates" (v). And in fact, each entry is illustrated with an example from a literary source—Thomas Chandler Haliburton's stories of Sam Slick, the Yankee clockmaker; Augustus Baldwin Longstreet's scenes of rural Georgia life; and, of course, the legends of Davy Crockett. Bartlett's American dialect derives from print, and more than that, from authors "whose writings relate to that class of people among which these words are chiefly found" rather than from that class of people itself. His selection of sources highlights the difference: Thomas Chandler Haliburton hailed from Nova Scotia, not New England; Longstreet, as noted earlier, was a state legislator and judge, not a rural Georgian; and Bartlett draws all of his Crockett quotations from *An Account of Col. Crockett's Tour to the North and Down East*, a piece of Whig campaign propaganda cobbled together by party operatives.[31]

Appropriately—which is to say, ironically—enough, Bartlett calls upon Crockett to demonstrate the meaning of "backwoodsman," citing the preface to the *Tour to the North and Down East*: "I presume, ladies and gentlemen, it is your curiosity to hear the plain, uneducated backwoodsman in his home style" (19). The quotation is illustrative of more than Bartlett probably recognized. Crockett acknowledges his polite audience's "curiosity" for his "home style," yet he does not actually speak in the "plain, uneducated" language they desire but in a genteel manner presumably much like their own. The *Dictionary of Americanisms* itself exemplifies this "curiosity" and the cultural alchemy it manages to perform, producing a national language out of a regional vernacular, and a regional vernacular out of its literary representation. To see the role Crockett plays in these transformations gives a sense of this figure's acrobatic signifying, which convincingly remade the backwoodsman into a figure for national authenticity.

The Counterfeit Presentment of the American National Opera

One can begin to access a similar history for Jim Crow by considering the
odd conjunction of terms—"blackface minstrelsy"—used to describe his
performance. Just as a backwoods caricature appeared as the epitome of
authentic "Americanism," so too did blackface minstrelsy at once embody
national alterity (blackface) and representativeness (minstrelsy). Originally,
"minstrelsy" referred to European traditions of folk poetry, the kinds of
repositories of cultural memory and identity that Americans felt themselves
sorely lacking. Katie Trumpener has shown how, in response to English
occupation, Anglo-Celtic antiquarians produced a rich archive of bards,
ballads, minstrels, and oral tradition.[32] Of course, the North American colo-
nies, as well as the antebellum United States, had a very different relationship to England than did Scotland, Ireland, or Wales. However, the brand
of minstrelsy developed in this former outpost of the British empire also
served nationalist purposes, including that of countering the invidious literary comparisons with England that continued to plague the nation. A series
of "Ethiopian" songsheets published in New York in the 1840s made the
analogy between blackface and European minstrels its signature motif. The
songsheets frame each song with a border featuring a black lute-player
wearing a cartoonish approximation of medieval garb: plumed hat, puffed
breeches, striped stockings, and pointed shoes. Open-mouthed and looking
toward the text, he appears to be singing the song printed within the frame.
Clearly, this black bard's function is humorous, and his comic value resides
in the perceived disparity between African Americans and true literary culture—a disparity that made burlesques of Shakespeare's plays standbys of
the minstrel stage. Yet the irony of the juxtaposition proves unreliable, for
the image also reminds readers of the serious belief that blackface minstrels
were the "American Shakespeares" literary nationalists so desperately
sought. How did audiences come to imagine actors smeared in burnt cork,
wearing manufactured rags and speaking in a spurious African American
vernacular, as the country's minstrels?

Eric Lott's landmark study, *Love and Theft: Blackface Minstrelsy and
the American Working Class*, argues that blackface minstrelsy accesses "a
peculiarly American structure of racial feeling" because audiences understood blackface performers, despite their obvious masquerades, as racially
black: "When, in the decades before the Civil War, northern white men
'blacked up' and imitated what they supposed was black dialect, music, and

dance, some people, without derision, heard Negroes singing."[33] Certainly, many blackface performers claimed that they learned their routines from actual African Americans (a claim that often competed with their simultaneous efforts to present themselves as creative artists, rather than copyists), and some credulous theatergoers may have failed to recognize the performances' extravagant counterfeits. But the evidence suggests that most audiences were well aware of, and even relished, the gap between white actors and black characters. In an especially conspicuous version of Neil Harris's "operational aesthetic," minstrel songs and plays continually placed their conditions of production on display in the jokes they told ("Why is a minstrel performer in the morning like a sheared sheep? Because the wool is all taken off") and in winking references to burnt cork, shoe polish, and white men's longing to be "Gentlemen ob colour."[34] The spectacle of fakery was likewise key to minstrelsy's publicity strategies: a songsheet of "Jump Jim Crow" from the late 1830s, for instance, features the title character holding a blacking brush and a script, while the cover to sheet music by the Virginia Serenaders contrasts two images of the troupe: the first in makeup and costume, playing their instruments in ludicrous contortions, and the second as white gentlemen in elegant suits and classic portrait-style poses.[35] This is not to say that minstrelsy's exaggerated disguises prevented American audiences from investing it with racial meaning, but to emphasize that audiences did so *nonetheless*. One does not have to conclude that audiences failed to distinguish between blackface and blackness in order to see minstrelsy as the antebellum era's most influential theater of racial production. I am interested in an even more incredible version of this story: that even as audiences delighted in blackface for its outlandish impostures, they mined it for improbable forms of authenticity. For Lott, the institutionalization of minstrelsy as a "national cultural form" depends on audiences' understanding of blackface as blackness, "no matter how distorted or weak this material may appear."[36] But how does our understanding of blackface change if we think of its fraudulence not simply as the most astounding evidence of white Americans' appetites for blackness, but as itself crucial to minstrelsy's appeal?

As W. T. Lhamon points out, minstrelsy was actually an international phenomenon, which in part grew out of an earlier British stage tradition of blackface characters.[37] Yet while minstrelsy was transatlantic in practice, it remained doggedly national in theory, and its numerous British incarnations did not stop American writers from declaring it "our only original

American institution."[38] "Who says we have no American Poetry? No
American Songs?" James K. Kennard, Jr., demanded in an 1845 article in
the *Knickerbocker*. It is true, he admits, that the best-known American
poets, such as Bryant and Longfellow, have nothing about them that
"savors *peculiarly* of America." But "the Jim Crows, the Zip Coons, and the
Dandy Jims" of the minstrel stage "have electrified the world. From them
proceed our ONLY TRULY NATIONAL POETS."[39] (Nor was Kennard alone in
this view of blackface minstrelsy's place in American poetry. As if to illustrate his point, a scrapbook at the American Antiquarian Society contains
a songsheet of "Gumbo Chaff," one of the earliest minstrel songs, pasted in
amidst poems by Bryant, Lydia Sigourney, and Nathaniel Parker Willis.)[40]
Kennard singles out for praise Thomas Dartmouth Rice, the white performer who originated the character of Jim Crow—or as Kennard, borrowing
one of nineteenth-century Americans' favorite phrases from Shakespeare,
puts it, "gave to the world his counterfeit presentment of the American
national opera."[41] Far from damning the minstrel show's fraudulence, however, here the phrase "counterfeit presentment" indicates its verisimilitude.
Specifically, Kennard retains the possibility of imposture but dismisses its
connotations of derivativeness: "whether these performers are blacks, or
whites with blacked faces does not appear; but they are doubtless meant to
represent the native colored population of 'Old Varginny,' and as such
should be judged."[42] American fans of blacked-up minstrel performers
agreed that the "true secret of their favor with the world is to be found in
the fact that they are genuine and real," and in particular, they were genuinely, really American. When Rice first performed his trademark song,
"Jump Jim Crow," another magazine writer recounts, "It touched a chord
in the American heart which had never before vibrated, but which now
responded to the skillful fingers of its first expounder, like the music of the
Bermoothes to the magic wand of Prospero."[43] Here again, as in Kennard's
quotation from *Hamlet*, blackface minstrelsy conjures visions of an American Shakespeare. Moreover, the writer's allusion to *The Tempest*, meant to
illustrate the harmony between minstrelsy and nationality, goes even further: it imagines minstrels emanating from the "American heart" itself, as
music does from Prospero's island. It is as if America always had "Jump
Jim Crow" in its heart, and T. D. Rice simply released it. Several years later,
another writer captured minstrelsy's convoluted nationalism by characterizing "Jump Jim Crow" as "a national or 'race' illustration," a description
that leaves in doubt what the word "or" could possibly mean in the face of

Jim Crow's emphatic production of racial difference.[44] Do the quotation marks frame "race" as a synonym for "nation"? Or are they scare quotes, admitting the artificiality of blackface? The phrase, like the historical formation it describes, holds race and nation in tense conjunction, quite literally rendering antebellum nationalism's strained efforts to articulate itself to (and through) minstrelsy's patently dubious "race."

Eric Lott, Alexander Saxton, David Roediger, and others have deftly dissected the fraught relationship between minstrel shows and the construction of white working-class culture.[45] Yet the literary nationalists' interest in blackface, like their interest in the backwoods, compels us to expand the scope of these inquiries in order to understand the immense attraction minstrelsy held for the antebellum bourgeoisie, as well. Despite blackface minstrelsy's exaggerated performances of race and class, it produced the sort of heterogeneous cultural mingling that plays out on the pages of the anonymous scrapbook I described above, which placed Gumbo Chaff alongside the celebrated dandy Nathaniel Parker Willis and Lydia Sigourney, "the sweet singer of Hartford." In 1855, an article in the thoroughly respectable *Putnam's* looked back on the preceding decades of blackface minstrelsy and recalled an entire nation singing and dancing "Jump Jim Crow."

> The schoolboy whistled the melody on his unwilling way to do his daily tasks. The ploughman checked his oxen in mid-furrow, as he reached its chorus, that the poetic exhortation to "do just so," might have the action suited to the word. Merchants and staid professional men, to whom a joke was a sin, were sometimes seen by the eyes of prying curiosity in private to unbend their dignity to that weird and wonderful posture . . . and of the thoroughly impressive and extraordinary sights which the writer of this article has in his lifetime beheld, the most memorable and noteworthy was that of a young lady in a sort of inspired rapture, throwing her weight alternately upon the tendon Achilles of the one, and the toes of the other foot, her left hand resting upon her hip, her right, like that of some prophetic sybil, extended aloft, gyrating as the exigencies of the song required, and singing Jim Crow at the top of her voice.[46]

We do not have to take the *Putnam's* writer at his word when he depicts "Jump Jim Crow" uniting rich and poor in order to appreciate his clear

investment in blackface. Accounts of numerous other privileged observers
likewise attest to the appeal of minstrelsy. While the members of the *Yale
Literary Magazine* ventriloquized Davy Crockett, their classmates in the college's elite secret societies capped a holiday performance of short plays, "a
comic oration and a comic poem, both relating to college life," with "a
display of negro minstrelsy."[47] Minstrelsy troupes even became fixtures at
the White House, where they entertained presidents Tyler, Polk, Fillmore,
and Pierce.[48] As the *Knickerbocker*'s cozy "Gossip with Readers and Correspondents" section reported,

> The amateur who introduced negro-melodies into our house has
> much to answer for. They are echoing all day *somewhere*. Even as
> we write, there is quite a sweet little voice (to our ear) singing:

> I'm going to Alabanjo,
>   With my 'bama on my knee!

> She hasn't got the words, but she has got the tune to a note.[49]

Theater historian Peter Buckley affirms, "Minstrelsy invaded almost all
grades of performance sites through the late 1840s and attracted, in ways
not yet appreciated by scholars, audiences of respectable families."[50] My
point here is not that blackface minstrelsy broke down class divisions,
which indeed became more rigid during these years, even as racial affilia-
tions increasingly replaced class ones. Yet neither do reports of minstrelsy's
contagious popularity merely reflect the paranoia of a protective cultural
elite. Rather, the recurring images of pretty white ladies singing and dancing to "Jump Jim Crow" remind us that class and race boundaries—often,
as here, structured by gender—were not forgotten in the class-traversing,
race-impersonating pleasures of minstrelsy, and were probably fortified by
it. In this respect, minstrelsy followed a path parallel to the theaters where
it played, which increasingly became "mixed class" establishments in the
1830s and 1840s but physically and socially produced class stratification in
their tiered seating structures. Along with Crockett, Jim Crow shuttled
between the popular and the populist, not only because a dominant group
used both to try to imagine some version of the "people," but because they
used this version of the "people" to try to imagine themselves.[51]

In Chapter 1's account of the backlash against literary nationalism, I cited the protests of critics who compared the state of American literature to a phantom, a monster, or as the *American Review* put it, to Poe's undead M. Valdemar, the mesmerized dying man who finally dissolves into a puddle of "loathsome . . . detestable putrescence."[52] This quotation makes an unexpected reappearance in the 1855 *Putnam's* article, troubling its nostalgic reminiscence of the previous two decades' "golden age of negro literature." The writer bemoans the passing of that age: "Hardly a song has been produced since that time which does not present the most glaring marks of barefaced and impudent imposition," he complains, and he cautions readers not to accept bogus substitutes: "If a gleam of the former light occasionally sparkles . . . it is but the phosphoric glimmer which beams from loathsome and decaying putrescence." The writer's lament for the debased state of 1850s minstrelsy, "forged in the brain of some northern self-styled minstrel," throws into relief its "former grandeur" of the 1830s and 1840s, when it was animated by the spark of authentic blackness.[53] Meanwhile, as writers compared (white) American literature to a preserved corpse, and the *Putnam's* article implicitly contrasted poor Valdemar's corpse with the vigor that properly belonged to minstrelsy, the minstrel play "Virginia Mummy" brought minstrelsy's vitality to life in the person of a corpse that had never been dead at all. The play tells the story of a doctor who, like the narrator in "The Facts in the Case of M. Valdemar," intends to reanimate a dead body. And like the literary critics to whom the *American Review* compared Poe's narrator, the doctor does so in pursuit of fame, declaring, "The world shall now acknowledge me!" Not surprisingly, his plan fails: instead of a dead Egyptian mummy, through a convoluted series of events he winds up with the "Virginny Mummy"—the blackface character "sassy Ginger Blue," packed in a box but very much alive.[54]

Much as literary nationalism's critics painted antebellum American literature as M. Valdemars and Frankensteins, the "mummified" Ginger Blue, painted over in "white, black, green, blue, and a variety of colors," appears as a hyperbolic embodiment of blackface (165). Indeed, in one of the minstrel show's typical eruptions of self-referentiality, another character drolly remarks that he "smells of shoe blacking" (172). The figure of the live blackface mummy stages a kind of inversion of literary nationalism's monstrous undead. M. Valdemar and Frankenstein, like the moribund American literature they metaphorize, are properly deceased, but they insist on thriving, on acting alive, nonetheless. Ginger Blue's regionally, racially marked Virginny Mummy reverses the situation: like the possums with which minstrelsy obsessively identified African Americans, he acts dead but is indeed exuberantly alive. Moreover, the Virginny Mummy lets the audience in on the joke, rather than making it at their expense. Whereas the case of M. Valdemar hoaxed readers on a national scale, the Virginny Mummy fools only the play's silly doctor, while the knowing audience gets to laugh at his gullibility. Routed through the power—not exactly of blackness, but of manifest blackface, doubly marked for emphasis in the form of both blacked-up mummery and painted mummy—the trope of revivification that haunted literary nationalism is itself reborn.[55] Instead of a preserved corpse we get a "live mummy," whose death has been a fake all along. American literature isn't dead; it's only playing possum.

The "Fox Poplar": Jim Crow/Davy Crockett

At least since Constance Rourke observed, "Western myth-making was woven deep in early minstrelsy, so deep that it can hardly be counted an alien strain," it has been customary for critics to acknowledge minstrelsy's debt to southwestern humor, especially the figure of Crockett.[56] Such genealogies helpfully counter tendencies to imagine these figures as self-contained regional creations, and undoubtedly both minstrelsy and the Crockett literary industry drew on accounts of backwoods roarers like Ohio river-boatman Mike Fink, established conventions of "Yankee" humor, and, indeed, stories about the historical David Crockett. However, the narrative of minstrelsy's backwoods inheritance rests on a basic chronological oversight: when, unlike their firmly regional predecessors, Davy Crockett and Jim Crow parlayed their outsized difference into national belonging, they did so in tandem.[57] T. D. Rice first appeared on the stage as "Jim Crow" in 1830, when David Crockett was serving his first term as a U.S. congressman, and three years before the first "autobiography" of Crockett, *The Life and Adventures of Colonel David Crockett, of West Tennessee*, appeared in print. The early era of minstrelsy, dominated by characters like Crow and his foils Zip Coon, Dandy Jim, Ginger Blue and Pompey Squash, lasted until about 1850; afterward, the minstrel show moved away from these character-based songs in favor of more straightforward plantation nostalgia. The first flush of the Crockett literary industry overlapped almost exactly with this period; the almanacs that were its most popular product dwindled in the early 1850s and finally ceased production in 1856. In the years since, however, the narrative of a progression from Davy Crockett to Jim Crow has managed to overwrite this history. Its sequential chronology has prevented critics from seeing that influence often flowed in both directions, and its focus on linear descent has obscured the more interesting implications of contemporaneity.[58]

The retrospective distancing of Crockett and Crow is not surprising. Despite their racial, cultural, and regional differences, the two resembled each other so closely that it is difficult to imagine them in the same place at the same time. To antebellum Americans, the two figures must have appeared as uncanny doubles. One of the earliest published versions of T. D. Rice's "Jump Jim Crow," a broadside printed in Boston, begins:

> I was born in a cane brake, and cradled in a trough,
> Swam de Mississippi, whar I cotch'd de hoopen coff.
>
> To whip my weight in wild cats, eat an alligator,
> And drink de Mississippi dry, I'm de very *critter*.[59]

For all his exaggerated alterity, Jim Crow's biography is lifted straight from Crockett's well-known boasts: the first line quotes the introduction to the 1838 almanac, which opens, "I was born in a cane brake, cradled in a sap trough," while the second verse cites his famously savage appetites and recapitulates his signature claim, "I can whip my weight in wild cats," a line that would continue to appear in versions of "Jump Jim Crow" for years to come.[60] Jim Crow goes on to rehearse one of Crockett's best-known stories, in which he attempts to grin an owl down (Crockett's trademark hunting technique), only to discover he is grinning at a pine knot.[61]

> I went to de woods, heard a debil of a howl,
> I look'd up a tree, and saw a great owl.
>
> I off wid my hat, stuck my heel in de ground,
> And then went to work to grin the owl down.
>
> I grinn'd wid my eyes open, and den wid um shut,
> But I could not diskiver dat I stirred de owl a foot.

Den I grinn'd slantendicular, den wid one eye,
'Twould have done your soul good to see de feathers fly.

Den I climb'd up de tree, and I wish I may be shot,
If I had'nt [sic] been grinning at a great pine knot.

Although minstrel humor relied on a caricatured African American vernacular, here Crow continually slips into a different dialect, as the western twang of "diskiver" ("discover") joins the standard stereotyped substitution of "d" for "th." In the song's most obvious appropriation, Crow borrows Crockett's favorite neologism "slantendicular," just as in the verse above, he imitates the backwoodsman's tendency to describe all living beings, including humans, as "critters."

One might conclude that the humor of the song lies in its sheer incongruity, in the shock of Crockett's words in Crow's mouth, were it not for the fact that such borrowings remained a fixture of minstrel songs for the next two decades, long past the point they might have retained any novelty. Crockett often turns up in person in early minstrelsy songs for no clear reason. In one of George Washington Dixon's versions of "Zip Coon," Zip Coon recounts the exploits of "dat tarnal critter Crockett" and then compares his own feats to the backwoodsman's, and allusions to Crockett and his exploits likewise pepper versions of "Gumbo Chaff" and "Jump Jim Crow."[62] At the same time, the Crockett literary industry's vision of the western frontier frequently incorporates unexplained references to Jim Crow and other minstrel figures. Among its various stories of backwoods adventures, the first Crockett almanac includes an illustration of a "Possum Up a Gum Tree," the title of a popular early blackface song, without comment. Jim Crow appears in person in one of the following year's almanacs, in a grotesque engraving of an African American man with the mock-dignified caption: "James Crow, Esq., of Kentucky; from a painting by Trumbull, in the Capitol at Washington" (a fictitious attribution to the painter John Trumbull, famous for his portraits of American dignitaries). In fact, the primary publishers of the Crockett almanacs, Turner and Fisher, used their success to launch a new genre of almanac: in 1845, Turner published *De Darkie's Comic All-Me-Nig*, and his partner Fisher followed with *Bone Squash's Black Joke Al-Ma-Nig* six years later. These almanacs translate the minstrel show onto the page, compiling stories, jokes, songs, and comic dialogues, but Turner and Fisher hardly bother to change the Crockett

almanacs' plots or settings. They simply transplant blackface characters to
the backwoods, where they hunt alligator and wildcats in "Snappen Turtle
Creek" and "Starvation Hollow."[63] Such appropriations and allusions,
which extract blackface characters from the northern city or southern plantation to place them in Crockett's shoes, lend new meaning to Ben Harding's boast that the Crockett almanac itself is "like a Jim Crow traveling
all over the Union."[64] As regionally and racially marked as blackface was, it
also proved highly portable, its markers of one form of alterity easily converting into markers of another.

Perhaps the most remarkable connections writers drew between Davy
Crockett and Jim Crow take the form of imagined encounters between
backwoods and blackface performance. The first Crockett autobiography,
The Life and Adventures of Colonel David Crockett, of West Tennessee, follows
the congressman to a campaign stop in "the far away west," where Crockett
himself "jumps" to the popular minstrel song "Clare de Kitchen." "Not
one in all the crowd moved with better grace, or shuffled with more spirit,"
and the banjo player accordingly adapts the song's lyrics to honor Crockett's convincing turn as a minstrel:

> Jay burd set 'pon de singin' lim'
> He look at me, I look at him,
> I raise my gun, he seed me cock it,
> An de way he flu was a sin to Crockit.
> > Old fokes, young fokes, clare de kitchin,
> > Old Firginny neber tire.[65]

Crockett's apparently natural gift for minstrelsy dramatizes the song's own
scene of doubling ("He look at me, I look at him") and posits blackface as
the flipside of the backwoods. Two years later, another Crockett autobiography, *An Account of Col. Crockett's Tour to the North and Down East*, staged
this doubling of Jim Crow and Davy Crockett even more explicitly at one
of T. D. Rice's Philadelphia performances. Much to the audience's delight,
Crockett attends the show: "Everyone seemed pleased, particularly when I
laughed; they appeared to act as if I knew exactly when to laugh, and then
they all followed."[66] The anecdote depicts the audience imagining a kind of
intrinsic connection between Crockett and Crow; perhaps it encourages the
reader to imagine one, as well. Furthermore, not only does the audience
believe that Crockett knows "exactly when to laugh" at Jim Crow, but this

projected mirroring of Crow and Crockett calls forth their own mirroring, for as Crockett notes, "they all followed."

At this point, it should come as no surprise that if anyone was the subject of as many pseudoautobiographies as Davy Crockett, it was Jim Crow. The first published autobiography (there were at least two more) hints that the parallel might, in fact, signal a family resemblance. *The Life of Jim Crow, Showing How He Got His Inspiration as a Poet* (1835) begins with a conventional authorial protest: Jim Crow explains that he never intended his manuscript for publication, but since he has come to be a "great literary character," his public demands he "make my infernal sensibilifications yieldify to de 'Fox poplar'" and "do like oder great actors, publish my account ob men and manners in dese blessed States, and I trus I shall be inable to do dem as much justice as dey desarve, on account ob my debility to use fasificationority as de foreignificated deatrical ladies do."[67] Crow's preface positions him as an ideal literary nationalist both in subject and in spirit: his autobiography will also be an account of "men and manners in dese blessed States" (a corrective to the unflattering reports of British visitors like the actress Fanny Kemble, who had published her journal of a tour to the United States that same year), and his writing is called into being by the "Fox poplar" (*vox populi*)—no matter that he substitutes "fox," slang for "deceive," for "vox." Indeed, the narrative that follows thoroughly inducts Jim Crow into American literary culture. Once he arrives in New York, he goes to "pay my devotions to de folks ob de lidderary hemporium," where he "sung and jumped to a pretty fine tune" and "git traduced to all de puff makers, blue stockings, &c." When he visits Mordecai Noah, the editor of the *Evening Star*, Crow learns something about puffery firsthand. Noah takes him out for punch, and once he has drunk "two bowls," "he took out he pencil an write a long puff bout Mr. Crow, which he said should shine in large caps in de Ebening Star. What kine ob caps do you wear in de Star office, says I—he laughed right merrily at my ignorance of de black art" (16). The autobiography's pun identifies printing, long known as "the black art," with the new "black art" of minstrelsy. Yet Crow's proximity to literary culture is also a joke, a pretension undercut by his malapropisms, ignorance, and thick dialect.

Later in this chapter, I discuss at greater length this push-and-pull between distinction and appropriation, which simultaneously sets Crow apart from literary culture and claims him as a part of it. For now, I am interested in the *Life*'s account of his family history. Born on a plantation in Kentucky, Crow relates that as an infant he frightened his mistress so much that she wrote to her husband to "cum home from Congress quick as lightnin," for "ole mudder brought to bed wid a young debbil." The story's identification of Crow's master as a Kentucky congressman makes him close kin to Tennessee congressman Crockett, a resemblance confirmed when he returns ("in a debbil ob a way," much like his young property) and "by gosh if he didn't roar out like ole Davy Crockett" (7). It is this Crockettesque figure who not only owns, and presumably fathers, but also names Jim Crow and, on the day he turns twenty, launches his career in show business, giving him a new suit of clothes and instructing him to "go seek my fortin" (10).

Perhaps the most remarkable evidence of Jim Crow and Davy Crockett's intertwined genealogies appears in the song "Pompey Smash," which both demonstrates the connections between blackface and backwoods in its history and dramatizes them in its lyrics. As popular music scholar Charles Wolfe has shown, "Pompey Smash" originated as a minstrel song, first published in *The Negro Singer's Own Book; Containing Every Negro Song that Has Ever Been Sung or Printed* (1846) and quickly reprinted in songbooks from New York to London. Following this initial success, however, "Pompey Smash" transformed into the folk song "Davy Crockett," variations of which musicologists have collected all over the north, south, and midwestern United States.[68] In fact, the song itself seems to authorize this transformation, as its own lyrics thematize the doubling of Pompey Smash (a Jim Crow-like blackface character) and Davy Crockett. In the mode of many other early minstrel songs, as well as backwoods humor, it consists of the speaker's string of outrageous boasts and tall tales, the most extensive of which involves a stand-off between Pompey Smash and Crockett.

> Now I'll tell you 'bout a fite I had wid Davy Crockett
> Dat haff hoss, haff kune, an haff sky rocket,
> I met him one day as I go out a gunnin,
> I ax him what he guine, an he say he guine a kunein,
> Den I ax him what he gun, an he say he got nun,
> Den I say, Davy, how you guine to hunt widout one.
>
> Den says he, Pompey Smash, just cum along ob Davy
> An I'll dam soon show you how to grin a koon crazy
> Well, I follow on arter, till Davy seed a squirrel,

Settin on a pine log, eatin sheep sorrel,
Den he stop rite still, and he gin for me to feel,
Says he, Pompey Smash, let me brace agin your heel.

I stuck out my heel, an I brace up de sinner,
An den Davy gun to grin hard for his dinner,
But de kritter didn't move—nor didn't seem to mine him,
But seem to keep a eatin, an neber look behine him.
At lass, Davy sed, he raley must be ded,
For I seed de bark fly all 'bout de kritter's hed.

Den we boph started up, de truth to diskiver,
An may de debil roast ole Pompey Smash's liber,
If it wan't a great not, 'bout as big as a punkin,
Saz I, kurnel Davy, does you call dis skunkin.
          Heah! heah!! heah!!!
Den sez he, you black kaff, now I tell you doan laff,
If you do I'll pin your ears back, an bite you in haff.

I throde down my gun, an I drop my amynishin,
Sez I, kurnel Davy, I'll cool you ambishun,
He back boph his years, and puff like a steemer,
Sez he, Pompey Smash, I'm a Tennessee skreemer,
Den we boph lock horn, an I tink my breph gone,
I was never hng [hug] so close, since de day I was born.

We fought haff a day, an den we greed to stop it,
For I was badly whipt, an so was Davy Crockett,
When we look for our heds, gosh we found 'em boph missen,
For he'd bit off mine, an I'd swallow'd hissen.
Den boph did agree for to leff de oder be,
For I was rather hard for him, an so was he for me.[69]

For all Pompey Smash and Davy Crockett's antagonism, from beginning to end, the song incessantly produces their equivalence. The subtitle identifies Pompey Smash as "The Everlastin and Unkonkerable Skreamer," a typically backwoods title that Crockett also uses in the verses above, where he identifies himself as a "Tennessee skreemer." Pompey Smash's adventures throughout—being pursued by "Big Sam," diving "eleben miles" under a river, taming an alligator—are lifted straight from the Crockett almanacs.[70] Most remarkably, the fight above culminates with Pompey Smash and Davy Crockett's physical merging, as each of them complacently discovers that he has swallowed the other's head.

I end this section with one last encounter between Jim Crow and Davy Crockett, one that is especially illuminating for the ways it not only couples these radically different subalterns as partners, but does so under the sign of the nation. In *The Life of Jim Crow*, the budding performer achieves his first success when Andrew Jackson overhears him singing, "If I war President ob dese United State / I'd eat molasses all de day, and swing upon de gate." Naturally, Jackson tells him "if I ebber come to Washington I mus gib him a call," and eventually Crow does visit Washington, where he "supped wid Davy Crockett" (9, 15). Indeed, various minstrel songs, with varying degrees of desire and trepidation, depict blackface characters instituting a regime change in Washington—a trope shared by the Crockett almanacs, which specialized in stories of Crockett galvanizing Congress with the invigorating spirit of the West.[71] In a version of "Zip Coon" from 1834, these federal fantasies converge as Crockett and Zip Coon arrive in Washington to fill the space left empty when the inflated nation explodes:

I tell you what will happin den, now bery soon,
De Nited States Bank will be blone to de moon;
Dare General Jackson will him lampoon,
An de bery nex President will be Zip Coon.

An wen Zip Coon our President shall be
He makes all de little Coons sing possum up a tree;
Oh how de little Coons will dance an sing
Wen he tie dare tails togedder cross de lindey swing.

Now mind wat you arter, your tarnel kritter Crocket [*sic*],
You shan't go head without Zip, he is de boy to block it
Zip shall be President, Crockett shall be vice,
An den dey two togedder, will had de tings nice.[72]

The nationalization of Jim Crow and Davy Crockett, which designated them as representatives of a longed-for American literature, gets spectacularly dramatized here in the installation of not one, but both of them, in the seat of national representation, the White House. Their pairing seems a fulfillment of the cross-racial, cross-cultural class solidarity that Eric Lott argues constituted the promise of white working-class audiences' investments in blackface minstrelsy. But if Lott's book is a study of what almost happened—a radicalized class alliance that might have led to an "American 1848"—I am interested in how the song evokes what happened instead: the sublation of the popular in the populist, the incorporation of difference. Even as the presidential plot of "Zip Coon" envisions a revolutionary upset, it is not at all clear whether the Zip Coon–Davy Crockett ticket works most as a national fantasy of the capital turned upside down, or as a joke that reassures white audiences that their sense of national belonging is, at any rate, less laughable than Coon's and Crockett's.

For all its raucously utopian possibilities, their bid for the presidency offers an early example of what Lauren Berlant has identified as one of the most enduring narratives of national interpellation, the "pilgrimage to Washington," a "test of citizenship competence" usually performed on "subaltern bodies and identities." (Those with power presumably need not undertake the pilgrimage because they already have a place in Washington, figuratively if not literally.) Thinking of Washington, as Berlant does, as a "borderland central to the nation" and thus "a place of national *mediation*" helps explain why the white frontiersman Crockett and the black metropolitan Zip Coon might converge there—and at the very center of national power, the White House, no less. It also brings to light the questions of national representation at stake in the pilgrimage narrative. Hyperbolic and patently incongruous, backwoods and blackface relocated to Washington become "fantasy norms of the nation form" that "create public spaces of exaggeration, irony, or ambivalence for alternative, less nationally focused, or just more critical kinds of political identification."[73] To imagine the Zip Coon–Davy Crockett presidential ticket is to critique a United States that has become indistinguishable from its eponymous inflated bank and to fantasize about a more authentic representation of the nation. Yet one must note that this fantasy undercuts the critique that invokes it, for it presumes that the United States Bank is *not*, in fact, representative of the nation, but an anomalous fraud that could be banished by a change in presidential leadership.

Indeed, Berlant's analysis suggests that the apparent challenge of a subaltern presidential ticket would inevitably resolve into normativity. Even as "subaltern style cultures" like minstrelsy or southwestern humor open

"new realms of sensation, technique, and cynical knowledge about power"
to dominant ones, "the very availability of these borrowed practices tends
to intensify the aura of incompetence and inferiority—the subaltern-
ness—of the subaltern subject. The subaltern body's peculiar burden of
national surrogacy enables many stories of minoritized citizenship to be
'included' in the self-justifying mirror of the official national narrative while
being expatriated from citizenship's promise of quotidian practical inti-
macy."[74] Berlant's identification of "national surrogacy" as the "subaltern's
body's peculiar burden" always exacts a punishing return: although subaltern bodies are invoked to represent the nation, this does not bring them
into the national fold but confirms their marginality, which the nation
depends upon to produce a story of inclusion. Little surprise, then, that
Zip Coon's dream of becoming president entails not transformation but
continuation; his campaign promise seems to be that he will make "all de
little Coons" (his biological children? African Americans in general?) put
on a never-ending minstrel show. The remainder of the chapter explores
this paradox, in which the nationalization of blackface and backwoods performances puts rural westerners and urban African Americans squarely in
their place. The allure of these performances lies in their doubled disidentification and identification with duplicity, as Jim Crow and Davy Crockett
drew fraudulence off from more official forms of literary production and,
in doing so, made fraudulence palatable, even American.

Authenticating Fakeness

White yeoman hunter of the western frontier and black plantation slave
gone north, Davy Crockett and Jim Crow could hardly have appeared more
distant from each other in the racial, regional, economic, and cultural terms
of the antebellum United States. Yet story after story and song after song
defied these obstacles to bring Crockett and Crow, or one of his blackface
counterparts, together. Minstrelsy and the Crockett literary industry set
Crockett wheeling and turning, sent Jim Crow into the backwoods to hunt
alligators, made Crockett a model for Jim Crow and Jim Crow a model for
the Crockett almanac, pitted the two against each other, and teamed them
up to lead the nation. The cavernous absence of any narrative logic behind
these stories intimates a preponderance of cultural logic. The final section

of this chapter looks back to investigate the links between its previous sections—between the conflation of Crow and Crockett and their nationalization—in order to grasp this cultural logic. It proceeds from the premise
that understanding the implausible fungibility of backwoods and blackface
can illuminate why two figures defined by the most exaggerated kinds of
fabrication became the heroes of a literary culture consumed by authenticity. The literati's enthusiasm for blackface and the backwoods performances, I argue, turned on two seemingly contradictory notions: that these
might be different from the literati's own cultural productions, and that
they might be the same.

Berlant's point that subordinated bodies are regularly conscripted for
national surrogacy emerges from a discourse (arguably still with us) that
will not or cannot imagine their personhood as such, but only their
embodiment of group traits. For those identities marked as different, this
difference often does not indicate unique lived experiences but rather functions as a placeholder for difference as a concept. Recognizing how cultural
difference might be exaggerated and diminished in the same gesture helps
explain why Davy Crockett and Jim Crow became virtually interchangeable,
as their difference from each other became subsumed in their difference
from the cultural mainstream that produced and consumed them.

At first glance, the literati's preoccupation with fakeness, detailed in
the previous chapter, makes their enthusiasm for these consummately fake
figures all the more bizarre. But fakeness does not apply to subaltern bodies
in the same way it afflicts those bodies that possess the integrity bestowed
by recognized personhood. In a culture fixated on authenticity, even the
most outlandish invention of African American and rural western figures—the ludicrously blacked-up white minstrel, the larger-than-life western roarer—fails to ruffle feathers because these identities always already
lack integrity. The popularization of mass cultural forms of fraudulence like
blackface minstrelsy and the backwoods tall tale, then, only solidifies the
association of the marginalized with the fraudulent—while under the pressure of difference, it usefully produces authenticity at the center. In doing
so, it transforms fraud from a national problem (in which the "nation" is
synecdochic for those in control of the means of literary production) into
a racial and regional marker.

These dynamics animate one of the great ironies of antebellum racialization: that at the very moment when white Americans began to imitate
African Americans, they also began to claim that African Americans

possessed an innate talent for imitation.[75] When the British actress Fanny Kemble overheard the slaves on her husband's Georgia plantation singing, for instance, she described it as "veritable negro minstrelsy," a phrase whose bizarre conjunction of the authentic ("veritable") and the fraudulent ("minstrelsy") portrays the slaves that minstrel performers mimicked as the true (that is, fake) minstrels themselves. Furthermore, the slaves practice a "very transparent plagiarism," Kemble complains: they borrow their songs from the "instrumentality" of white "overseers or masters whistling Scotch or Irish airs." These songs, in turn, become the "so-called negro melodies with which all America and England are familiar," a narrative of cultural appropriation that manages to overlook the white "so-called negroes" who made the songs famous, in order to charge black slaves with stealing white music.[76]

A still more gymnastic inversion takes place in Kennard's "Who Are Our National Poets?" which Kennard begins ironically, as befits the *Knickerbocker* house style, but ends, as Eric Lott puts it, "mastered by his own irony."[77] Initially, the article's celebration of blackface minstrels as "our national poets" serves as a *reductio ad absurdum* of literary nationalism, with its fetishization of the author who is "most secluded from foreign influences, receives the narrowest education, travels the shortest distance from home, has the least amount of spare cash, and mixes least with any class above itself." But the joke quickly gets away from Kennard, as his tributes to T. D. Rice, the African Melodists, and other blackface performers gain increasing momentum. Kennard's logic takes on a life of its own, and soon he is worrying about the corruption of this earlier blackface tradition, debased by the "base counterfeits" of "mean whites" that "pass current with most people as genuine negro songs."[78] At this point, however, the article takes another sharp turn, for Kennard's concerns about white counterfeiting abruptly dissolve in an account of black counterfeiting. In a strange commutation, the act of imposture absent from Kennard's account of blackface, at least in its nobler forms, reappears as a trait of the black slaves it imitates. "Like the wits of the white race, the negro singer is fond of appearing to extemporize, when in fact he has everything 'cut and dried' beforehand," Kennard explains, and as evidence, he tells the amazingly convoluted tale of what can only of described as a slave's minstrel show. Having learned various pieces of household gossip, "Sambo" puts them all to the tune of "Zip Coon" and practices the song while working in the field. That evening, he calls the household together for some musical entertainment, acting as if he will sing the familiar "Clare de Kitchen." However, "this is a feint, skillfully planned by Sambo," because then "suddenly, as if a new thought struck him, he makes an extraordinary flourish" and sings his new version of "Zip Coon" instead, to the delight of his audience. "Thousands at the South would recognize the foregoing as a faithful sketch of a not infrequent scene," Kennard concludes.[79] "Sambo's" pseudoauthentic folk performance presents a disconcerting reenactment of minstrelsy not only because the slave actually performs minstrel songs, but also because his performance hinges on a basic misrepresentation that passes off the manufactured for the vernacular. Its currency, moreover, goes beyond the article's individual act of transference: on the minstrel stage proper, this caricature of the dissembling slave performer finds its analogue in blackface characters' inevitable posing, from Jim Crow's tall talk to Zip Coon's gaudy pretensions to dignity. These characters shift the minstrel show's fakery from form to content, doubling and displacing its enabling impostures (white men in blackface) in enacted impostures, in which its black characters are themselves always pretending.

While blackface minstrelsy restaged fraudulence as a racial characteristic, Crockett and the backwoods culture industry likewise helped circumscribe it by defining it as a regional one. Crockett's stock in trade is, of course, the tall tale, a genre that antebellum Americans came to cherish as native to the west. Thomas Chandler Haliburton, no stranger to the ruses of regionalism, maintained that this tendency toward "tallness" had even become ingrained in western language. In his three-volume *Traits of American Humor, by Native Authors*, the Nova Scotian judge who gained fame as Yankee clockmaker Sam Slick wrote,

> Wholly unconstrained at first by conventional usages, and almost beyond the reach of the law, the inhabitants of the West indulged, to the fullest extent, their propensity for fun, frolic, and the wild and exciting sports of the chase. Emigrants from the border States, they engrafted on the dialects of their native places exaggerations and peculiarities of their own, until they acquired almost a new language, the most remarkable feature of which is its amplification. Everything is superlative, awful, powerful, monstrous, dreadful, almighty, and all-fired.

Haliburton continues, "As specimens of these extravagancies four narratives of the Adventures of the celebrated Colonel Crocket [*sic*] are given"—

four stories from the "Nashville" almanacs whose Boston origins make
their exemplification of frontier language questionable at best.[80] New Yorkers Timothy Flint and Charles Fenno Hoffman, both of whom did stints as
editors of the *Knickerbocker*, had a more familiar word for such "extravagancies"; they each referred to the West as a "paradise of puffers," saddling
it with a term more closely associated with their own brand of metropolitan
print culture.[81] Yet western fakery became an established fact, so much so
that when one of the Crockett almanacs tried to dispense with the tall tale
format, it was not only unsuccessful but, in the eyes of at least one reader,
actually a lie. In 1841, the Boston publisher S. N. Dickinson announced his
intentions to rid the almanac of "those wild and improbable stories which
have heretofore *graced* the publication" and fill it instead with "stories of
real adventures of huntsmen and others who have penetrated the wilder-
ness," which "children, as well as other persons, can read with profit and
instruction."[82] Accordingly, the following year Dickinson issued the *Crockett Almanac, 1842; Improved Edition, Containing Real Stories*, with great
hopes for its salubrious effect: "In introducing the present number of the
Crockett Almanac to the attention of the Public, the Proprietor would take
occasion to say, that, having assumed the entire charge of the work, it will
be his endeavor so far to elevate its character, as to render it every way
worthy of general patronage. The miscellaneous department has undergone
a thorough reform, in the substitution of articles relating to actual adventures in the Western country, for those heretofore published, of a less elevated character. Narratives are given of scenes, of not the less startling
interest, though depicted with the pencil of Truth."[83] The *Crockett Almanac;
Improved Edition* contains nothing about Crockett. Instead, it offers scrupulously factual accounts of historical pioneers, often with corroborating
names, dates, and places, and it replaces the earlier almanacs' exaggerated
dialect with high-toned lyricism ("It was a beautiful afternoon in the Indian
Summer, that season which, particularly in the Western portion of our
country, is of all others, the most enchanting"). "How to Capture a Bear,"
for example, relates the story of "Mr. William Halden, of New York," who
treed a bear while traveling through the western states. The situation
"would have made the blood of a Crockett run cold," but Halden acquits
himself admirably, and he "afterwards presented the bear to the editor of
the 'Grand River Times'" (a Michigan newspaper) to verify his story. Yet
somehow all this truthfulness failed to impress readers. "A great lie," one
wrote in the margin of his copy, and Dickinson did not publish another

Crockett almanac again.[84] Audiences simply refused to believe a more believable Crockett almanac.

The problem of fraudulence that plagued the center of antebellum literary culture became unproblematic—indeed, salutary—on its periphery to the extent that it produced a distinction between these two domains. Yet at the same time, as we saw earlier, antebellum Americans regularly erased that distinction by invoking blackface and backwoods performances as national. The point here is that Jim Crow and Davy Crockett thrived on two contradictory but not mutually exclusive logics: one that hinged on social identity, described above, and one that hinged on literary genre. The tall tale and the minstrel show turned fraudulence from a literary problem into a literary form, and a national literary form, at that. In their embrace of Crow and Crockett (and for that matter, their role in the production of these figures), antebellum literary culture not only displaced fraudulence while preserving it at a flattering distance, they also reappropriated it in the renovated shape of racially and regionally specific genres. Having struggled with little success against accusations of American literature's fraudulence, the literati made fraudulence itself American.

Literary nationalism, which seemingly offered a means of fixing and disseminating the identity of the expanding United States, had proven to be as much a problem as a solution; the eagerness to produce a genuine American literature threatened to manufacture an artificial one and, thus, to generate a national imaginary that was all too imaginary. The tall tale and the minstrel show, however, established the convincing "home literature" that literary nationalism, despite its assiduous efforts, had not satisfactorily produced, and they did so by transforming the problem into its own solution. Stretching the truth became a native trait; as Johnson Jones Hooper's backwoods anti-hero Captain Simon Suggs would famously declare, "It is good to be shifty in a new country."[85] The fame of Suggs's motto is as telling as the motto itself, for the value of the backwoods and blackface performances lay in their transformation of fraudulence from a shameful fact into a point of pride. Whereas the taint of fraudulence undermined more polite literary productions, minstrelsy and the tall tale inverted this action so that fraudulence heightened literary value rather than debasing it—the taller, the better, as Crockett and Crow demonstrated by raucously topping each other's yarns. In short, blackface minstrelsy and the backwoods tall tale made fraudulence generic, both in the sense of making it a defining literary feature instead of a debilitating one, and in the sense of making it reassuringly normal.

Chapter 3

"Slavery Never Can Be Represented": James Williams and the Racial Politics of Imposture

> By far the larger part of the slaves know as little of their ages as horses know of theirs, and it is the wish of most masters within my knowledge to keep their slaves thus ignorant. I do not remember to have ever met a slave who could tell of his birthday.
>
> —Frederick Douglass, *Narrative of the Life of Frederick Douglass, An American Slave, Written by Himself*

> I was born in Powhatan County, Virginia, on the plantation of George Larrimore, sen., at a place called Mount Pleasant, on the 16th of May, 1805.
>
> —James Williams, *Narrative of James Williams, An American Slave, Who Was for Several Years a Driver on a Cotton Plantation in Alabama*

If Frederick Douglass's *Narrative of the Life of Frederick Douglass* (1845), the source for the first epigraph, enjoys the distinction of being the most canonized American slave narrative, perhaps James Williams's *Narrative of James Williams* (1838), the source for the second, earns the distinction of being the most disgraced. Whereas Douglass's narrative launched its author to international fame as an anti-slavery activist, newspaper editor, and statesman, Williams's narrative, which was discredited as a fraud and hastily withdrawn from publication several months after it appeared, remained a sore spot for the anti-slavery movement for years afterward. But for a brief moment early in his career, Douglass was in danger of repeating Williams's fate. When his white abolitionist supporters famously warned him to avoid analysis or political critique and simply "give us the facts," they did so not only because they believed "philosophy" to be outside the intellectual province of a former slave, but because, as one explained, "People won't believe you ever was a slave, Frederick, if you keep on this way." Indeed, Douglass recounts, soon "I was in a pretty fair way to be denounced as an imposter." It was exactly this threat that prompted Douglass to write "such a revelation of facts as could not be made by any other than a genuine fugitive": the *Narrative of the Life of Frederick Douglass*.[1]

Underwriting the most famous and the most infamous of slave narratives alike, the problem of imposture was closely and often confoundingly tied up with the anti-slavery movement. It even spawned a small but vigorous subgenre of the slave narrative, the pseudo-slave narrative. Pseudo-slave narratives are now largely considered embarrassing irregularities in the genre, when indeed they are considered at all. But for contemporaneous readers, divisions between the two proved disconcertingly leaky: as Douglass's anecdote suggests, the abolitionist movement found it at once imperative and impossible to monitor the fraudulence of slave narratives. This chapter investigates the panic around imposter slaves as a theater where the racialization of fraudulence described in the previous chapter plays out in unexpected ways. It takes up the contradictions embodied in blackface minstrelsy—the casting of African Americans (and particularly enslaved African Americans) as both inherently authentic and innately fraudulent, as both central to national literary culture and tangential to it—and shows how easily they could explode. To do so, it juxtaposes the *Narrative of James Williams*, the only known (or believed) pseudo-slave narrative by an African American author, with two pseudo-slave narratives by white authors, Richard Hildreth's *The Slave: or Memoirs of Archy Moore* (1836) and Mattie Griffith's *Autobiography of a Female Slave* (1856), which met with very different fates.[2] Hildreth and Griffith's impersonations were accepted even after they were exposed, a reception that contrasts sharply with the deep-seated suspicion surrounding the testimonies of fugitive slaves, including James Williams's narrative. The second half of the chapter, however, unfolds an unexpected twist to this story. While many white readers treated the *Narrative of James Williams* skeptically and some actively attempted to disprove it, once it was debunked they reversed course, refusing to believe Williams could have crafted such a persuasive fiction. As the racialization of fraudulence evolved, it also manifested a disconcerting tendency to back-fire, as white readers unintentionally extended to African Americans the elusive capacity for original literary creation.

Imposture Along the Color Line

The term "pseudo-slave narrative" itself should invite suspicion, since as numerous critics have pointed out, the line between fact and fiction in slave narratives was both heavily policed and difficult to draw. Fearing recapture, many fugitive slave authors changed names and other information in order to protect themselves, but the conventions of anti-slavery print culture destabilized distinctions between truth and falsehood as well. Slave narratives were usually solicited, transcribed, or subjected to rigorous editing by white abolitionists, whose own literary tastes often eclipsed the voices of the former slaves. Even as editors inevitably insisted that narratives had fallen directly "from the lips" of their narrators, they exaggerated the sensationalism of the fugitives' accounts or excised incidents they judged too incendiary for public taste, inserted flights of sentimental fancy or anti-slavery polemics, and regularized and regulated authors' language. Less concerned with individual life stories than with establishing a unified picture of slavery, they jettisoned or massaged details in favor of representative experience. Even when abolitionist editors did not directly intervene in slaves' narratives, the movement's public relations imperatives and the conventions of white literary culture almost inevitably mediated their production. In a pioneering essay questioning the relevance of authenticity to the slave narrative, John Sekora explains, "Editors and sponsors sought not merely facts but facticity—the careful layering of heterogeneous material into a collective and invulnerable whole."[3] Consequently, while white northerners incessantly scrutinized slave testimonies for their authenticity, that authenticity relied on an ability to reproduce existing accounts, as Frederick Douglass discovered when William Lloyd Garrison commended his willingness not to "overstate a single fact in regard to SLAVERY AS IT IS"—the title of Theodore Dwight Weld's widely read 1838 collection of documentary evidence from southern newspapers.[4] As Dwight McBride puts it, "The slave is the 'real' body, the 'real' evidence, the 'real' fulfillment of what has been told before."[5]

Perhaps no writer was as painfully aware of the traps of abolitionist reading as Harriet Jacobs, who begins the preface to *Incidents in the Life of a Slave Girl*, "Reader, be assured this narrative is no fiction." But neither is it a strict adherence to the facts, as she goes on to explain: "I am aware that some of my adventures may seem incredible; but they are, nevertheless, strictly true. I have not exaggerated the wrongs inflicted by Slavery; on the contrary, my descriptions fall far short of the facts."[6] Readers would never accept "the facts" as anything but fabrication, Jacobs implies, leaving her no choice but to defraud them in the other direction—to write scant of the facts, rather than in excess of them. As William Andrews puts it, Jacobs must be "sufficiently insincere" to guarantee that she has not fictionalized her story.[7] Critics of *Incidents* and other slave narratives have noted that the documentary demands of the genre frequently run aground on the inexpressible nature of physical and psychic pain, but alongside the impossibility of representing slavery's extremes of violence, Jacobs alerts us to the dilemma that awaits at the other end of the transaction: the tautological character of readers' belief. Indeed, some anti-slavery activists suggested that slavery itself bankrupted designations of fraud and authenticity before the fact. Douglass, whose own narratives cannily play with problems of plausibility, pronounced the institution a "gross fraud" ratified by state- and church-sponsored lies and at odds with "natural" morality.[8] Other anti-slavery activists also figured slavery as a large-scale confidence game. An 1843 article in the *Emancipator*, for example, begins, "*Stop the Swindler! What swindler?*—AMERICAN SLAVERY!"[9] Garrison took the metaphor a step further, arguing that slavery had made the whole United States "a stupendous republican imposture."[10]

Given this history, can categories of fraud and authenticity retain any usefulness for understanding slave narratives? Such a question becomes more worrisome when we see how faithfully the debates that dogged the slave narratives' original publications have been reenacted in more recent scholarship, most notably the ongoing controversy over Olaudah Equiano's *Interesting Narrative*.[11] My point here is not that all attempts to verify or question the factual basis of slave narratives are inherently racist, futile, or both; in fact, I put the *Narrative of James Williams* under a similar lens later in the chapter. But I do want to underscore the risk such attempts present of ensnaring critics in the terms of the narratives' initial production and reception among the self-appointed guardians of the anti-slavery movement. This history reminds us that we can usefully discuss slave narratives

in terms of fraud or authenticity only by understanding these as instrumen-
talized categories, rather than definitive ones. As Williams Wells Brown, in
a lecture before the Salem, Massachusetts Female Anti-Slavery Society, told
his assembled listeners, "Slavery has never been represented; Slavery never
can be represented."[12]

Slave narratives had circulated in Europe and the Americas since the
eighteenth century, but their popularity surged in the late 1830s and 1840s:
whereas four slave narratives appeared in the United States and Britain
between 1820 and 1829, between 1830 and 1839 that number climbed to nine,
and between 1840 and 1849 it shot up to twenty-five (twenty-eight, if we
include fictionalized slave narratives).[13] Primarily, the growing influence of
the abolitionist movement motivated their popularity, although as Saidiya
Hartman has pointed out, many readers no doubt also enjoyed them for
their sensationalism.[14] But slave narratives possessed a further attraction:
ironically, given the enduring debates around imposture the genre spawned,
slave narratives were seen to possess unique claims on literary authenticity.
White Americans entertained romantic fantasies of African Americans'
essentially artless nature, holding them out as an antidote to the hard-nosed
commercial and social machinations corrupting white culture. Like blackface
minstrelsy and backwoods tall tales, slave narratives helped to make up the
nation's fetishized literary periphery—a periphery that, as I suggested in the
last chapter, many believed might redeem the literary center. Thus literary
critics celebrated slave narratives for the salutary potential they held for moribund American writing to a degree that often feels peculiarly aestheticized,
depersonalized, and depoliticized. As critic and Unitarian minister Theodore
Parker wrote with evident relief, "There is one portion of our permanent
literature, if literature it may be called, which is wholly indigenous and original. . . . We have one series of literary productions that could be written by
none but Americans, and only here; I mean the Lives of Fugitive Slaves. All
the original romance of Americans is in them, not in the white man's
novel."[15] Parker's literary-clerical colleague Ephraim Peabody concurred,
observing, "There are those who fear lest the elements of poetry and
romance should fade out of the tame and monotonous social life of modern
times," but "there is no danger of it while there are any slaves left to seek
for freedom, and to tell the story of their efforts to obtain it."[16] Parker and
Peabody's disturbing sanguinity testifies to the importance African American
slave narratives held for national literary culture during the period. By 1853,
an article in *Graham's Magazine* fulminated that slaves had inundated the

literary market: "The shelves of booksellers groan under the weight of Sambo's woes, done up in covers! What a dose we have had and are having! The
population of readers has gone a wool-gathering! Our 'Helots of the West'
are apparently at a premium with the publishers just now; and we have
Northern folks as anxious to make money of them, as the Southrons can be,
for their lives."[17] The passage's final jab implies that slaves are as exploited
by white northerners' literary enthusiasms as they are by southerners' laws.
The writer's concern, however, lies less with the suffering slaves than with
"the [white] readers of the North," who he contends have been subjected to
their own kind of slavery—the slavery of the reigning obsession with slaves.
"We cannot tolerate negro-slavery of this sort—we are abolitionists on this
question!" the writer declares archly. "If we are threatened with any more
negro-stories—here goes!" The writer does not share any belief in slaves'
literary authenticity; indeed, he compares the literature of slavery to Barnum's "Woolly Horse, Tom Thumb, and [Feejee] Mermaid" and the ubiquitous "Locke's moon hoax."[18] But his zeal to prove that "nothing has a slower
growth than *truth*" and that "black letters" must therefore be false suggests
exactly how many people thought otherwise.

The bilious *Graham's* writer is far from an abolitionist. Yet even as
many sympathetic northerners hailed African American slaves and the
narratives they wrote as touchstones of authenticity, paradoxically they,
too, remained convinced of these authors' inevitable duplicity. Boston
abolitionist Samuel Gridley Howe put it this way: "The negro, like other
men, naturally desires to live in the light of truth; but he hides in the
shadow of falsehood, more or less deeply, according as his safety or wel-
fare seems to require it."[19] As numerous critics have noted, the anticipa-
tion of black deceit literally frames slave narratives in the form of the
vast quantities of authenticating materials—letters of recommendation,
reprinted advertisements for runaways, excerpts of state slave codes—that
routinely buttress them. This racial double casting, which assigned African Americans seemingly contradictory roles as both genuinely artless
and consummately artful, forms part of a broader belief in the "duality
or instability of Negro character" that George Frederickson has identified
as one of the most lasting legacies of slavery.[20] As the previous chapter
suggests, that concept of "duality" may have originated with the "Negro
characters" of the minstrel stage, or at least taken shape there. But white
readers readily applied it to actual African Americans, in part because, as
I argued earlier, minstrelsy itself conflated theatrical "Negro characters"

with innate "Negro character," presenting the genre's operative impostures as a (black) racial disposition for fakery.

Attempts to adjudicate the truth of fugitives' words reached a fever pitch in the pages of northern newspapers, which bristled with warnings against false slaves preying on towns with known anti-slavery sympathies. Newspaper alerts about imposter fugitives were such a fixture of antebellum print culture that they demand analysis as a genre of their own, as David Waldstreicher has done for runaway slave advertisements. Although space does not permit such a full examination here, the warnings do offer a fascinating barometer of northerners' panic about imposter slaves, while unintentionally revealing the profound instability of this category. In early 1858, for instance, the *New York Tribune* complained, "The trade or profession of a fugitive from slavery has proved so lucrative, that quite a number of black and copper-colored scoundrels are prosecuting it on speculation, some of them (we think) with white villains who corroborate their lies and share their gains. We very often receive letters narrating the arrival, in this or that Northern neighborhood, of an alleged fugitive, who tells long and startling yarns about his escape from bondage in some heroic or wonderful way, his arrival in this city, what was said and done for him here by so and so, &c.—much of which we know to be utterly false."[21] Even professedly abolitionist newspapers urged skepticism towards freemen "speculating" in slavery. "Once for all, we earnestly caution our anti-slavery friends to be less credulous, and more searching, in every case where one presents himself as a fugitive slave," William Lloyd Garrison wrote in the *Liberator*. "Imposters may naturally be expected to abound with the growing sympathy for the enslaved, and the strongest evidence should be required before giving any heed to the representations that may be made, in all such cases."[22] But the abolitionists' rigorous credibility tests often placed fugitives in impossible situations. "Whenever one comes along, who pretends to have been helped through this city as a fugitive, just ask him to show the documents," the *Tribune* writer (probably editor Horace Greeley) counseled; "If he cannot, set him down as a swindler, and you will scarcely ever be wrong."[23] The *Tribune*'s breezy tone suggests exactly how quickly a fugitive who had neglected to procure certificates from the right sources might have been consigned to the category of "swindler" and dismissed accordingly. "Note also that the real fugitives always seek counsel and sympathy from men of their own race, while the bogus are sure to give them as wide a berth as possible," the article continued, thereby damning every fugitive

108 Chapter 3

who asked the assistance of a white person to immediate suspicion. Yet we know from well-authenticated narratives like those of Frederick Douglass and William Wells Brown that real fugitives frequently sought aid from white abolitionists, whether through chance (statistically, any person a fugitive encountered in the North was more likely to be white than black) or because white abolitionists were usually the most prominent members of the movement. Such accounts reveal that the ostensibly open public sphere of the abolitionist movement—the freedoms of mobility and expression it promised fugitive slaves and freemen—required vigilant upkeep, an ongoing drawing and redrawing of its borders.

The racialization of fraudulence we can glimpse in the newspaper warnings against imposter slaves comes into sharp focus when one compares the panic surrounding black impersonators of fugitive slaves with the warm reception that pseudo-slave narratives by white authors Richard Hildreth and Mattie Griffith enjoyed, even once they were exposed as fictions. Reading Hildreth's *The Slave: or Memoirs of Archy Moore* and Griffith's *Autobiography of a Female Slave* today, one can only wonder that they were not exposed sooner. Both closely follow novelistic conventions: long and floridly written, they hang their narrators' journeys to freedom on melodramatic love plots. Archy Moore escapes slavery to become a pirate (with a specialty in raiding the U.S. coastline), but he vows to return to save his wife and child, who remain in slavery. After enduring years of physical and psychological cruelty as a slave on a Kentucky plantation, Griffith's narrator Ann is bought and emancipated by a sympathetic Bostonian, but not before her lover commits suicide in despair.[24] Both narratives also cover considerable geographic terrain, offering a sort of written panorama of slavery that spans plantations mean and prosperous, elite urban households, slave pens, auction blocks, and swamp-based runaway slave insurgencies. But as generically anomalous as they may seem today, *The Slave* and *Autobiography of a Female Slave* were hardly the only antebellum pseudo-slave narratives. They are simply the best remembered, perhaps because *The Slave* went through so many editions that it remains relatively easy to come by, and University Press of Mississippi published a paperback reprint of *Autobiography of a Female Slave* in 1998. In their own time, they vied with Jabez Delano Hammond's *Life and Opinions of Julius Melbourn* (1847), Peter Neilson's *Life and Adventures of Zamba, an African Negro King* (1847), and Emily Catherine Pierson's *Jamie Parker, the Fugitive* (1856), among others.[25]

The genre's popularity during the antebellum years and afterward raises an unavoidable question: why were free white authors so eager to impersonate black fugitive slaves? Sheer zeal for the anti-slavery cause obviously constituted a major factor. Hildreth advocated tirelessly for the movement for years, publishing an influential economic argument against slavery, *Despotism in America* (1840); organizing against the Fugitive Slave Law in Boston; and denouncing the institution in his various roles as newspaper editor, journalist, and historian. Griffith, the daughter of a Kentucky slave-holding family, flouted her community and sacrificed her own interests to support abolition. Orphaned and left to support her invalid sister and three young nieces, Griffith's only financial assets lay in the slaves she inherited from her father. She thus wrote the *Autobiography* at once to condemn slavery and to end her own dependency on it, intending, according to her friend the Boston educator and editor Elizabeth Peabody, "*to return* to her poor people the money they had earned for her—to establish themselves in freedom."[26] Indeed, Charles Nichols and Augusta Rohrbach have argued that white slave impersonators generally were actuated as much by the prospect of financial gain as from any ethical imperative.[27] Certainly, slave narratives became immensely popular in the antebellum years, much to the disgust of the *Graham's* critic quoted earlier, but this estimation of the profits of anti-slavery publishing seems high in an era when very little publishing at all earned a profit. In fact, *The Autobiography of a Female Slave* was a financial failure, prompting Elizabeth Peabody to solicit aid for Griffith more directly. "'The Autobiography' has not sold well," Peabody confided to a friend, "& she is brought to a standstill."[28] Hildreth optimistically sold his share in the newspaper he edited, the *Boston Atlas*, before writing *The Slave*, but even though the book went through eight editions, Hildreth was obliged to resume his duties at the *Atlas* soon after it was published.[29]

Furthermore, white abolitionists stood to gain more than economic rewards from impersonating black slaves. As Christopher Castiglia has shown, nineteenth-century abolitionist organizations like the American Anti-Slavery Society routinely "interiorized" claims to social equality by appealing to the sufferings of disenfranchised persons rather than critiquing the structural injustices that disenfranchised them. These African American interiors, Castiglia argues, in turn became the basis for new forms of interiority by white abolitionists, who acquired "civic depth" through sympathetic identification with "black virtue."[30] As extraordinarily literal examples of white abolitionists' interiorization of black slaves, Richard Hildreth's and Mattie Griffith's impersonations offer their authors a remediated whiteness, at once dignified by blackness and safely differentiated from it. Such convoluted dynamics of subject formation, in which identifications with blackness enhance whiteness, certainly go far in explaining the insistent whiteness of both Hildreth's and Griffith's "black" narrators, which otherwise seems to undermine the authors' assumed identities. Archy Moore, as the title of subsequent editions of the book announced, is a "White Slave," with "some imperceptible portion of African blood."[31] Similarly, Ann is quick to inform us that her skin "was no perceptible shade darker that that of my young mistress."[32] In fact, *Autobiography of a Female Slave* constantly flirts with self-disclosure, as the fictitious author Ann repeatedly conjures up the real author Griffith. At one point, another slave on the plantation admiringly tells Ann, "Yes, chile, you does talk so pretty, like dem ar' great white scholards. Many times I had wondered how a poor darkie could larn so much." Elsewhere Ann encounters a woman whose biography exactly parallels Griffith's: "The lady's entire wealth was in six negroes [who] were hired out at the highest market prices, and by the proceeds she was supported. She had been raised in a strongly conservative community; nay, her own family were (to use a Kentuckyism) the 'pick and choose' of the pro-slavery society . . . yet she, despite the force of education and the influence of domestic training, had broken away from old trammels and leash-strings, and was, both in thought and expression, a bold, ingrain abolitionist. She defied the lions in their chosen dens."[33] We might read Griffith here as resisting her own cross-racial performance, playfully dropping hints to her identity, or simply patting herself on the back. But more than anything, *Autobiography of a Female Slave*'s successive identifications and dis-identifications, its imposture and its exposure, leave the impression that there was little in pseudo-slave narratives to reveal.

Indeed, when the real authorship of both *The Slave* and *Autobiography* ultimately did emerge, the reception was notably anticlimactic. Hildreth had taken pains to present *The Slave* as a true account, adopting the pose of editor rather than author. In a prefatory "Advertisement" he explains, "It is unnecessary to detain the reader, with a narrative of the somewhat singular manner in which the MS. of the following memoirs came into my possession," and he carefully distances himself from the memoir-writer Archy Moore: "I would not be understood . . . as implicitly adopting all the writer's feelings and sentiments; for it must be confessed that he sometimes expresses himself with a force and freedom, which by many will be thought extravagant."[34] But readers were quick to see through the ruse. The very first review of *The Slave*, in the *Boston Atlas*, referred to it as a novel, and the second, in the *Boston Daily Advocate*, "a fiction woven out of terrible truths."[35] Despite positive reviews, in March 1838 (probably not coincidentally, less than a month after publishing the *Narrative of James Williams*) the American Anti-Slavery Society dropped *The Slave* from the catalog of books sold at its office. A statement in the *Emancipator* condemned its blasphemous language and sexually graphic content, but considered the book's most damning feature the fact that "*it is a work of fiction*, without the readers being admonished that such is its character."[36] Few shared the American Anti-Slavery Society's concern, however. As a review of the narrative in the *New York Plaindealer* averred, "Fiction never performs a nobler office than when she acts as the handmaid of truth," and *The Slave*'s office was deemed noble enough to see it through seven more editions, including, in 1852, a significant expansion. The 1852 edition, moreover, carried the imprint of Tappan and Whittemore; apparently even American Anti-Slavery Society cofounder Lewis Tappan changed his mind about the virtue of Hildreth's deception.

Like Hildreth, Griffith had assured her readers, "This book is not a wild romance to beguile your tears and cheat your fancy. No; it is the truthful autobiography of one who has suffered long, long, the pains and trials of slavery."[37] But even from the earliest reviews, few appear to have given much credence to her claims. The *Liberator* unhesitatingly assumed that it was not the autobiography it purported to be, but rather "recognize[d] it as the production of an elevated and a philanthropic heart," while the *Boston Evening Transcript* informed its readers, "Its title indicates that it is an autobiography, yet it is not precisely so." Instead, "It is a work of the 'Uncle Tom' and 'Ida May' school," that is, a novel about slavery by a white female author.[38] Subsequent reviews in the *Christian Inquirer*, the *Christian Examiner*, and the *Louisville Journal* all evinced familiarity with the narrative's authorship, which caused little stir.[39] Instead, its reviewers insisted on an emotional, rather than technical, distinction between truth and fiction. The *New York Independent*, which seems to have been the first outlet to reveal the identity of the *Autobiography*'s author, nevertheless followed this disclosure with the declaration, "The book is a story of fact throughout."[40] Similarly, the *Christian Examiner* affirmed, "We have confidence in the truth of the narrative," and the *Christian Inquirer* maintained, "If a tenth part of it be true, it ought to make Abolitionists of us all."⁴¹ If the fiction of *The Slave* made it "the handmaid of truth," the fiction of *The Autobiography of a Female Slave* was as true as truth itself. The sanction, even welcome, the abolitionist community gave these impersonations stands in stark contrast to the furor raised by false fugitive slaves and, as we shall see, the *Narrative of James Williams*. What appeared as authenticity—metaphysical, if not physical—on one side of the color line, appeared as unambiguous fraud on the other.

"A Portrait and Other Embellishments"

James Williams's life, like the life of his narrative, began promisingly. Raised as a house slave in Powhatan County, Virginia, "comfortably clothed and fed, kindly treated by my old master and mistress and the young ladies, and the playmate and confidant of my young master, I did not dream of the dark reality of evil before me."⁴² Williams's fortunes change dramatically, however, when his master dies and his master's son, George Larrimore, removes all the field slaves to a cotton plantation in rural Greene County, Alabama. Larrimore lures Williams into accompanying him to the planta-tion in the capacity of a body servant and then abruptly leaves him there, under the supervision of a drunken, brutal overseer, to be the other slaves' driver. Surreptitiously, Williams works to subvert the overseer's authority, dodging whipping assignments and conveying vital information to the field slaves, but eventually the overseer discovers these tactics. When he tells Williams to prepare to be whipped himself, Williams takes off. Befriending slave-catching hounds, fending off wolves, and outpacing pursuers, he makes his way north, and when he reaches Philadelphia he falls in with a group of abolitionists, who send him to New York. Eventually his hosts there conclude that it is not safe for him to remain in the United States, and they dispatch him on a ship to Liverpool, England.

Williams, according to his own account, arrived in New York on Janu-ary 1, 1838. Three days later, the Executive Committee of the American Anti-Slavery Society authorized John Greenleaf Whittier to transcribe his story, to be published by the Society's Publishing Committee "with a por-trait and other embellishments"—a description that the American Anti-Slavery Society would have reason to regret in the following year.⁴³ The public at large first learned of Williams on January 25, 1838, when the *Emancipator* announced the imminent publication of his narrative, promising, "no work more interesting has been published, since the beginning of the Anti-Slavery discussion."[44] No previous slave narrative had ever been accompanied by such an extraordinary publicity campaign: the item's headline, "James Williams—The Fugitive Slave," with its direct article (*"The Fugitive Slave"*) and attendant associations of singularity, suggests just how unprecedented an event the narrative's publication was. Over the next several months, numerous articles appeared trumpeting the power of Williams's narrative, its electrifying portrayal of plantation life, its potential to galvanize the movement, and, above all, its authenticity. The *Liberator* proclaimed it "incontrovertibly true"; *Human Rights* certified, "we are convinced of its truth and accuracy"; and the *Pennsylvania Freeman* assured readers, "It is no *fiction*."[45] An advertisement for its sale trumpeted, "AUTHENTIC NARRATIVE OF AN AMERICAN SLAVE!" and went on to tout the "truth and accuracy" of "the simple and unvarnished story" (figure 8).[46]

This designation was partly recursive: Williams's narrative was judged to be factual because it shored up the movement's existing knowledge. Another writer to the *Pennsylvania Freeman*, enumerating the reasons he believed the *Narrative* to be true, placed this at the top of his list: "it is just what we might expect from the known laws and usages of the South. (See *Stroud's Sketches of Slave Laws*.)" Likewise, the *Liberator* review judged it "an important addition to the documentary evidence respecting the secrets of the slaveholder's prison-houses" "because it so powerfully corroborates other evidence and facts which have been published." Both writers' circular logic, in which Williams contributes to the available body of evidence by replicating it, betrays the tightly controlled definition of "knowledge" within the movement. As the first writer puts it, "if we would see the hearts of tyrants relenting, fetters bursting, and righteousness flooding the land, we must *draw out and multiply* specific facts"—not add to them.[47] If, as seems likely, Williams borrowed some of the events of his story from published sources (as the *Liberator* appreciatively remarks, at least two of its incidents also appear in George Bourne's *A Picture of Slavery in the United States of America*), he was only following the abolitionist movement's established rules of evidence.

From the outset, abolitionists recognized the importance Williams's narrative held for the cause. A writer to the *Herald of Freedom* predicted, "The *Narrative of James Williams* is doubtless destined to work a very great

AUTHENTIC NARRATIVE

OF AN

American Slave!

NARRATIVE of JAMES WILLIAMS, an American Slave; who was for several years a driver on a cotton plantation in Alabama. Published and sold by ISAAC KNAPP, at 25, Cornhill—price, bound, 25 cts; paper covers, 18 3-4 cts.

This work contains the simple and unvarnished story of an American Slave,—of one whose situation, in the first place, as a favorite servant in an aristocratic family in Virginia, and afterwards as the sole and confidential driver on a large plantation in Alabama, afforded him rare and peculiar advantages for accurate observation of the practical workings of the system. His intelligence, evident candor, and grateful remembrance of those kindnesses which in a land of slavery made his cup of suffering less bitter; the perfect accordance of his statements (made at different times and to different individuals) one with another, as well as those statements themselves, all afford strong confirmation of the truth and accuracy of his story.—EDITOR.

———

NOTE. The reader is referred to John G. Whittier, of Amesbury, Mass., or to the following gentlemen, who have heard the whole or a part of his history from his own lips : Emmor Kimber, of Kimberton, Pa., Lindley Choates, of Lancaster Co., do ; James Mott, of Philadelphia, Lewis Tappan, Elizur Wright, Jr. Rev. Dr. Follen, and James G. Birney, of New York. The latter gentleman, who was a few years ago a citizen of Alabama, assures us that the statements made to him by James Williams were such as he had every reason to believe, from his own knowledge of slavery in that State.   mar 30.

Figure 8: "Authentic Narrative of an American Slave!" Advertisement for the *Narrative of James Williams*, from the *Liberator*, 30 March 1838. (Courtesy of the Newberry Library) revolution in the feeling of community on the subject of American slavery," detailing at length the conversions to abolitionism it would effect from northern apologists, mob members, fence-sitters, and defenders of slavery on biblical grounds.[48] (Indeed, two weeks earlier, the newspaper had published an effusive appeal for emancipation entitled "Suggested by Reading the Narrative of James Williams.")[49] In numerous letters to the editor, correspondents attested their confidence in Williams's account. One contrasted its genuineness with Hildreth's fiction, calling it "the tale of the real fugitive, the real Archy Moore," while another declared, "That the narrative is authentic I have not the least doubt."[50] Williams's narrative quickly became the standard by which other slave narratives were measured; in September 1838 the *Michigan Observer* enticed readers with "the promise of another Narrative, fresh from the lips of a fugitive slave, which, in some respects, will equal in interest that of Williams."[51] A correspondent for the *Emancipator* advised, "James Williams should be published on a sheet and sold by the thousand—by the tens of thousands;—I think it could be printed for 10 or $15 the thousand;—Do think of this. . . . I should like to have this narrative placed in every family."[52] The American Anti-Slavery Society immediately acted on this suggestion, issuing the narrative in two cheap formats: as an eight-page pamphlet edition of the *Anti-Slavery Examiner*, which printed the entire text in three columns of small type, and as a similar pamphlet in its Abolitionist's Library series.[53] In the meantime, the *Michigan Observer* serialized Williams's narrative, while the American Anti-Slavery Society extended its geographic reach even further by sending a free copy to every member of Congress.[54]

Through some one of these channels, the *Narrative* found its way to Greene County, Alabama, the setting for its events, igniting an explosive exchange between the local paper and the *Emancipator*. In the March 29 issue of the *Alabama Beacon*, the newspaper's editor, J. B. Rittenhouse, fired the opening salvo of the controversy. "We have been politely favored by our correspondent with the lying Abolition pamphlet entitled the 'Narrative of James Williams,'" he fumes, and although he admits that he himself has not read the narrative fully, he has been assured that it is "a foul fester of falsehood" and "a miserably 'weak invention of the enemy.'" He concludes by promising threateningly, "We shall pay it our respects in our coming number."[55] Lewis Tappan, of the American Anti-Slavery Society, responded in the next issue of the *Emancipator* with a lengthy open letter to the *Beacon*. Tappan initially took a conciliatory tone, acknowledging, "If it is 'a foul fester of falsehood,' we shall be glad to be undeceived, for we know, as well as they can tell us, that falsehood cannot help our cause." It wasn't long, however, before a note of anger crept in: "But we beg our Alabama friend to bear in mind, that in the sober judgment of many thousands of intelligent people, the narrative appears *prima facie* to be true, and to refute it you must give us something more than naked denials or evasions."[56] From there, the debate erupted and the two newspapers traded insinuations, insults, and accusations over the next several months. Each brought forward fresh evidence, only to be quickly dismissed by the other; each charged the other with prevaricating or falsifying information; each offered competing theories, variously sympathetic to Williams's honesty and literary endeavors.

Why did the American Anti-Slavery Society defend Williams so assiduously, rather than cutting ties at the first sign of trouble? The possibility that Williams had invented the narrative—that is, reinvented himself as a slave—held at least as many dangers for the abolitionist movement as it did for Williams himself. These were due in part to the ingrained racism that expected black Americans to lie but white Americans to adjudicate their deceptions. Such logic shifted the responsibility for fugitives' testimony to the white gatekeepers of abolitionism's public relations. Moreover, the movement was already fending off accusations that its representatives regularly exaggerated or even invented slavery's worst abuses, and an exposure on the scale that the *Beacon* threatened would set its efforts back significantly. Even more disturbingly, Williams's apparent decision to exchange his status as a freeman for that of a fugitive slave implied that there was more cultural (and even financial) capital to be had within the anti-slavery movement in being black and enslaved than in being black and free.

Ordinarily, authors of slave narratives were called upon to demonstrate their veracity through public performances. Audiences flocked to lecture halls to hear former slaves' stories firsthand, to cross-examine them, and to see scars from whippings or other traces of plantation violence.[57] But Williams's flight to England foreclosed that possibility, and in the absence of his testifying body, his narrative's claims quickly unraveled. On April 5, the *Beacon* announced that its sources reported that no George Larrimore had ever resided in either Powhatan County, Virginia, or Greene County, Alabama. Tappan, this time joined by James Birney, the corresponding secretary of the American Anti-Slavery Society, objected that the inquiries were misleading in tone and wording and, moreover, such statements could not be trusted in the absence of authenticated certificates. Maintaining "we are far from charging [Rittenhouse] with intentional misrepresentation," they nonetheless insisted that his zeal for the slaveholding cause did not recommend him as a fair judge of the situation: "We may safely say, that his eagerness to injure those to whom he assumed the status of an adversary, disqualified him much for soberly investigating truth." In consequence, they opined, the American Anti-Slavery Society was under no obligation to accept the testimonies presented. "They *may* be all that we could insist on their being *proved* to be—we assert nothing to the contrary—but the proof, which ought not to be denied us, has not, as yet, been exhibited."[58]

Yet others were more readily convinced. The *New-York Commercial Advertiser* joined the fray on September 19, comparing the "jesuitism by which the public were gulled" by the American Anti-Slavery Society to the publication of *The Awful Disclosures of Maria Monk*, the sensationalist (and fabricated) exposé of convent life that had sent shivers through the American public two years before.[59] Even John Greenleaf Whittier, Williams's amanuensis, appeared somewhat tentative about the matter, writing in the *Pennsylvania Freeman* that "we candidly admit that it has created a doubt in our mind of the accuracy of some particulars," although "we are still disposed to give credit in the main to his narrative."[60] And in the privacy of his diary, Lewis Tappan now put James Williams's name within quotation marks.[61] When the *Beacon* first attacked the narrative, the Executive Committee of the American Anti-Slavery Society had tried to defend it on grounds of general rather than personal veracity, announcing that the picture of slavery presented there, "if not drawn from life, was certainly true to nature."[62] But apparently Williams's deceptions could not sustain the claim to representative truthfulness that had made Richard Hildreth's and Mattie Griffith's deceptions "authentic." The American Anti-Slavery Society finally deemed the campaign to deflect the investigation impracticable: on October 25, 1838, the Executive Committee issued an official statement in both the *Emancipator* and the *Liberator* discontinuing the sale of the work.[63]

For many years, studies of slave narratives likewise found little value in the *Narrative of James Williams*. Gilbert Osofsky dismisses the *Narrative* as one of a "number of slave narratives [that] are of such doubtful validity that they may be shelved at the start," while John Blassingame excludes it from his anthology *Slave Testimony* as "an outright fraud."[64] Recently, several scholars have returned to the incident with a more critical eye, treating

Williams's narrative as a limit case to illustrate tensions within the slave narrative as a genre. According to William Andrews, for example, the American Anti-Slavery Society's defense of Williams "reveals how important the 'performative' feature of a slave's narrative was to securing the credence of its . . . audience." Ann Fabian, too, reads Williams as a reminder of "how difficult it was in the late 1830s to incorporate the testimony of slaves into the cultural fabric of the antebellum north," as his fabrications violated the genre's mandate "to convince audiences and readers that former slaves, so notorious in bondage as skilled liars, had been converted in freedom to tellers of truths." Laura Browder, who mistakenly assumes that Whittier was the actual author of the *Narrative of James Williams* and Williams simply his invention, groups the narrative with pseudo-slave narratives by white authors, which she reads as manifesting the abolitionist community's anxieties about controlling black voices. She points out that by establishing certain conventions of authenticity, such anxieties inflected the production of "genuine" slave narratives, as well.[65] By using the *Narrative of James Williams* to illuminate the slave narrative's acutely unstable protocols of authenticity, such symptomatic readings find new significance in a book that had been consigned to irrelevance. But whereas earlier critics tended to dismiss Williams's narrative as anomalous, these more recent accounts equally risk effacing it by reading it as representative. Specifically, they read controversy that surrounded the narrative, rather than the narrative itself.

    In the remainder of this chapter, I look closely at Williams's narrative, not just as an event but also as a text, in order to understand why the suspected imposture provoked such a crisis. Of course, it is difficult to understand what Williams's book *does* without understanding what it *is*. Did he write a true history, altering minor details for self-protection? A wholesale fabrication? A fictionalized frame relating true incidents, lived or reported? Such questions threaten to return us to the binary opposition of fraud and authenticity. Yet for all the dangers these categories pose, they prove indispensable to our understanding of Williams's work simply because, historically, they were the terms under which he wrote. Abolitionism managed the voices of fugitive slaves in these terms; whatever Williams did, he did through them. It becomes necessary, then, to situate the *Narrative of James Williams* in these terms without reducing it to them—to demonstrate that the question of whether Williams falsified his narrative or not should interest us for reasons that cannot be satisfied by either an affirmative or a negative answer to that question.

Other slaves whose narratives came under suspicion—which were most of them, for reasons suggested earlier—were able to establish their stories in traceable facts. When abolitionists raised doubts about the *Narrative of the Life of Frederick Douglass*, verification of Douglass's history came from an unlikely (and unwitting) source. A. C. C. Thompson, a Delaware planter, printed a lengthy refutation of Douglass's statements in the *Delaware Republican*, in which he asserted, "Although I am aware that no sensible unprejudiced person will credit such a ridiculous publication, which bears the glaring impress of falsehood on every page, yet I deem it expedient that I should give the public some information respecting the validity of this narrative, because I was for many years a citizen of the section of the country where the scenes of the above mentioned narrative are laid; and am intimately acquainted with most of the gentlemen whose characters are so shamefully traduced." Thompson denied Douglass's allegations that slave children were commonly separated from their mothers and that it was not unusual for masters and overseers to murder slaves, insisted on the humanity of his former neighbors, and finally disputed the idea that Douglass had written the narrative at all.

> About eight years ago, I knew this recreant slave by the name of Frederick Bailey, (instead of Douglass). He then lived with Mr. Edward Covey, and was an unlearned, and rather an ordinary negro, and I am confident that he was not capable of writing the Narrative alluded to; for none but an educated man, and one who had some knowledge of the rules of grammar, could write so correctly. Although, to make the imposition at all credible, the composer has labored to write it in as plain as style as possible; consequently, the detection of the first falsehood proves the whole production to be notoriously untrue.[66]

Douglass quickly published a widely reprinted response to Thompson's allegations, in which he thanked his accuser for rendering him a valuable service. In confirming the existence of Frederick Bailey, Edward Covey, Mr. Gore, and Colonel Lloyd, by way of refuting the narrative's assessment of their characters, "You thus brush away the miserable insinuations of my northern pro-slavery enemies," he informed his inadvertent assistant.[67]

Williams opens his narrative with an informational onslaught that likewise seems calculated to aid his readers in verifying his account. He names his owner, his wife's owner, each of his siblings' owners, and, in some cases, incidents in which they played a part and witnesses to the event. He cites the names of his owner's friends and the planters from whom he purchased slaves, and he identifies each by city or county. But none of these names lead anywhere. Some can be matched to real people: for instance, Williams notes that his brother belonged to "the late Mr. Brockenbrough, of Charlottsville [sic]," presumably Arthur Brockenbrough, proctor of the University of Virginia, who died in 1832. Mr. Brockenbrough, Williams continues, married a sister of Williams's master, while another sister married "a gentleman named John Roane, one of the most distinguished men in Virginia," whose sister Jane Roane Williams's master married in turn (28). In fact, a Virginian named John Roane served in Congress at the time, but he did not have a sister named Jane, nor do the other family connections lead to anyone resembling George Larrimore in family situation, property holdings, or location. None of the other names or any variations (for example, Lorimer or Larimore for Larrimore) appears in the 1830 Virginia census, nor do the names of any of the neighboring planters in Alabama appear in the 1840 census for Greene County.[68]

False names alone, though, hardly make for conclusive evidence that Williams fabricated the rest of the account, given fugitive slaves' need to avoid identification. If names were too dangerous to reveal, dates may supply more reliable information. Early in the narrative, Williams recounts the death of his first master in 1832, recalling, "He died on the 14th of July. There was a great and splendid funeral, as his relatives and friends were numerous" (34). However, none of the obituaries listed in the *Richmond Enquirer*, the major paper for the region, during June, July, or August of that year match the description of George Larrimore. If this is a simply an omission, it is a surprising one, given Williams's account of the lavish funeral and the fact that, according to Williams, Larrimore "had a fine house in Richmond, and used to spend his winters there with his family" (30).

The most promising clue to the facts of the narrative is the unusually large number of slaves the Larrimores owned, as well as the size of the cotton plantation on which Williams worked in Alabama. One of the American Anti-Slavery Society's correspondents confirmed that an estate named Mount Pleasant did exist in Powhatan County. However, not only was it apparently never owned by a Larrimore, but, contrary to Williams's

depiction, it was "of but little value," and none of the owners' circumstances correspond with those Williams describes.[69] Williams estimates
that "about 300" slaves lived there (31), but no estate with this many
slaves appears on the 1830 census for Powhatan County. Out of 517 households, most have fewer than twenty slaves, and only one family, with 103,
has over 100. The situation was equally anomalous in Greene County
where, according to Williams, George Larrimore installed 214 slaves on
an enormous plantation of 2,000 acres (37). Such a large slave workforce
was almost as rare in this area, however. The 1840 census for Greene
County shows that most households owned between one and fifty slaves.
Out of 1,326 households, only fifteen owned more than 100 slaves, and
only two of these owned more than 200. A property as immense as the
one Williams describes would have been conspicuous, and since the narrative was publicized in the local newspaper, it seems odd that no resident
or visitor would have appeared to defend—and thus identify—its owner,
as A. C. C. Thompson unwittingly did for Douglass's Colonel Lloyd. In
addition, Williams's position as a driver supervising so many slaves would
have made him a valuable asset to the plantation, and common practice
would have dictated that his owner advertise for him when he ran away.
(Jean Fagan Yellin discovered an advertisement for the capture of Harriet
Jacobs in a Norfolk, Virginia paper, for instance, which helped her
authenticate *Incidents in the Life of a Slave Girl*.)[70] But no advertisements
for a runaway from Alabama resembling Williams (whose physical
appearance Tappan and Birney describe, and whose portrait opens the
Narrative) appear from the summer of 1837 to the end of the year in any
of the major newspapers of the South I have examined.[71]

Perhaps we should not be surprised when the highly detailed, documentary style of Williams's narrative leads nowhere. Susan Stewart suggests that
a totalizing historical impulse is the hallmark of imposture, for the "imposter is, of course, self made" and, thus, must create a "new, invented genealogy" full of proper arbitrariness.[72] In other words, Williams's abundance of
factual detail may not only prove unverifiable but indeed mark the narrative as a fake. Thus while Frederick Douglass maintains that slaves, as a
general rule, do not know their birthdays, a claim other slave narratives
bear out, Williams opens his narrative with this very information (25).[73] In
fact, Williams furnishes a bewildering array of exact dates throughout, from
the death of his master on July 14, 1832 (34), to one of the overseer's

drunken rages "about the first of September," 1835 (57), to his August 1, 1837 escape (81), to his October 7, 1837 crossing of the Roanoke River (95). Such precision is particularly odd given Williams's assertion that he can neither read nor write (not to mention that, in the last instance, he has been traveling for months with no human contact). Other statements raise doubts on their own terms. "Sleeping thus by day and traveling by night, in a direction toward the North star, I entered Georgia," Williams writes (89). Yet he begins his journey in northwestern Alabama; a northern route would take him to Tennessee, not Georgia. Nevertheless, when he loses sight of the path during an overcast period, and several days later "turned around and saw the North star, which had been shining directly upon my back" (92), he is once again in "the dreaded frontiers of Alabama" (93). Indeed, Williams's adventures stop just short of the fantastic. He endures numerous hairbreadth escapes and enjoys great strokes of luck, such as an ability to encounter familiar landmarks in any city he has ever visited, even once. His preternatural facility with animals rivals Davy Crockett's: he successively turns the hounds on his trail into fawning traveling companions (a scene depicted on the front cover of the *Narrative*'s New York edition); is surrounded by a pack of wolves, but left unharmed; and is similarly unmolested by two bears.

Finally, there is the matter of Williams's disappearance in England. On February 8, 1838, the *Emancipator*, announcing the imminent publication of the *Narrative*, added, "He has gone to England, where his intelligence and honesty will win him friends, and make him a useful assistant to [anti-slavery activist] George Thompson."[74] But Williams seems to have done no such thing. In late March the *Pennsylvania Freeman* briefly notified its readers of Williams's safe arrival in England, and that is the last we hear of him. This fact is particularly surprising given that Tappan directed him to John Cropper, Jr. and Joseph Sturge in Liverpool, both leaders of the British anti-slavery movement.[75] Many fugitive slaves found a livelihood lecturing on the well-attended British anti-slavery circuit, but Williams appears never to have joined the movement at all. In a letter to Angelina Grimké Weld, Lydia Maria Child wondered, "Where *is* James Williams? Can he not be found and cross-examined?"[76] No doubt the same thought occurred to Tappan and Birney when the *Narrative* first came under attack. The two men kept up a regular correspondence with Sturge, in particular; it seems impossible that they did not attempt to locate Williams through him. That Williams never materialized to make his own defense suggests that he had deliberately evaded his only contacts in England, successfully disappearing without a trace.

If Williams did not invent the narrative entirely, it seems clear that he fabricated significant parts, fabrications that served no purposes of self-protection. Nor, apparently, did he manufacture the story for profit. As Tappan and Birney protest in one of their statements in the *Emancipator*, "There seemed to be present with him none of the ordinary motives to practise deception. His wardrobe was but scanty—yet he seemed careless about replenishing it except in so far as actual comfort required. He had no money, nor did he ask for any. He borrowed nothing."[77] What Williams had to gain from falsifying the story of his life remains a mystery.

The Author Malfunction

Williams's elusiveness with regard to the narrative is only matched by his elusiveness within it. One searches in vain for clues to the historical James Williams in the text only to find that, despite its claims to autobiography, Williams barely emerges into intelligibility within its pages. A comparison with another slave narrative published the same year, *A Narrative of the Adventures and Escape of Moses Roper, from American Slavery*, underscores the extent of his absence. Roper foregrounds his body, reminding the reader frequently of his nearly white complexion (which sometimes allows him to pass) and noting how well his height served him while crossing rivers on his way north. We might assume that this information is simply necessary to the story of his escape until Roper adds parenthetically, "I have grown three inches since"—an aside whose irrelevance to the narrative suggests the generic importance of visualizing the slave's body.[78] Williams, on the other hand, never pictures his body; our only clue to his appearance comes from the engraved portrait that his publishers append to the narrative. Williams suppresses, too, all traces of his physical labor. Although he describes the work of the slaves he supervises, he tells us almost nothing of his own work on the plantation. Roper, by contrast, recounts the agony of pulling fodder, "without any shirt, in the cotton field, in a very hot sun, in the month of July," the grueling work of felling trees in a swamp, and the year he spent in the employment of a slave trader, dressing, feeding, and oiling slaves in preparation for auction (9, 11, 68).

Williams's interiority proves as elusive as his exteriority. He stages none of the demonstrations of sincerity Ann Fabian describes as indispensable to winning over an audience unconvinced of African Americans' qualifications for liberty. The omission is particularly strange because Williams has especially pressing reasons to do so. His role as a double agent working both for and against an overseer foregrounds his duplicity, giving special impetus to the slave narrative's generic requirement to convert "slaves who 'by nature lied' into freemen who by obligation told the truth."[79] Moreover, his complicity in the brutal discipline of the plantation, where his responsibilities included whipping other slaves, makes it urgent for him to prove his humanity to the reader. But the *Narrative of James Williams* records very few moments of emotional response or self-reflection. Again, here it stands in contrast to *A Narrative of the Adventures and Escape of Moses Roper*—most obviously so when the two authors find themselves in similar positions. After Roper's master discovers that he and another slave have attempted to run away, he punishes the two together by linking a heavy chain around both of their necks. "It was most harrowing to my feelings thus to be chained to a young female slave, for whom I would rather have suffered 100 lashes than she should have been thus treated," Roper recalls. "Words are insufficient to describe the misery which possessed both body and mind whilst under this treatment, and which was most dreadfully increased by the sympathy which I felt for my poor, degraded fellow sufferer" (16–17). Williams is implicated even more closely in the pain of other slaves, but where Roper dwells on his anguish, Williams remains, on the page, at least, impassive. Here, for example, is his account of a hunt for a runaway:

> While going over our cotton picking for the last time, one of our hands, named Little John, ran away. The next evening the dogs were started on his track. We followed them awhile, until we knew by their ceasing to bark that they had found him. We soon met the dogs returning. Their jaws, heads, and feet, were bloody. The overseer looked at them and said "he was afraid the dogs had killed the nigger." It being dark, we could not find him that night. Early the next morning we started off with our neighbors, Sturtivant and Flincher; and after searching about for some time, we found the body of Little John lying in the midst of a thicket of cane. It was nearly naked, and dreadfully mangled and gashed by the teeth of the dogs.

They had evidently dragged it some yards through the thicket: blood, tatters of clothes, and even the entrails of the unfortunate man, were clinging to the stubs of the old and broken cane. Huckstep [the overseer] stooped over his saddle, looked at the body, and muttered an oath. Sturtivant swore it was no more than the fellow deserved. We dug a hole in the cane-brake, where he lay, buried him, and returned home. (50–51)

Even in the midst of the grisliest scenes, when his integrity is most at stake, Williams refuses the reader any performance of subjectivity. Indeed, he neither grammatically nor emotionally distinguishes himself from the white slave-catchers here, speaking in a flat first-person plural throughout the passage. The narrative furnishes us with almost no sense of Williams as an individual; within as without the text, he eludes identification.

In his preface to the *Narrative of James Williams*, John Greenleaf Whittier extols Williams's textual absence as the narrative's greatest recommendation. Although much has been said about slavery as an institution, Whittier regrets that "we have lost sight of the victims of avarice and lust." Williams, however, corrects our vision, graciously dematerializing himself in order to provide the reader with an unobstructed view of slavery. "But in this narrative the scenes of the plantation rise before us, with a distinctness which approaches reality," Whittier notes approvingly, going on to recount all the gruesome sights "we see" and sounds "we hear" as a result (xix–xx). As William Andrews observes, Whittier's preface implies that "for [Williams's] story to be taken seriously as something approaching reality, he must become transparent, unsubstantial."[80] The inverse relation between narrating subject and narrative reliability that Andrews describes suggests that in some sense, abolitionist literary conventions ironically made an imposture like Williams's not so much a transgression of generic requirements for authenticity as a *fulfillment* of them—although ultimately, of course, one whose fulfillment transgresses.[81] Not only does the evacuation of the slave narrative's body guarantee credibility; as Karen Sánchez-Eppler suggests, it also facilitates the sympathetic identification that constituted another requirement of abolitionist reading. Sánchez-Eppler points out that abolitionist writers sought to render slavery intelligible by rendering it familiar to white readers. Thus the sentimental fiction that formed a staple of anti-slavery newspapers and annuals blurred the difference between free white readers and enslaved black characters through the call-and-response of tears, the coding of virtue as "the obliteration of blackness," and the metaphoric collapsing of the institutions of marriage and slavery. By contrast, the prominent authorial presence generally found in slave narratives resists the dissolution readers required, threatening to derail abolitionist reading strategies—a tendency that Williams's textual absence, according to this analysis, would helpfully correct.[82]

Yet where Andrews's and Sánchez-Eppler's analyses of the vanishing acts abolitionist readers demanded of slaves lead us to expect that Williams's audience would welcome his narrative disembodiment, in fact we find the opposite to be true: readers responded to the *Narrative* by doggedly reconstructing Williams's presence. The American Anti-Slavery Society prefaced the text with an engraved portrait of Williams wearing a waistcoat and cravat and glancing off to the side with a furrowed brow (an expression that, in retrospect, it is tempting to read as the contemplation of flight from yet another attempt to fix his identity), and in the narrative's reception, this picture threatened to eclipse the rest of the book. One writer to the *Liberator* claimed to read Williams's whole story through the image. "That fine portrait, bearing on it the sad impress of soul-conquering slavery, is the picture of a *real* MAN," he insisted. "On the cover of the little book, you see the fugitive slave, in his extremity, standing alone on the earth, against the world. . . . See his garb—his attitude! how utterly man-forsaken! not guilty but fugitive, the very living and speaking personification of helplessness and flight and utter despair of escape."[83] This reader absorbs the narrative (and, finally, the entire institution of slavery) into the portrait's "sad impress," leaving it no independent content. By investing Williams's "garb—his attitude" with a book's worth of meaning, he effectively renders Williams's words superfluous, while imagining the illustration as "living and speaking." Others negotiated the gaps between Williams, his narrative, and his portrait by collapsing the three; a review in *Human Rights* remarks that Williams "left his own portrait (a good likeness) on the title page," as if Williams actually marked the finished book with his own impression.[84] And those who encountered Williams in the flesh proved no less determined than those who encountered his text not only to recuperate his body, but also to locate his eloquence there. Tappan and Birney, defending the narrative against Rittenhouse's accusations, find Williams's strongest credentials in his physical form: "He was there before us—the actor in the scenes he so vividly described—in the prime of life—with a fine head—an expressive countenance shadowing forth 'sorrow' rather than 'anger'—a symmetrical figure, graceful in its movements," they recall, referring the narrative's authenticity to the embodied charge of Williams's initial delivery.[85] Meanwhile, the *Pennsylvania Freeman* advertised *A Narrative of the Adventures and Escape of Moses Roper, from American Slavery* as "about the size of James Williams," suggesting that if the latter's narrative shared none of the former's attention to personal presentation, it could at least be made, itself, a person.[86] Such extratextual supplementary measures imaginatively reincarnate Williams, restoring his absent body to the text.

The insistently embodied terms in which audiences read the *Narrative of James Williams*—so at odds with text itself, where the narrator hardly leaves a trace, and indeed with the conventions of abolitionist veracity and sentimentalism, which stipulate that his presence there would work against him—return us in an unexpectedly literal register to the questions Michel Foucault raised many years ago in his influential essay, "What Is an Author?" Our desire to attribute a text to an author is neither inevitable nor invariable but ideological, Foucault contends; it slots texts into a social order by "separating one from the other, defining their form, and characterizing their modes of existence." Discerning the functions an author serves, he proposes, allows us to reexamine the privileges of a "free" and "originating subject" more generally by addressing a now well-known but still pressing set of questions: "Under what conditions and through what forms can an entity like the subject appear in the order of discourse; what position does it occupy; what functions does it exhibit; and what rules does it follow in each type of discourse?"[87] These questions of authorial presence and absence prove vital to understanding the functions of James Williams, who both appeared and disappeared in the order of discourse, and whose occupation of the position of an unfree subject struck his readers as all too originating.

In light of Foucault's reminder to interrogate the perceived relation of author to text, the reception of *The Narrative of James Williams* among abolitionist readers sounds a new resonance in what Toni Morrison has famously termed the "real or fabricated Africanist presence" that threads through the work of white American authors, by asking us to think about the ways in which "Africanist" and "presence" are often automatically linked, such that African Americans are assumed to be *present* in the texts they write.[88] Put bluntly, abolitionist literary culture rested on the misrecognition of texts as people—specifically, the interchangeability of fugitive slave narratives and fugitive slaves themselves. Such conflation of texts and fugitive slaves occurred all the more easily because abolitionists regularly understood fugitive slaves *as* texts, a congruence they performed every time they displayed scarred or maimed bodies on the lecture circuit to be read for the story of plantation violence, or referred the evidence of a slave's testimony to extant published authorities. While earlier I described abolitionists' desire for authorial transparency as being at odds with their expectation that the author manifest his or her presence in the text, in fact this is only an apparent contradiction. For what abolitionist reading denied was precisely the opacity of black authors.

In the *Narrative*'s most harrowing episode, Williams stages the peculiar violence of such modes of reading. Although he devotes the bulk of the book to recounting the torture and terrorism that reign on the plantation—the overseer Huckstep's cruel whippings and other abuse, his repeated rape of a female slave, his surprise attacks on slaves in their homes, his murder of attempted runaways and resisters—the scene of bodily requisition that Williams dwells on the longest is a specifically textual one. During one of his drunken rages, Huckstep seizes a collection of religious books belonging to an elderly slave named Uncle Solomon. He then calls the man into his house and demands that he deliver a sermon. When Uncle Solomon refuses, Huckstep forces him to swallow a glass of brandy "and then told him to preach and exhort, for the spirit was in him. He set one of the Bibles on fire, and after it was consumed mixed up the ashes of it in a glass of water, and compelled the old man to drink it, telling him that as the spirit and the word were now both in him, there was no longer any excuse for not preaching" (74). Studies of African American writing, especially works by former slaves, tend almost automatically to equate literary production with empowerment, but here Williams emphasizes the eagerness with which readers could press black expression into the service of white authority. The scene links this ideological incorporation with a requirement for textual incorporation; with hideous literalism, Huckstep unites author and "word" by demanding that Uncle Solomon actually ingest his text. In underscoring the oddly *literary* character of the scene's violence, which reproduces a mode of reading that, as I have been arguing, also structured abolitionist literary culture, I do not mean to equate the violence of abolitionist literary culture with that of slavery. Slavery's abuses were worlds removed from the abuses enacted by its vehicles for representation. At the same time, however, it is easy to reproduce the logic by which abolitionist writers, buttressed by the binaries of north and south, free and enslaved, anti- and pro-slavery, localized racial oppression and thus acquitted themselves of it. What Williams's narrative points up is that white supremacy was not so neatly contained, especially when the problem of slavery was translated on to the page.

In his examination of the crisis the *Narrative of James Williams* sparked, William Andrews emphasizes Williams's ability to project a character whose "emotional restraint, reticence about personal feelings and judgments, and apparent propensity to forgive and pity . . . either played to or, through lucky coincidence, conformed to his audience's expectations of the fugitive slave as autobiographer."[89] Andrews's assessment of Williams's self-awareness, as it manifested itself in an ability to anticipate his interlocutors' expectations and craft a persona to match, makes it tempting to read this scene as a canny swipe at the fungibility of text and author foisted on African Americans' literary production—a fungibility that actually assisted Williams's own imposture by assuming that Williams must be co-identical with the *Narrative* in the first place. Such an interpretation would hold that Williams did more than play to his audience's expectations. It would hold that he turned those expectations against them, making the *Narrative of James Williams* not just a fraud but a hoax, a joke at its audience's expense. We might then see Williams's fabrications as evincing the "distrust of the American reader and American acts of reading" that Robert Stepto has identified as a "primary and pervasive" convention within African American literature. Declaring the reader, not the author, to be "the principal unreliable factor in the storytelling paradigm," authors construct their texts so that "the reader gets 'told'—or 'told off'—in such a way that he or she finally begins to *hear*."[90] Understanding the elusiveness of the *Narrative of James Williams* as a metacritique of abolitionist acts of reading is undeniably appealing. However, even if one is reluctant to pursue such an intentionalist interpretation, it is nevertheless clear that Williams's text generated a set of problems for its audience whose intractability calls out abolitionist literary culture's reliance on a stiff—but brittle—racial formulation of literary production.

In assuming an equivalence between authors and text, misrecognitions of Africanist presence construe African American literature as confessional by definition. All expression becomes an expression of self, foreclosing the possibility of other kinds of literary production that are neither inward-looking nor factual. As Ann duCille has put it, "African American literature is forever fixed in a documentary relation to the real world."[91] In our own time, these imperatives continue to shape perceptions of writing by African Americans and, for that matter, other authors of color—appearing, for instance, every time book reviewers expectantly scrutinize works by these writers for traces of autobiography. If we have moved past the conflation of author and text, we have done so in part simply by reserving it for specific racialized texts, in whose words we continue to try to apprehend their author. But what happened when suspicions that African American writers naturally told stories collided with convictions they could not—when a writer assumed unable to speak beyond his own life was debunked as an impostor?

Fraud or Fiction?

From 1849 to 1879, Josiah Henson, the pastor of the black Ontario colony Dawn, repeatedly remade himself through a series of narratives whose fictions rivaled James Williams's. While the first version of his history was fairly straightforward, subsequent versions "showed substantial alterations, extensions, and fabrications," according to Henson's primary biographer, Robin Winks.[92] But concurrent with Henson's self-invention, another legend began to take shape around him, courtesy of his editors and sponsors on the lecture circuit: Henson became known as the inspiration for Harriet Beecher Stowe's Uncle Tom. In fact, the association was purely mythical, but it gained wide currency nonetheless. Henson was introduced to audiences as Uncle Tom, the title page of his 1879 autobiography parenthetically identified him as such, and John Greenleaf Whittier, gullible to the last, supplied a preface noting that the narrative "proves that in the terrible pictures of 'Uncle Tom's Cabin' there is 'nothing extenuate or aught set down in malice.'"[93] When Henson took the opportunity his narrative afforded to construct a new character for himself, abolitionists did him one better: they absorbed him into an existing fictional character. In doing so, they defused the threat of self-authorization he presented, rewriting his fiction-making as fictionality.

The *Narrative of James Williams*, however, resists such incorporation. It was not only that no convenient part was available for Williams to play; even if there were, he could not possibly have filled it. Unlike Henson, his authorship could not be contained by reducing him to a character, for his narrative provides no character to employ this way. And because slave narrators play two roles—as both protagonists and authors—this disappearance raises further problems. If Williams's absence as a character barred his narrative from the type of assimilation into the reigning literary culture that Henson experienced, his concomitant disappearance as an author threatened the very terms of that culture. As the author of a slave narrative, Williams's disappearance in the text signaled the text's reliability, as Whittier's preface demonstrates. But as the author of a fiction, by disappearing in the text Williams availed himself of the narrative privileges of high-cultural authorship: the elite novel's omniscient, objective narrator. If Richard Hildreth and Mattie Griffith made literary imposture virtuous (not technically but "really" true) Williams made it uncomfortably *literary*— "really" fiction.

When suggestions arose that Williams had fabricated the narrative, therefore, they ignited a panic not only because of the embarrassing position in which they placed the American Anti-Slavery Society, but because they also raised disquieting implications for the racialized literary hierarchies on which a dominant but embattled literary culture relied. Far from functioning as a sorting mechanism that would distinguish the mainstream from the marginal, Williams's fraudulence blurred the differences between the two, eroding rather than shoring up the integrity of the literary core. Thus Lewis Tappan insisted that Williams could not possibly have fictionalized the narrative because whereas as an autobiography, it would simply be accurate, as a work of fiction it would be ingenious. "It will be a wonder of the age if a fugitive slave could invent what is recorded in the narrative of James Williams!" he protested.[94] "Memento," writing in the *Liberator*, agreed, observing of the portrayal of Master George's New Orleans wife, "No slave could have depicted such a complex and contradictory creature, if he had not so closely watched the living reality."[95] The reviewer refers the vividness of Williams's representation instead to African Americans' much vaunted mimetic capacity. This explanation echoes the laboriously inverted responses to minstrelsy recounted in the last chapter, which misattributed the performers' mimicry to the African Americans being mimicked. White literary culture embraced African American writers as naturals at replication, the mode of testimonial and confession, but not capable of originality. As another writer in the *Liberator* put it, "it seemed incredible to suppose an unlettered slave could *make* such a story out of his own head."[96] To admit that Williams invented the narrative—thereby combining the practice and techniques of fiction—would be to admit him to the highest ranks of literature.

Consequently, the abolitionists' inability to imagine that Williams was capable of crafting such a fiction became the strongest evidence he had told the truth. "A large number of gentlemen were well satisfied that there could be no imposition in the story without attributing to its author such powers of mind, as few men, either white or black, could justly lay claim to," the Executive Committee of the American Anti-Slavery Society noted in their annual report, and the *Liberator* was even more incredulous: "Does it not occur to persons that if an unlettered fugitive slave could *invent* such a narrative the fact would evince a genius of the first order! Why, he would be another Walter Scott! But they will be forced to confess that the narrative is authentic, or that American negroes surpass the generality of whites in genius."[97] Likewise, "He may have fallen into some errors of fact or exaggeration," the *Pennsylvania Freeman* protested, "but that the material portion of his narrative is correct, we must either believe, or give him credit for inventive powers almost equal to a Cooper or Brockden Brown."[98] Williams's imposture, it seemed, granted him not just personal agency but cultural authority. In the end, the newspaper reports suggest, it was difficult to assess which was the more disturbing legacy of the affair: the conclusion that Williams was a liar, or the conclusion that Williams's fictive powers placed him in the company of the nation's greatest literary artists.

Chapter 4

Mediums of Exchange:
Fanny Fern's Unoriginality

Who is FANNY FERN? and, What is FANNY FERN?
—"Interesting to Ladies," *Pittsfield Sun*, 22 September 1853

In 1849, the prolific anthologizer and industrious puffer Rufus Wilmot Griswold followed the success of his collections *The Poets and Poetry of America* (1842) and *The Prose Writers of America* (1847) with *The Female Poets of America*, an expanded version of his *Gems from American Female Poets* (1844). Griswold's was one of three popular anthologies of women's poetry that appeared in quick succession in the late 1840s, signaling an unmistakable shift in the gender composition of the American literary marketplace. In his introduction, Griswold commends women for showing "indications of the infusion of our domestic spirit and temper into literature" and for their affinity for pursuits that "beautify existence but do not consolidate power."[1] Yet once again, we find the literati's appreciation for a new addition to American literary culture tinged with suspicion. However impressive, women's literary accomplishments nonetheless discomfit Griswold's critical faculties.

> It is less easy to be assured of the genuineness of literary ability in women than in men. The moral nature of women, in its finest and richest development, partakes of some of the qualities of genius; it assumes, at least, the similitude of that which in men is the characteristic or accompaniment of the highest grade of mental inspiration. We are in danger, therefore, of mistaking for efflorescent energy of creative intelligence, that which is only the exuberance of

personal "feelings unemployed." . . . The most exquisite susceptibility of the spirit, and the capacity to mirror in dazzling variety the
effects which circumstances or surrounding minds work upon it,
may be accompanied by no power to originate, nor even, in any
proper sense, to reproduce.[2]

Women's emotional susceptibility, according to Griswold, uncannily mimics the effects of men's artistic talent, putting the critic's habitual discernment "in danger." One could unpack Griswold's anxieties about the
interchangeability of literary greatness and female sentiment, not to mention his fear that literary women do not "reproduce" in the "proper sense,"
at some length. For my purposes, what is most interesting about his ambiv-
alent introduction is its nervousness about the origins of women's writing—or, more to the point, its concern that this writing has no origins at
all but simply "assumes . . . the similitude" of "mental inspiration."

Whereas the previous chapters explained how antebellum literary
fraudulence became regionalized and racialized, in this chapter I argue that
beginning at mid-century, literary fraudulence also became gendered.
Accounts of nineteenth-century women's writing often emphasize the
eagerness with which readers imagined women writers instantiating an
authentic selfhood free from the posturing of conventional (male) authorship. But Griswold's doubts about recognizing the "genuineness of literary
ability in women" point to a countervailing discourse that associated
women writers with intrinsic fraudulence. In order to reconstruct that discourse, this chapter focuses on the novelist and newspaper columnist Fanny
Fern, the pen name of Sara Payson Willis, whose enormous popularity put
her at the center of debates around women's authorship. Fern belonged to
a rash of mid-century newspaper writers whose flowery, alliterative, *obvious*
pseudonyms—Fanny Forrester, Grace Greenwood, Minnie Myrtle, Lily
Larkspur, Bell Bramble, Jenny June—embody Griswold's concerns by
defining their owners as "purely fictional," "hothouse products," and "ref-
ugees from history," as Ann Douglas puts it.[3] Indeed, until quite recently,
Fern's writing has largely escaped discussions of American literary history.
But this omission would have greatly surprised her contemporaries, who
devoured her writings in the *New York Ledger*, where she was the highest
paid newspaper columnist of her time (at a newspaper that boasted the
highest circulation of its time); who made her novel *Ruth Hall* a runaway
bestseller; who enthusiastically named waltzes, boats, and children after her;

who made her true identity the subject of heated debate and, even after it was revealed, energetically impersonated her in print, photographs, and on the lecture circuit. As one of the many articles catering to popular curiosity announced, the question of the day was "Who is FANNY FERN? and, What is FANNY FERN?"[4]

My account of the feminization of fraudulence proposes that the writer's shift from "who" to "what"—from human to thing, from subject to object, and the very uncertainty the slippage implies—is just as revealing as the rest of the article's disclosures about Fern. Griswold's image of women writers who "mirror in dazzling variety" their surroundings itself rather dazzlingly mirrors Marx's account of exchange value, in which "the body of commodity B acts as a mirror to the value of commodity A," such that "the commodity A converts the value in use, B, into the substance in which to express its, A's, own value."[5] The likeness suggests that women writers' perceived fraudulence derived not only from the commodification of women's writing as it entered the literary market, but from an alleged affinity between commodities and women writers themselves. While I am interested in discovering the ways that a language of commodified fraudulence framed mid-nineteenth-century women's literary production, however, this is not a straightforward story of victimization. I argue that even as such gendered constructions regulated Fern's career, their institutional force proved susceptible to recoding, as Fern embraced such associations so forcefully as to splinter the disciplinary logic they initially sustained. In other words, if this chapter tells a story about the almost literal objectification of women writers, it also tells the story of why a writer like Fern might have delighted in imagining herself as an object.

The Feminization of Publicity

Literary histories of the mid-century influx of women into the U.S. literary marketplace have generally begun from the proposition that femininity and publicity constituted a historical binary. Accordingly, these accounts are structured around the clash between the very public character of authorship and a widespread belief that women naturally and properly inclined toward privacy. In her pioneering study of nineteenth-century women writers, *Private Woman, Public Stage: Literary Domesticity in Nineteenth-Century America*, Mary Kelley argues that these assumptions dictated the terms of authorship to an extent that sometimes taxed logic, so that mid-nineteenth-century women writers consistently downplayed their public stature to assert their "primary identity as private, domestic females."[6] Richard Brodhead's *Cultures of Letters: Scenes of Reading and Writing in Nineteenth-Century America* complicates Kelley's analysis while retaining its basic premises, by pointing out that these writers did not strive to withdraw from the public eye but rather sought to publicize their privacy. Thus "the same contemporary cultural processes that worked in one direction to delimit women to dephysicalized and deactivated domestic privacy also helped open up an enlarged publicity that women could inhabit in the entertainment field," making the relation between celebrity and privacy cooperative rather than antagonistic.[7] In highlighting—one might even say advertising—their "private, domestic" selves, these writers fulfilled a gendered mandate to protect themselves from the public jostling of the literary marketplace even as they participated in it.

Versions of this model, which align women with privacy—however convoluted the means—have dominated literary criticism of Fanny Fern, almost against the odds for a woman whose private life remains something of a mystery.[8] Although some critics have faulted earlier accounts for underestimating the extent to which women writers crafted their literary identities, they nonetheless have assumed that private selfhood remained the basis for those literary identities and that when women writers challenged its precepts, they did so as covert operatives.[9] But during the same period, another configuration of femininity competed with this one, whose gendered ordering of the literary marketplace positioned women not as synonymous with authentic private selfhood but with excessively public circulation. As Catherine Gallagher, writing in the context of nineteenth-century Britain, points out, "When women entered the career of authorship, they did not enter an inappropriately male territory, but a degradingly female one" organized by "the metaphor of the author as a whore."[10] Gallagher challenges assumptions that women's entrance into the field of authorship was seen as wholly inappropriate by uncovering a reinforcing logic of gender and commerce that made women eminently compatible with the literary marketplace, or at least with its more distasteful commercial aspects. Her essay thus intervenes in the critical "association of writing with creative generativity" by recovering a discourse that pictures women's literary production occurring not within the self but outside of it.[11]

Gallagher's suggestive analysis can help us trace a new genealogy for the mass market that emerges in tandem with its so-called "feminization" in the 1850s. Gallagher herself does not address the transformation of the literary marketplace during the time she examines; in fact, her essay rests on the premise that literature and prostitution have always gone hand in hand. But the association was never so strong as in this period, when literature became a thoroughly commercial article buoyed by a host of advertising techniques and dominated by the new category of the best seller.[12] Critics like Janice Radway and Andreas Huyssen have powerfully argued that the emergence of a literary mass market coincides with its identification with women; certainly, as Susan Geary explains, taking Fern as her example, "The scribbling women were the first group of American writers to succeed under this new system."[13] But Gallagher's essay suggests that the convergence of femininity and the mass market might not be simply a historical coincidence. Indeed, it raises the possibility that women writers' mass-market share may have been overstated. As Radway and Huyssen have noted, gender gave disapproving commentators an idiom for characterizing the undifferentiated fecundity of the mass literary market, its perceived artifice, and the threat it posed to "authentic" writing. But while the language of feminization may have been intended to condemn the new mass market, it also proved *useful* to it in at least two ways. First, feminization helped circumscribe the threat of commodification by resignifying the resemblance between literature and commerce *as* gendered. For worries about the increasingly commercial nature of literature affected male writers as well, and this is just the point: commodification happened across the board, but the language of feminization made it gender-specific. The story of women dominating the mid-century literary marketplace may not be a reflection of real economic history, then, so much as an artifact of this bifurcation of literary production, which divided "authors and women authors," as Nina Baym puts it, by placing artistic integrity and originality on the one side, and commerce and imitation on the other.[14] Second, this theoretical delimitation of literary commerce conveniently allows it to flourish in practice. That is, even as it disparages the mass market, by relieving male writers of the burden of commerce, the language of feminization smoothes the way for its development.

A vituperative article entitled "Literary Lion Hunting" that appeared in the *United States Review* (successor to the *United States Magazine and Democratic Review*) in 1855 vividly illustrates the concatenation of women, the market, and literary fraudulence. The author, identified by the initials "J.F.C.," excoriates the debased state of literature, which under "the dominion of the dollar" has become a "sphere wherein natural falsity, ecstatics, exotics, and all the other exes of rationality, are chiefly sought by those beleaguering quacks of quality who daily deal in flimsy fiction and desperate doggerel." J.F.C.'s hyperbolic alliteration hints that he may have had Fanny Fern and her colleagues in mind; certainly he identifies this "natural falsity" as feminine, as he goes on to describe the "quacks" in question as the "full-plumed and half-fledged . . . *male and female sister-hood.*"[15] Picturing this new breed of fraudulent authors, men and women alike, as fundamentally feminine, J.F.C. links fraudulence and femininity so closely that their conjunction overrides biological sexual distinctions.

J.F.C.'s fury ran to two articles and twenty-six pages. But it is clear from even this short excerpt how his scorn for the literary mass market takes shape in the figure of the commodified female author, or as he puts it, the "authoress" "before the world in hundreds of pages, 12mo, cloth"—that is, the authoress made indistinguishable from a book for sale. Much as J.F.C. locates this new breed of feminized quackery under "the dominion of the dollar," Fanny Fern's contemporaries overtly aligned her with the world of commodities. Robert Bonner, Fern's editor at the *New York Ledger*, made the unprecedented price he paid for her story "Fanny Ford" (a hundred dollars a column) key to its promotion, boasting that the newspaper was "always willing to pay well for a good article," and Fern was "worth her weight in gold."[16] Whether or not Bonner's pun on "article" is intentional, it renders Fern's writing indistinguishable from merchandise, an association that his cash valuation of the author only confirms. Others imagined Fern more literally as a marketable commodity: as Fern herself remarked, she had "a mud-scow and a hand-cart, a steamboat and a hotel, a perfume and a score of babies, not to mention tobacco and music, named for her."[17] In an anonymous, slanderous biography of Fern, William Moulton, her former editor at the Boston newspaper the *True Flag*, pictures his introduction to her as follows:

ANOTHER SCENE. TRUE FLAG OFFICE, TEN O'CLOCK, A.M. . . . Enter jaunty bonnet, with gay feathers, elegant veil, rich broadcloth cloak, and silk dress—rather magnificent, if not more so. . . .

Jaunty Bonnet, (in a low, half-whisper, under the veil)—Excuse me—I'm a little out of breath, running up stairs. I've brought Mr. Snooks to introduce me.

Mr. Snooks turned out to be a Fern manuscript. The jaunty bonnet carried him in an elegant reticule, in close proximity to a
coquettish handkerchief, redolent of perfume. The jaunty bonnet
turned out to be—Fanny herself![18]

Gender directs this remarkable drama of reification and commodity fetish-
ism, as Fern becomes a disembodied bonnet and her manuscript, even
more bizarrely, becomes a man. Fern's commodification in this scene signals her essential artifice; she literally amounts to nothing more than a
bonnet, showy clothes, and "coquettish" accessories. The literary ramifications of such a transformation become apparent when we remember that,
according to Marx, a commodity "can only tell us . . . its own value" in "the
language with which alone it is familiar, the language of commodities," or
the grammar of exchange by which one commodity puts itself in relation
to another.[19] As comically garrulous as Marx's talking coats and bolts of
linen are, they cannot speak for themselves; like Fern, at least in the eyes of
her critics, they can only speak in the language of others.

Disappearing in Print

I have been emphasizing the ways in which our attention to women writers'
roles as representatives of private, inviolable selfhood has tended to obscure
their alternate roles as representatives of excessively public exchange, a role
that cast them not as guarantors of personal authenticity but as "purely
fictional." According to this model of women's literary production, women
writers did not so much produce as *re*produce each other's words, exchang-
ing conventions and clichés without originating any material themselves.
The reduction of women's writing to a traffic in formulas thus empties
women writers themselves of any authorial identity; ironically, the extent
of their circulation in print correlates directly with their personal disappearance. This logic placed women writers in a strange relation to their literary
success: the more widely their writing circulated, the more they found
themselves unable to imagine their connection to it, or even unable to
imagine themselves at all.

In the preface to her first collection of newspaper pieces, *Fern Leaves*
(1854), Fern pictures the writing that has made her such a celebrity—that
has demanded the book's publication—as a kind of vanishing act.[20]

> I never had the slightest intention of writing a book. Had such a thought entered my mind, I should not long have entertained it. It would have seemed presumptuous. What! *I*, Fanny Fern, write a book? I never could have believed it possible.
>
> How, then, came the book to be written? some one may ask. Well, that's just what puzzles *me*. I can only answer in the dialect of the immortal "Topsy," "I 'spect it growed!" And, such as it is, it must go forth; for "what is written, is *written*," and—*stereotyped*.[21]

Fern's incredulous retrospective self-address ("What! *I*, Fanny Fern, write a book?") seems absurd. If Sara Payson Willis is already "Fanny Fern," she has already identified herself as a writer. But her explanation continually places her authorship in question. She goes on to rephrase her question in the passive voice ("How, then, came the book to be written?"), eliding her own agency in the book's production. But she can no more offer a response than she can frame the question. Instead, she borrows another's words, modifying Topsy's famous answer to Miss Ophelia in *Uncle Tom's Cabin*.[22] The reference further alienates Fern from the book she has written because Topsy cannot imagine her own production; she insists that she "never was born" because she "never had no father nor mother."[23] Moreover, the reference calls forth but leaves unspoken the question that enlists this response from Topsy, which is not, as one might expect from Fern's own query, "How were you made?" but the more pointed, "Who made you?" These paragraphs, which initially seem poised to describe the conditions of the book's production, finally leave the identity of its author in doubt. Jarred by the counterintuitive temporality of the first inquiry, Fern syntactically drops out of the equation, reverts to another's words, implicitly disclaims her own authorship, and finally, silently, poses the question that these gestures beg: not "How was this book written?" but "Who wrote it?"

Fern links this authorial disappearance to her appearance in print—to the production of the author Fanny Fern, whose presence sets this strange dialogue in motion, and whose words, mysteriously alien to their ostensible author, are always already "*stereotyped*." More specifically, she links it to a mode of reading her circulation entails. "Stereotype" denotes the contemporaneous printing process for books, but at the time *Fern Leaves* was published, the word had also begun to acquire its now more familiar meaning of a widespread preconceived idea.[24] In fact, Fern uses "stereotype" in this sense twice in the first seven pages of the book.[25] "Stereotype" thus conjoins the material and the metaphoric at this moment, and it is just this conjunction that structures her alienation from her book. Her authorship, she suggests, is indissociable from others' constructions of it, producing words that she no longer recognizes as her own. At the same time, this stereotype of women's writing is precisely that women's writing is itself inherently stereotyped—not original literary production but the reproduction of artificial conventions. The preface follows a circular logic, as the pseudonymous author's surprise at her authorship predicts, so that Fern's initial disconnect from her book derives from the circulation in print that concludes it.

Although at first glance Fern's predicament resembles the disembodiment that Michael Warner argues characterizes writing in the Habermasian print public sphere, on closer inspection it points us to a very different mode of print disembodiment: a compulsory rather than voluntary identity, commercial rather than civic, typical rather than provisional, explicitly female rather than implicitly male. Fern's inability to recognize her own words is not mere coyness but reflects contemporary accounts of her mode of production, or lack thereof. As John S. Hart, the editor of the popular anthology *The Female Prose Writers of America*, wrote of Fern, "she is probably often surprised at the excellence of her own articles." His entry on her goes on adduce the reasons for this disconnect, finally quoting at length from a review of her work in the *Boston Post* that asserts, "FANNY FERN is not a legitimate writer. She is a literary accident—a most happy one, certainly; but still an accident."[26] One of Fern's fellow female writers, Rose Terry Cooke, made the illegitimacy of women's writing and the personal blankness that results the subject for her story "The Memorial of A.B., or Matilda Muffin," which owes something, I think, to the details of Fern's particular experience. As with so much "light" fiction by mid-nineteenth-century women writers, this story is both funny and strangely unsettling. Its titular narrator is "what is popularly called a literary woman," although, anticipating her readers' disgust, she is ashamed to admit it.[27] Like Fern, she adopts a pseudonym, and she shares with Fern a conversational writing style, humorously poised between resignation and despair, which leads critics to "rebuk[e] [her] for alluding lightly to serious subjects" (188). Like Fern, too, she suffers from a peculiar disembodiment brought on by literary circulation. After she receives a writing assignment for the "Monthly Signpost" on short notice,

Miss Muffin's head looks her in the face, (metaphorically,) and
says, "You can't!"—but last year's bonnet creaks and rustles from
the bandbox, finally lifts the lid and peeps out. . . . The bonnet
retires to the sound of slow music; the head slinks back and holds
its tongue; Miss Muffin sits down at her table; scratch, scratch,
scratch goes the old pen, and the ideas catch up with it, it is so
shaky, and the words go tumbling over it, till the *ts* go out without
any hats on, and the eyes—no, the *is* (*is* that the way to pluralize
them?)—get no dots at all; and every now and then the head says,
softly, "Oh dear!" (186)

In a bizarrely disjointed scene of writing that conjures up Fern's preface to
Fern Leaves, Matilda finds herself severed from her own authorship and
even from her own body, as her face splits off from her head.[28] Moreover,
she sees her agency transferred to an animate bonnet, much as Fern did in
Moulton's *Life and Beauties of Fanny Fern*. As in all these scenes, however,
such distresses do not prevent writing but are the conditions of possibility
for it. "The old pen," "the ideas," and "the words" operate independently
of Matilda, as she herself drops out of the picture, leaving her disembodied
head to comment on it. These dramas of authorial disappearance crystallize
in Matilda's inability to write the letter "I" properly; she can only render
the letters as watchful "eyes," a problem that ultimately becomes one not
just of orthography but of ontology, "*is*."

Appropriately, Cooke's story hinges on the revelation of Matilda Muffin's true identity. After she begins to publish as "A.B.," she finds that "who
and what I was" has become a matter of public discussion.

Somebody told me she was a lady living on the North River, very
wealthy, very haughty, and very unhappy in her domestic relations.
Another said she was a young widow in Alabama, whose mother
was extremely tyrannical, and opposed her second marriage. A third
person declared to me that A.B. was a physician in the navy,—a
highly educated man, but reduced in circumstances. . . . There were
other romances, too tedious to mention, depicting me sometimes as
a lovely blonde, writing graceful tales beneath a bower of roses in
the warm light of June; sometimes as a respectable old maid, rather
sharp, fierce, and snuffy; sometimes as a tall, delicate, aristocratic,
poetic looking creature, with liquid dark eyes and heavy tresses of

raven hair; sometimes as a languishing, heart-broken woman in the prime of life, with auburn curls and a slow consumption. (188)

The episode closely mirrors the speculations around Fern's own authorship, which one admirer distilled in poetic form:

Oh mirth-provoking Fanny,
Pray tell me if you will,
What sort of a being you really are,
And whether a Jack or a Gill;
And much I wonder, Fanny,
If you are maid or wife;
On the shady side of forty,
Or in the bloom of life.

If you are blonde, or brunette,
With ringlets dark as night,
Or soft and wavy tresses
That flash in the morning light;
If you are tall and stately,
With the bearing of a queen,
Or short, and fat, and dumpy,
Or the two extremes between.[29]

I will return to these conjectures later in this chapter; for now, I simply want to emphasize the multiplicity of Fanny Ferns and A.B.s imaginatively available to their readers. In response to the public speculation around "A.B.," Cooke's heroine abandons her pseudonym and begins to write as "Matilda Muffin," at which point "the question naturally arose,—'Who *is* Matilda Muffin?'" (189). Her present article, we learn, is intended to answer exactly this question. Although her readers assume that "Matilda Muffin" is a pseudonym proper to the "great alliterative ranks of female writers" (187), we learn that it is, in fact, the writer's actual name. "My name, my own, that would have been printed in the marriage-list of the 'Snapdragon' before now, if it had not appeared in the list of contributors, and which will appear in its lists of deaths some day to come,—my name, that is called to breakfast, marked on my pocket-handkerchiefs, written in my books, and done in yellow paint on my trunk, is—Matilda Muffin. 'Only that, and nothing more!'" (189). The punchline of the story is the revelation that its literary heroine is intrinsically pseudonymous; there is no "true identity" to be discovered beneath her artifice. The passage's final line underscores the irony, as Matilda Muffin announces her authorship by way of another author, citing Poe's famous lines from "The Raven."[30] Or a more precise reading might interpret "The Memorial of A.B." as a satire not on women's authorship but on its reception, for rather than assuming a fiction to hide the reality, Matilda Muffin finds her reality *read* as fictional.

Fanny Fern's and Matilda Muffin's tendencies literally to write them-selves out of the picture echo unexpectedly in a more recent and apparently more sober text. In 1968 Roland Barthes proposed, "Writing is that . . . space where our subject slips away, the negative where all identity is lost, starting with the very identity of the body writing." This foundational state-ment of poststructuralism, which dispatched the possibility of a writing subject and erected a de-centered field of language in its place, would be repeated and modulated by numerous critics to come, most famously by Jacques Derrida.[31] These insights have constituted some of the most lasting legacies of poststructuralism, but Fanny Fern's abortive account of her own authorship, written more than one hundred years before Barthes's essay, suggests that his revelation of the death of the author might not have come as much of a surprise to mid-nineteenth-century women writers. My point here is not to make another gibe at poststructuralism but to suggest that this century-spanning echo, in which Fern oddly seems to prefigure Barthes, may have something to tell us about the larger operations of capi-talism I gestured toward earlier in proposing that a gendered logic of exchangeability helped construct the literary mass market. If postmodern-ism is, as Fredric Jameson has influentially stated, a "cultural dominant" of late capitalism, and poststructuralism is, in turn, a "sub-variety of the postmodern," Fern's experience seems to call the terms of this periodiza-tion into question.[32] Jameson identifies the "constitutive features of post-modernism" as "a new depthlessness, which finds its prolongation both in contemporary 'theory' and in a whole new culture of the image or the simulacrum" and "a consequent weakening of historicity, both in our rela-tionship to public History and in the new forms of our private temporal-ity."[33] But the case of Fanny Fern and her literary colleagues demonstrates that there is nothing inherently "new"—at least for some—about the sensa-tion of depthlessness and the culture of the simulacrum, for Douglas's "ref-ugees from history" (whom I have suggested we might better understand as exiles from history) were well acquainted with something like Jameson's "weakening of historicity." To be clear, I am not claiming that these experiences are identical; late capitalism has transformed its subjects in ways beyond anything Fanny Fern and her readers could have imagined. Nonetheless, it seems worth considering the strange correspondence that emerges between popular mid-nineteenth-century female writers and late twentieth-century male critical theorists. This historical stutter might attune us more closely to the linked formations of gender and capitalism—that is, to the role that gender plays in producing a cultural logic of capitalism, and to the discontinuous effects of capitalism that might result.

Losing Sight of the Woman in the Authoress

The fact that Fanny Fern, Matilda Muffin, and their pseudonymous colleagues all wrote for newspapers is telling. The periodic character of newspaper publishing entails that its writers exist iteratively, while bringing them in continual contact with their own circulation. Unlike a book, a regular newspaper column has no material integrity (it cannot, for example, be held in the hand in its entirety), and it continually folds public reception into itself through reference to its readers' responses. This was especially true at the *New York Ledger*, which derived its very identity as a newspaper from its enviable circulation, the largest in the country at the time.³⁴ But Fern also published a novel, *Ruth Hall* (1855), a *Künstlerroman* of equal parts pathos and sarcasm that possessed unmistakable parallels to her own life. The move from newspaper to novel, particularly a semi-autobiographical novel, seems like an odd one for Fern, for critics have traditionally considered the novel a genre that both arises from and thematizes ideas of individual agency and uniqueness. Although women novelists also adopted pseudonyms, they preferred ones that sounded like real names (for example, Susan Warner's pseudonym, Elizabeth Wetherall), rather than ones that announced their fictitiousness. Yet against generic expectations, *Ruth Hall* persistently refuses the emergence of an individualized writing subject in the form of either the heroine or her quite obviously interchangeable author.³⁵ It thus offers a useful test case for Fern's writing, foregrounding its discontinuities in ways that we might lose sight of amid the customary spatial and temporal intervals of the newspaper medium.

These statements may seem misplaced with regard to a novel that seems to chart such an emphatic narrative of self-fulfillment, in which the heroine prevails over poverty, sickness, misuse, and the iniquities of the literary market to become a celebrated author and "a regular business woman."[36] Indeed, the back cover of the current American Women Writers series edition of *Ruth Hall* describes Ruth as a "woman who realizes the American Dream solely on her own, becoming the incarnation of the American individualist." Yet in the book that bears her name, in which she figures as the main character, and whose plot revolves around her literary celebrity, Ruth has surprisingly little voice. Instead, Fern unfolds her story through the numerous characters that surround Ruth, from her cruel in-laws to her lecherous fellow boarders to the editors, critics, publishers, and booksellers who thwart her literary efforts. Moreover, in a book about a writer, we never see Ruth's writing. We only hear others' opinions of it, in numerous reported conversations on the subject and in the stacks of letters that, as "Floy," she receives from her readers, which Fern "reproduces" in full. Such absences, in which Floy's readers' words crowd out those of Floy herself, peculiarly reenact Fern's preface to *Fern Leaves*, where Fern's circulation erases the scene of her writing.

Even more troubling, considering these strange silences, is the novel's conclusion. Literary heroines were not uncommon at this time, but their authors usually punished them for their efforts, so that by the novels' endings they have renounced their vocations (as do Beulah Benton in Augusta Evans Wilson's *Beulah* and Fleda Ringgan in Susan Warner's *Queechy*) or simply died (as does Mercy Philbrick in Helen Hunt Jackson's *Mercy Philbrick's Choice*). Both Joyce Warren and Susan Harris emphasize that *Ruth Hall*, however, proves an exception to this rule.[37] Indeed, the novel's last words, spoken to Ruth by her friend and editor Mr. Walter, are "Life has much of harmony yet in store for you." Yet these consoling words immediately follow a more somber scene, where Ruth, Mr. Walter, and Ruth's children visit the grave of Ruth's late husband, which seems to portend a very different future. "Old memories were thronging, thick and fast, upon her;—past joys—past sorrows—past sufferings;—and yet the heart, which felt them all so keenly, would soon lie pulseless amid these mouldering thousands. There was a vacant place left by the side of Harry. Ruth's eye rested on it—then on her children—then on Mr. Walter. 'So help me God,' reverently murmured the latter, interpreting the mute appeal" (400). We might take Fern's prediction that Ruth's "heart . . . would soon lie pulseless amid these mouldering thousands" as a commonplace about the ephemerality of human life, except for the quite practical implications that follow. As Fern looks to the burial spot marked out for her, at her children, and at Mr. Walter, she sends him a "mute appeal"—presumably, an appeal to take care of her children after she dies, which he accepts. Like Ruth's conspicuous absences from the text, these final hints at her impending death suggest new meanings in the novel's contemporary nickname, "Ruthless Hall."

Blanks mark the form of *Ruth Hall* as well as its plot, perforating its narrative in disorienting ways. In a novel in which each chapter brings a change of scene, Fern eschews transitions, abruptly relocating her readers without explanation. Often she moves from setting to setting within chapters as well, separating each from the other with an empty space. Samuel Otter has suggested that such gaps play a special signifying role for Fern: "The intervals between words, sentences, paragraphs, chapters—Fern points to these and fills them with meaning. They become spaces of implied authorial comment and understood exchange between writer and reader."[38] Chapter 61, for example, recounts a luxurious meal at Ruth's father's house before breaking, skipping a line, and relocating to Ruth's rented room for a final sentence, in which Ruth's little daughter "vainly plead[s]" for "some more supper" (239). The space between the two scenes becomes a breeding ground for irony. If here, as elsewhere, Fern's narrative of authorship exhibits a disconcerting number of blanks, it also foregrounds her ability to make something out of nothing.

A review of *Ruth Hall* in the *Southern Quarterly Review* registered the heroine's absence with horror, wondering how the author could "have forgotten and lost sight of the woman Ruth in the authoress Floy." In the remarkable transaction the reviewer describes, Floy's authorship supersedes her private identity, dissolving it in the medium of print. Worse, the reviewer continues, Fern "parted from her with that triumphal wave of the Seton Bank stock banner."[39] He takes exception here to *Ruth Hall*'s most novel physical feature: a replica of a bank stock certificate worth $10,000, complete with decorative type, an ornamental border, and a notice of conditions, which appears in the final pages, made out to Ruth as the product of her book's earnings (figure 9). The reviewer's outrage over such a blatant display of commercial success seems to confirm Gillian Brown's contention that "the real scandal of *Ruth Hall* lies in its unabashed commitment to market individualism," but the *Southern Quarterly Review*'s concern that female authorship evacuates identity problematizes any naturalized relation

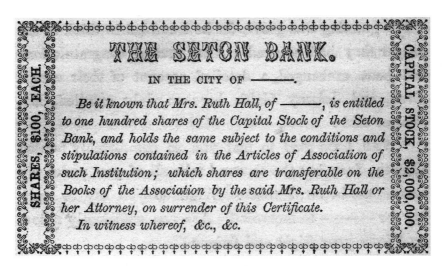

Figure 9: Bank certificate, from *Ruth Hall: A Domestic Tale of the Present Time* (1855). (Courtesy of the Newberry Library)

between "market" and "individualism."[40] While "the real scandal" of the novel undoubtedly lies in "its unabashed commitment" to the market, it is not in the individualism the market enables but in its capacity for *de*individualization, which the novel embraces in its willingness to lose "the woman Ruth in the authoress Floy." Indeed, the final flourish of the stock certificate threatens structurally to eclipse Ruth *and* Floy, and logically to subsume both in its cash appreciation. A peculiar plot point to visualize, the certificate, with its metonymic relation to Ruth, Floy, and Fern (who likewise reaped the royalties of her first book), almost seems to stand in for the conventional engraved portrait of the author, absent here. Troublingly cognate with the female author, the certificate quite materially crystallizes her as a medium of exchange. If *Ruth Hall* tells a story of female independence and social mobility, then this story exists by imagining female authorship as having no content but only form, no message but only medium. The stock certificate foregrounds the distinction in the elaborate display of typefaces and borders that ensures its value; like the female author, its meaning inheres in its very printedness. But of course, the startling realism of the certificate also conspicuously approaches counterfeit, linking women's authorship not only to market intelligibility but also to a brazen fraudulence.

Faking It

Over the past twenty-five years, Fanny Fern has enjoyed something of a literary historical renaissance. *Ruth Hall*, long out of print, was republished in 1986 along with a selection of Fern's newspaper writings, and Fern has been the subject of a hefty biography, a book-length critical study, and numerous articles and book chapters.[41] Yet her critical recovery has yielded a scarcely more coherent subject than before. Readers remain confounded by Fern's schizophrenic writing style, which was capable of sentimental effusions one day and acerbic social satire the next—a doubleness strangely inscribed, as several critics have noted, in the abrupt tonal shifts of *Ruth Hall* and the bipartite organization of *Fern Leaves*, whose "Part I" eulogizes angelic dying children, sorrowful widows, and patient wives, while "Part II" mocks domineering husbands, clerical hypocrisy, and literary pretensions. The split becomes acutely bizarre when Fern tackles the same subject in both modes, extolling marital self-abnegation, for example, in "Self-Conquest," "Elsie's First Trial," "How Husbands May Rule," "All's Well," "How Woman Loves," and "The Test of Love," and skewering it in "The Tear of a Wife," "An Interesting Husband," and "Owls Kill Humming-birds." In an effort to find some sort of footing, Fern's critics have often focused their attentions on one mode and simply ignored its obverse, tried to identify a linear progression between the two, or read one as a kind of crypto-version of the other. Ann Douglas and Nancy Walker, for example, see *Ruth Hall* as discarding its early sentimentality in favor of hard-nosed satire, while Susan Harris reconciles the apparent contradiction by interpreting Fern's sentimentalism as a "disguise, a deliberate strategy rather than evidence of a split consciousness."[42] Fern's use of sentiment, she contends, is merely a ruse that enables her real critical project.

Recent critics have taken a stronger interest in the multiple versions of Fern that circulated during her career, from her irregular tone to other writers' raids on her name and writing style to her own surprisingly enthusiastic embrace of this fluid literary persona. Yet even as they place Fern's authorial mobility at center stage, these studies have worked to buttress her coherence as a subject. Laura Laffrado, for example, asserts that Fern used the transience of the newspaper medium "to explore scenarios of self-representation," explaining her shifting tone and frequent accounts of her imposters and imitators as strategic deployments of identity that fostered, rather than fractured, a sense of self. Thus Laffrado delinks the author Sara

Payson Willis from the character Fanny Fern, whose migrations constitute deliberate manipulations by Willis, who "grew to know her self through writing Fern's weekly essays."[43] Melissa Homestead is more interested in the instability of the literary marketplace Fern entered, in particular the "game of so-called exchange publication" that characterized antebellum periodical circulation. Yet she, like Laffrado, sees Fern as a self-conscious "player" in the game who "successfully exploit[s]" its hazards for her own benefit.[44] Both writers, then, assume that Fern faces off with an inherently tumultuous literary world from a stable subject position. However, I want to take seriously Fern's literary irreducibility, rather than attempting to explain it away, in order to suggest that Fern's relation to the literary marketplace might be as constitutive as it is antagonistic.

As both Laffrado and Homestead note, Fern's writing spawned numerous imitators, prompting her to issue an ironic call to arms for would-be copyists in her newspaper column. "Borrowed light is all the fashion," she announces. "Borrow whole sentences, if you like, taking care to transpose the words a little. . . . If anybody has the impertinence to charge you with being a literary pirate, don't you stand it. Bristle up like a porcupine, and declare that it is a vile insinuation; that you are a full-rigged craft yourself, cruising around on your own hook, and scorning to sail under false colors. There's nothing like a little impudence!" Yet for all Fern's apparent indignation, these cases of identity theft may not be as straightforward as they appear, for she goes on to dispense some advice that lands strangely close to home. "In choosing your signature, bear in mind that nothing goes down, now-a-days, but *alliteration*. For instance, Delia Daisy, Fanny Foxglove, Harriet Honeysuckle, Lily Laburnum, Paulena Poppy, Minnie Mignonette, Julia Jonquil, Seraphina Sunflower, etc., etc."[45] If Fern takes aim at the notoriously derivative conventions of female authorship here, her barb doubles back in self-recrimination, given her own flowery and alliterative choice of a pseudonym. The turn raises a puzzling question: how does Fern distinguish herself from her imitators, if at all? By pitting Fern against fraudulent claims to "her" literary property, we risk losing sight of her readiness to puncture the claim to originality usually seen to authorize literary production.

Fern's exceptions to originality become even more pointed if we turn from the form of her pseudonym to its content. Fern claimed that she had chosen her pseudonym for its sentimental associations, explaining, "I think the reason I selected the name 'Fern' was because, when a child and walking with my mother in the country, she always used to pluck a leaf of it, to place in her bosom for its sweet odor."[46] Ann Douglas, however, has suggested that she chose the name in order simultaneously to capitalize on the already established trend for alliterative, flowery pseudonyms, and to ridicule it. "Thus [she] could get her audience both going and coming; work on their sentimentality, then satirize it."[47] Joyce Warren, too, emphasizes the subversive possibilities of Fern's pseudonym, pointing out that sweet ferns, unlike their feathery cousins, are "sturdy" and "tenacious," capable of growing under conditions "where more delicate plants cannot survive."[48] But as one of Fern's literary contemporaries, the poet and essayist Lucy Larcom, noted, ferns possess another distinguishing feature: they cannot reproduce directly, as flowers do. Instead, they produce asexual spores that, in turn, grow into tiny plantlets, which become fertilized and develop into new ferns. Larcom made this feature the central conceit of her poem "Fern-Life," which Cheryl Walker has read as a commentary on nineteenth-century women's writing lives.[49] "Yes, life! though it seems half a death," the poem begins, and the remainder portrays the agonizing inability to originate of "we fern-folk."

> No blossom—scarce leaf—on the ground,
> Vague fruitage we bear,—
> Point upward, reach fingers around,
> In a tender despair.
>
> . . . . . .
>
> Yet why must this possible more
> Forever be less?
> The unattained flower in the spore
> Hints a human distress.
>
> . . . .
>
> To fashion our life as a flower,
> In weird curves we reach,—
> O man, with your beautiful power
> Of presence and speech![50]

The final two lines explain Larcom's earlier identification with "we fern-folk," as she links ferns' fruitless strivings to women and specifically to women's would-be literary production, which she distinguishes from men's full powers of "presence and speech." We cannot know if Larcom took her extended metaphor for the barrenness of women's writing specifically from Fanny Fern, although Fern was a household name during this period and the confluence certainly is suggestive. But her association of ferns with creative unproductivity offers another possible valence for Fanny Fern's pseudonym, one that resonates with both cultural norms and Fern's own peculiar portraits of the artist.[51]

Eschewing originality, Fern frequently recycled her own work, including plots, language, and names. For instance, one early sketch, "Look on This Picture, and Then on That," which contrasts the arrival of one father, who prompts his children to flee as their mother anxiously quiets the baby, with that of another, who inspires his family's gleeful welcome, enjoys multiple incarnations over the course of Fern's career.[52] In *Ruth Hall*, Fern reuses the story for Ruth's recollections of her childhood, when her mother "always looked uneasy about the time her father was expected home; and when his step was heard in the hall, she would say in a whisper. . . . 'Hush! hush! your father is coming'" at which point Ruth would "run up into her little room" (17). Two years later, in Fern's second collection, *Fresh Leaves*, she returned to the story in "A Business Man's Home," where the news "There's your father, children" sends the children scurrying to tidy up as their mother casts "an anxious glance . . . around the room." One of the children responds by wistfully conjuring up the other half of the *Fern Leaves* story, asking, "I wonder what makes our father so different from Tom Hunt's father? Tommy always runs down street to meet his father when he comes home, and tells him what has happened on the play-ground."[53] Other earlier stories, too, reappear in *Fresh Leaves*: "A Business Man's Home" also lifts "Mother's Room" wholesale, while "Our First Nurse" rewrites "The Invalid Wife" (without changing the original names), and "Fanny Ford" borrows its embezzlement plot from "How Woman Loves" and the full names of two characters from "Mary Lee." Fern's recycling is particularly interesting considering that she evidently expected readers to be acquainted with her previous work, referring to them familiarly as her "parish" in the preface to *Fresh Leaves*.[54] Such acts question habitual assumptions that authors strive for originality, as Fern openly embraces acts of copying, imitation, and recirculation.

Fern's preference for proliferating over preserving authorial identity also challenges critics' tendencies to read her use of a pseudonym as an appropriately feminine demurral to public circulation that protects her private self. While this may have been true early in her career, Fern quickly ceased to cloak herself in her pseudonym and began to immerse herself in its public persona. She signed her letters to friends and family "Fanny Fern," and even her husband called her "Fanny." Her gravestone, at Mount Auburn Cemetery in Cambridge, Massachusetts, bears only the inscription "Fanny Fern." Fern's identification with her pseudonym requires us to revise the usual understanding of the term and imagine pseudonymity not as a negation of something—not *not* naming—but a positive claim to artifice. In her writing, as well, Fern energetically facilitated and drew attention to her circulation in print. In an article written soon after the publication of *Fern Leaves*, for example, she describes encountering her own celebrity in a train car:

> A boy came into the car with armful of *Fern Leaves* for sale, thrust a copy into my hand and assured me it was "*the* book of the season—forty thousand copies already sold!—presses running night and day, but the demand not supplied," &c., &c.
> "Who wrote it?" I asked.
> "Fanny Fern," replied the boy.
> "Who is she?" said I.
> "Don't know," said the peripatetic little bookseller. "She's first this person, and then that; now a man, and then a woman; somebody says she's everybody, and everybody says she's *some*.—Here's y'ur *Fern Leaves*, forty thousand sold in sixty days."
> I bought a copy.[55]

Far from disavowing her public circulation, Fern here advertises its extent, repeating the commercial feats of *Fern Leaves*—its enormous sales, its status as "*the* book of the season," the ubiquitous question of her identity. Finally, she literally buys into this public circulation.

Indeed, Fern actively encouraged the debates over her identity that kept her continually before the public eye, and perhaps even helped manufacture them. Soon after she began writing for the Boston *Olive Branch*, the newspaper ran a flurry of letters to the editor inquiring into her real name, her sex, her age, her appearance, and her marital status. Many offered projections of their own; as one admirer wrote, "I long ago pictured sweet Fanny to myself, and this 'counterfeit presentment' of the imagination is now an old acquaintance."[56] But rather than using the ensuing confusion to call

attention to a unique self who eluded public scrutiny, Fern simply continued to multiply "counterfeit presentments." "*Such* a dance as I shall lead
you!" she told her admirers. "I'm a regular 'Will o' the Wisp;' everything
by turns, and nothing long. Sometimes I'm an old maid, then a widow,
now a Jack, then a Gill, at present a 'Fanny.' If there's anything I abominate
it's *sameness.* . . . That's *what* I am, and as to the '*who*,' I'm rather mystified
myself, on *that* point. Sometimes I think, and then again I don't know!!"[57]
Fern brought the "disputed point, 'whether *I be I*'" to a head several
months later in a mind-boggling letter to the editor from "Miss Jerusha
Clutterbuck."[58]

> *Mr. Norris,*—I had an *anonymous* bunch of "Sweet Fern" sent me
> this morning. ME! (Miss Jerusha Clutterbuck!) Now I'm no more
> *Fanny Fern* than I'm *Jehoshaphat*! (if *that's* the pith of the joke;)
> however, it's just as acceptable as if it went to the *right person;* and
> is very *odor-o-fe-re-ous* as it stands in the vase before me. Now I
> know the floral signification of a sunflower, a hollyhock, a poppy,
> or a potato blossom, and am *quite conversant* with DANDY-*lions!*—
> but what Flora meant when she christened that herb "sweet fern,"
> is beyond *me*; I "pause for a reply"! The donor will probably be
> greatly distressed to learn that I am only "*a medium*" through which
> the *real bona fide* Fanny "raps" the public; but "mistakes will occur
> in the best regulated families," and I can only say that from my
> intimate acquaintance with the *real* "Fanny," it is my firm convic-
> tion that whoever expects to *get round her*, must "get up *early in the
> morning!*" FANNY FERN. (?)[59]

The style of the piece is manifestly Fanny Fern's: it combines her trademark
cantering prose; profuse italics, capitalizations, and exclamation points
(which her critics frowned upon as "clattering"); manic punning; and
patchwork citations from other sources. But the writer insists that she is
"no more *Fanny Fern* than [she's] *Jehoshaphat!*" and although she signs
Fern's name, she immediately follows it with a question mark, at once
claiming and disavowing it. As an alternative, she identifies herself as "Miss
Jerusha Clutterbuck," unmistakably the name of an elderly spinster—but
she brackets even this name in parentheses. Her explanation of the discrep-
ancy is hardly clarifying: "the *real bona fide* Fanny," she reveals, uses her as
a medium. A pseudonymous author ("the *real* 'Fanny'") who speaks

through a medium, who alternately identifies herself as "Miss Jerusha Clut-terbuck" and "FANNY FERN (?)," and whose writing strings together quota-tions, Fern here possesses a dizzying mobility that ultimately proves impossible to trace back to any single individual.

Lauren Berlant has described "female complaints" like Fern's as broker-ing an unacknowledged peace with the culture they ostensibly critique, "expressing the frustration of being generic" while at the same time "pass-ing off generic female self-identity as itself a commodity, a thing to be bought and shared."[60] Berlant offers an illuminating model of the devia-tions of political critique, especially its capacity to be rerouted into incorpo-ration and assent. But Fern's writing, and the responses it elicited, suggest that genericity does not necessarily produce "modes of containment," as Berlant contends.[61] With her outsized generic pseudonym and exuberant recirculation of her work and her persona, Fern does not "express . . . the frustration of being generic" so much as she takes it and runs with it. Where Fern's contemporary Emily Dickinson declared "I'm Nobody!" and her friend Walt Whitman proclaimed himself everybody, Fanny Fern insisted she could be anybody.

Reification as Utopia in Mass Culture

In this chapter, I have been arguing that mid-nineteenth-century readers constructed women writers as mediums of literary exchange, as authors who practiced something less like creation and more like fraud. From this vantage point, the proliferation of women's writing during this period per-versely leads to a mass disappearance of women writers. But Fern's repre-sentations of her authorship are jarring because they almost *too closely* exemplify these modes of reading. Refusing the coherence of the individual subject, she performs her own authorial disappearance, her own inter-changeability, her own fakery. Over the past two decades, performances like these have increasingly moved to the forefront of feminist and queer stud-ies. The film theorist Mary Ann Doane, drawing on the work of Luce Iri-garay, has evocatively described such reenactments of femininity as a "double mimesis" in which an already "'respoken' femininity is subjected to a respeaking in its turn" that "mak[es] these gestures and poses *fantastic*, literally *incredible*."[62] This notion of iterative femininity would find its most influential formulation in Judith Butler's concept of "parody," which thrives on the logic that "it is only *within* the practice of repetitive signifying that a subversion of identity becomes possible." For Butler, parody constitutes a mode of feminist and queer politics, "the site of a dissonant and denaturalized performance that reveals the performative status of the natural itself."[63] Butler's and Doane's paradigms, which usefully illuminate the ways in which hegemonic constructions of gender may be reinhabited, allow us to see Fern's embrace of her own fraudulence as a disruption of those constructions, rather than a capitulation to them. But I would suggest that Fern's iterations do even more. For Doane, "double mimesis" makes representations of women visible as misrepresentations. Likewise, for Butler, "parody" is a "subversion" that "exposes . . . the illusion of gender identity as an intractable depth and inner substance."[64] While both constitute powerful actions, their work is essentially negative: given a cultural construct, such practices deconstruct it. But surely negation is a limited pleasure. Although these deconstructions challenge hegemonic formations, they do not offer alternative modes of existence, and thus in some sense they remain confined within the terms of the representations they would negate. Fern's exuberant fakery, however, does not just negate representations of women writers' fraudulence but emphatically *reuses* them. In *Uncle Tom's Cabin*, St. Clare sums up Topsy's comic catechism by telling Miss Ophelia, "You'll have to give her a meaning, or she'll make one."[65] Fern, who borrows Topsy's answers for her preface to *Fern Leaves*, likewise makes unauthorized meanings for the language of fraudulence.[66]

We can detect the effects of this recoding in the often comically contradictory responses Fern's writing elicited from her readers, particularly her male ones. As I have observed, such readers accused Fern and other nineteenth-century women writers of a kind of counterfeit authorship, leading one writer to the *Olive Branch* to fret, "One hardly knows in these days of inflated and extravagant trash, the spurious from the genuine, the false from the true coin," adding that he was been "led to these remarks from reading" Fern and her pseudonymous colleagues.[67] Yet even while accusing Fern of inherent fraudulence, of writing as a mere medium of exchange (ambiguously "false" or "true coin"), these critics drew back from the implications of commodified artifice. Such conflicts are apparent even in the much-quoted compliments of Nathaniel Hawthorne, who notably exempted Fern from the women authors he believed hampered his book sales. Hawthorne's uneasiness with his female competitors extended at least as far back as 1830, when he used the ostensible subject of Anne Hutchinson to launch an attack on "public women" in general. "The press . . . is now the medium through which feminine ambition chiefly manifests itself," Hawthorne complains, and he looks toward the future with apprehension. "There are obvious circumstances which will render female pens more numerous and more prolific than those of men, though but equally encouraged; and (limited of course by the scanty support of the public, but increasing indefinitely within those limits) the ink-stained Amazons will expel their rivals by actual pressure, and petticoats wave triumphant over all the field."[68] Hawthorne oscillates wildly between assurance and agitation, certain that women writers can never achieve popular success but convinced that they will somehow come to dominate the literary marketplace nonetheless. In this fantasy of grotesque female reproduction, "female pens" multiply uncontrollably and the "ink-stained Amazons" themselves "increas[e] indefinitely" to the point that they push their male counterparts out of the literary marketplace.

Given the frantically sexualized language in which Hawthorne envisions this female literary takeover, it is no surprise that he associates women's writing with indecent exposure. He finds "a sort of impropriety in the display of woman's naked mind to the gaze of the world, with indications by which its inmost secrets may be searched out."[69] Twenty-five years later, Hawthorne feared that women's authorial exhibitionism had achieved its anticipated results. As he wrote to his publisher, William Ticknor, "America is now wholly given over to a d——d mob of scribbling women, and I should have no chance of success while the public taste is occupied with their trash—and should be ashamed of myself if I did succeed."[70] Two weeks later, however, he qualified his earlier statements.

In my last, I recollect, I bestowed some vituperation on female authors. I have since been reading "Ruth Hall"; and I must say I enjoyed it a good deal. The woman writes as if the devil was in her; and that is the only condition under which a woman writes anything worth reading. Generally women write like emasculated men, and are only to be distinguished from male authors by greater feebleness and folly; but when they throw off the restraints of decency, and come before the public stark naked, as it were—then their books are sure to possess character and value. Can you tell me anything about

this Fanny Fern? If you meet her, I wish you would let her know
how much I admire her.[71]

Hawthorne revisits his earlier image of women authors' exhibitionism here,
but it has undergone a dramatic shift in value: whereas earlier it signaled
the impropriety of women's authorship, now, in reference to Fanny Fern,
it becomes the highest recommendation. Fern somehow changes the terms
of Hawthorne's worries about women's authorship, making the exposure
of a private self something to be desired rather than deplored.

What we should conclude from this is not, I think, that Hawthorne
became an enthusiastic supporter of women's literary ambitions in the
interim. The most interesting thing about the admiration he expresses for
Fern is how peculiarly misplaced it is: he praises the pseudonymous writer
for her willingness to expose a private self, to "come before the public stark
naked, as it were." One logical conclusion is that Hawthorne had learned
of *Ruth Hall*'s autobiographical content, which Fern's embittered former
editor, William Moulton, had made public, along with Fern's real name,
two weeks earlier in the Boston-based *True Flag*. Yet Hawthorne's plea for
more information ("Can you tell me anything about this Fanny Fern?")
and his apparent unawareness of her given name indicate that he knew
nothing of her real identity. Given the strange irrelevance of Hawthorne's
compliments, not just inapposite to Fern but actually opposite, we might
see his revaluation of women's literary "nakedness" as a kind of wish fulfillment—an anxious response to her *lack* of a private self, one that he
here reflexively constructs. Hawthorne's comments themselves enact this
substitution in their abrupt shuttling from an image of the evacuation of
selfhood ("The woman writes as if the devil was in her") to the display of
selfhood, in which Fern "come[s] before the public stark naked, as it were."
Perhaps it should come as no surprise, then, when he ends the letter with
precisely the kind of curiosity to "search out" Fern's "inmost secrets" that
he earlier censured women authors for improperly inviting. By holding out
the threat of a purely public existence with no "innermost secrets" to maintain the integrity of the individual, Fern sends Hawthorne running to the
very possibilities for personal violation he once shuddered at—precisely
because they assume the existence of a private person. His projection of
Fern's body recalls abolitionist readers' responses to James Williams, which
likewise sought to rectify the author's disidentification with the text by
treating the text as an embodiment of the author.

Fern's harsher critics shared Hawthorne's tendency to careen from the overly public to the wholly personal when they attempted to assess her writing. Even as they dismissed it as imitative and artificial, a recirculation of conventions, they simultaneously insisted on its revelatory intimate content. In his slanderous biography *The Life and Beauties of Fanny Fern*, William Moulton sounds a familiar note when he writes of Fern: "Her manner is that of a consummate actress. And it is not long before you discover that she is little else than an actress. Her tears are regular stage tears. If she desires to excite your sympathy, she knows better than anybody else, how to do it. She'll improvise a 'Ruth Hall' story for you, inventing wrongs and sufferings to fit the occasion, and drop a few ready tears, like hot wax, to seal her testimony,—sometimes sobbing a little, and pressing your hand convulsively, to heighten the effect."[72] Fern is all artifice here; she simply does not exist beneath the staged postures she affects. Yet Moulton is torn between his desire to portray Fern as entirely superficial and his refusal to believe that she can fabricate anything. "Fanny writes well only when giving the concentrated spice and vinegar of her own experiences," he sneers, and the centerpiece of *The Life and Beauties* is a long section called "A Key to *Ruth Hall*," which reads Fern's novel as a self-deluding autobiography. Moulton's competing desires for Fern's writing to reveal both a scandalous private life and a lack of any private life at all pull his interpretation in opposite directions, so that he asserts that Fern is a master coquette, well-versed in artifice, *and* that her writing is unwittingly transparent, a "veritable transcript of the writer's own mind."[73]

The *Southern Quarterly Review*'s scathing review of *Ruth Hall*, which censured the book's willingness to "los[e] sight of the woman Ruth in the authoress Floy," displays a similar desire to recover the woman it contends has been lost in the act of writing. The reviewer initially dismisses Fern's novel as a derivative work of "inspired mediocrity" perfectly suited to the "immense middle class of ordinary readers of average intelligence," which is "composed four-fifths of women." He announces, "Until the advent of 'Ruth Hall,' no writer had hit the nail precisely on the head," but Fern's novel distinguishes itself by being indistinguishable, "never rising above the key note, never sinking below it; always intelligible; always correct and proper; not one new thought is introduced from first to last." The novel simply pieces together well-worn conventions, making it as false as a "glittering string of inflamed paste." Yet just as the reviewer recoils from Ruth's disappearance in "Floy," he cannot bear to part with the woman behind

Ruth Hall, and so while he denounces the book for being wholly "extrinsic," he also maintains that it discloses a (distasteful) female interiority. "How much of auto-biography may be found in the work, we know not, inasmuch as we have no inkling of who is meant by the vegetable pseudonym of 'Fanny Fern.' But there must be much self-infusion in the book, for even inspired mediocrity could not have so completely forgotten and merged the woman Ruth in the authoress Floy."[74] For all his accusations of derivativeness, the reviewer is ultimately reluctant to believe in the textual alienability he initially condemns, and the review ends with a hasty reunion of author and text. Fern's reviewers turned their critical gazes on her person so persistently that it became a running feature of her columns, where she lamented, "What a pity when editors review a woman's book, that they so often fall into the error of reviewing the *woman* instead."[75] Fern sees this "error" as a symptom of professional jealousy, but it may be as wishful as it is vengeful, for recovering the figure of the author keeps at bay Fern's more unsettling mode of female literary production. These critics, who strive to rein in Fern's overproduction of personality, can help us discern the double edge of literary fraudulence. Fern's critics deride her artificiality, but they also flinch at its unmoored vitality.

Fern's male critics, as I have noted, responded to her work with mixed scorn and outrage, and many of her female critics were equally hostile. But others responded in ways that suggest Fern not only activated the generative possibilities of literary exchangeability herself but extended them to her readers, as well. At times she did so quite explicitly, as in one of *Ruth Hall*'s stranger moments, when "Floy" receives a letter from "Mary R——." "It was in a delicate, beautiful, female hand; just such a one as you, dear Reader, might trace, whose sweet, soft eyes, and long, drooping tresses, are now bending over this page" (260). Addresses to the reader, of course, constitute a commonplace of nineteenth-century women's novels, but Fern does not address a generalized, unmarked reader; she projects a stock sentimental heroine, instantly recognizable by her "sweet, soft eyes, and long, drooping tresses." In effect, Fern interpellates her female reader into the world of fiction. Tellingly, this transformation is literary in origin as well as nature, as the reader's (imagined) handwriting initiates her metamorphosis. In this moment, Fern holds out the astonishing possibility that you are what you write, or perhaps what she writes.

The debates over Fern's identity that unfolded in the *Olive Branch* offer a glimpse of how Fern's female readers responded to this invitation. When the newspaper began publishing Fern's column, it received a slew of demands for her real name, portrait, and hand in marriage from infatuated male readers. These men, like Fern, adopt pseudonyms, but theirs empha-size facticity rather than fakery—"Frank Real," for example, and "Jack Plane," whose "plain" intentions Fern puns on in reply.[76] Fern received an equal number of letters from women, but instead of making claims to fac-ticity, these readers affect the patently artificial pseudonymity she models, and they reject the personalizing interventions of "Frank Real" and "Jack Plane." "Patience Pepper," for instance, advises Fern against marriage, and "Jenny Jessamine" asserts, "As long as you are *Fanny Fern*, I do not care to have you *anybody* else. I don't in the least know whether you are a maiden lady of a certain age, or a fat matron; I do not feel a bit envious if you are young and beautiful; I care not whether you are sweet sixteen, or venerable twenty-five."[77] Unlike "Frank Real" and "Jack Plane," Fern's female readers embrace her existence as a print fiction and even, as their choice of pseud-onyms implies, aspire to it themselves. Some female readers did personalize Fern. But their letters, perhaps more than any others, suggest that they found possibilities in her hyperbolic conventionality, for she inspired love letters from women as well as men. Initially, these proposals stem from rumors that Fern actually was a man, so that "Eva" addresses her suit to "Jack Fern." But when Fern responds explaining that she is a woman, "Eva," unperturbed, replies that they will "love one another, anyway."[78] Likewise, "Eliza," the author of the poem to Fern quoted earlier, ends her tribute, "Oh mirth-provoking Fanny, / If the genius of your pen / Can stir the hearts of women thus, / How is it with the men?" That "Eliza" is stirred by Fern's play with(in) convention to apparently unconventional affections seems to call for a queer reading of Fern. But if she did not elicit same-sex desire, she would be no less queer. That the fraudulent identity she inhabits wreaks havoc with normativity reminds us that the term "queer" has its origins in counterfeit.[79] To be "queer as a three-dollar bill" is to be queer as the verisimilar bank certificate that infuriates Fern's reviewer in the *Southern Quarterly Review*, or as the shinplasters that at once contaminated and sustained the antebellum economy. The ambiguous legitimacy of these counterfeit bills suggest something of the currency Fanny Fern found in her own counterfeit, which was neither wholly subjugated by the market nor subversive of it, but carried some queer value in between.

Conclusion

The Confidence Man on a Large Scale

As for the "Confidence Man" . . . he is a cheat, a humbug,
a delusion, a sham, a mockery!
                                        —*New York Herald*, 11 July 1849

If there is any antebellum text that seems to exemplify the version of
fraudulence I have been trying to challenge in this book, it is surely *The
Confidence-Man: His Masquerade* (1857), Herman Melville's obliquely satirical chronicle of the ruses practiced aboard a Mississippi steamboat over the
course of a single April Fool's Day. Critics have long understood fraudulence in Melville's final novel to be a topic for literary representation rather
than a function of it, exceptional rather than endemic, a rift in the social
fabric rather than its warp and weft. Whereas this book has emphasized the
ubiquity of antebellum fraudulence, which could not be confined to deliberate acts of con artistry, critics typically identify all of the *Fidèle*'s slick
talkers and charlatans as manifestations of a single protagonist, the Confidence Man of the novel's title. Most influentially, in her 1954 edition of the
novel, which initiated its critical revival, Elizabeth S. Foster theorized that
the Confidence Man was actually the devil himself, for who else could
assume so many disguises so convincingly? Generations of critics have followed Foster's interpretation of satanic shape-shifting, while others have
inverted it but preserved its unifying schema by arguing that the Confidence Man is not the devil but God.[1] Less allegorical interpretations have
nonetheless taken similar paths. Helen Trimpi, for example, has painstak-
ingly identified each character with a contemporary political figure, defying
awkward fits in order to assimilate the novel's anarchic uncertainty to a
coherent whole.[2] Critics who have not focused on the novel's characters

have nonetheless sought to unify it thematically, reading it as illustrative of a particular principle, such as the hypocrisy of Christianity or the untrustworthiness of language. All of these interpretations present *The Confidence-Man* as a riddle to be solved by the discerning reader who can find a hidden order beneath Melville's baggy disorder.

Given the approaches to fraudulence these critics have taken, it may seem odd to end this book with a discussion of *The Confidence-Man*. But my intention is to perform a kind of experiment that tests whether my argument can make sense of a text that to all appearances contravenes it. I begin from the observation that, despite the promising particularity of the title and the efforts of generations of critics, isolating a singular confidence man in Melville's novel proves remarkably difficult. Fraudulence, while everywhere aboard the *Fidèle*, remains bewilderingly elusive precisely because of its ubiquity. And fraudulence is not only unlocatable on the crowded decks of the *Fidèle* but inextricable from the novel itself, a formal problem that it thematizes as a rather disorienting tendency to thread discussions of literature through its narrative of deception. Continually folding in on its own plot, *The Confidence-Man* cannot be said to represent antebellum con artistry because it fails to make the crucial distinction between literary representation and con artistry that would enable such a feat, leading at least one contemporaneous reviewer to conclude that the novel itself must be "a hoax on the public, an emulation of Barnum."[3]

Countersigns of Confidence

The *Fidèle*'s microcosm of "free Ameriky" (as one of the passengers, an imposter wounded soldier, calls it) will appear familiar to readers of this book.[4] The sham currencies of an expanding nation are in full effect, much to the dismay of one passenger, who tries desperately to sort his counterfeit money from his valid notes, and the delight of another, who exploits the opportunity to sell the first a counterfeit detector, which Melville hints is also counterfeit. Elsewhere on the boat, a western land agent solicits speculators in the "*bona fide*" paper town of New Jerusalem (50). Several of this book's major players even make an appearance. A ringer for Davy Crockett arrives, "a rather eccentric-looking person" wearing "a high-peaked cap of raccoon-skin, the long bushy tail switching over behind," whom the narrator, adopting Crockett's trademark phrase, declares "half cynic, half wildcat" (106, 107). Edgar Allan Poe, too, turns up as a "crazy beggar" peddling

a "rhapsodical tract" (194), physically recognizable by his "broad, untanned
... brow" (Poe's most noted feature for contemporary admirers, for whom
it physiognomically denoted his massive intellect), and allusively so by his
"disheveled mass of raven curls" (195). Having gained notoriety for
debunking others' literary pretensions, here Poe appears undone by suspicions of his own fraudulence, his "picturesque" insanity "heightened by
what seemed just one glimmering peep of reason, insufficient to do him
any lasting good, but enough, perhaps, to suggest a torment of latent doubts
at times, whether his addled dream of glory were true" (195).

     Predictably, however, given the racialization of fraudulence I charted in
Chapters 2 and 3, the character who first attracts suspicion is a "grotesque
negro cripple" (10) named Black Guinea, who lacks both his legs and a
master—deficiencies that prompt the other passengers to request "any documentary proof, any plain paper . . . attesting that his case was not a spurious one" (13). Their requests place Black Guinea in a predicament similar
to that of the authors of slave narratives in Chapter 3, who likewise found
that white print culture constituted the horizon for their authenticity.
Another passenger's suspicions, however, suggest that Black Guinea may be
best compared to Jim Crow; the passenger accuses the performer, who plays
a tambourine and "shuffle[s] about, making music, such as it was" (10), of
being "some white operator" (14) like "the negro-minstrels" (31). Yet "these
suspicions came from one who himself on a wooden leg went halt" (12),
and the scene's ironic mirroring of their missing legs recalls the eagerness
with which white impersonators of African Americans represented African
Americans as chronic mimics. Indeed, although the man with the wooden
leg attempts to expose Black Guinea, he also allows that Black Guinea is no
different from anyone else. "Tell me, sir, do you really think that a white
could look the negro so? For one, I should call it pretty good acting,"
another onlooker objects. "Not much better than any other man acts," the
man with the wooden leg responds, "To do is to act; so all doers are actors"
(31). Yet his companions ignore his critique, and the resemblance between
accuser and accused "did not appear to strike anybody present" (12)—a
response that anticipates the novel's own scholarly reception, as critics have
likewise confined its profusion of fraudulence to a single miscreant.

     Similarly, for all critics' efforts to trace the novel's fraudulence back to
what Michael Paul Rogin felicitously terms an "authentic confidence
man," the closer one looks at *The Confidence-Man*, the more difficult it
becomes to pin down the con artistry it represents.[5] Indeed, the novel

rejects mimesis as a general rule; as Sianne Ngai points out, its characters staunchly remain literary *characters*, whose exteriors enclose no interiors.[6] Melville's refusal to distinguish between surface and depth makes it hard to think about the novel in terms of disguises, either real disguises or the kinds of textual masking amenable to a hermeneutics of suspicion. Thus even as Melville encourages us to connect the dots between the confidence men (beginning with his title), he constantly undermines our ability to do so definitively. For instance, while numerous critics have noted that Black Guinea's list of guarantors seems to forecast the novel's confidence men, hinting that he will authenticate his own deception in this succession of guises, they have puzzled over the fact that Black Guinea's list does not name all of the Confidence Man's ostensible manifestations, while it names some who never appear. This ostensible key to the novel's mysteries does not fit the lock. Frustrating as these apparent red herrings may be for modern readers, they aptly characterize an era when, as Karen Halttunen puts it, "The confidence man personified the pervasive duplicity of the rising generation."[7]

Indeed, the second half of the novel foregoes a clear demarcation between confidence men and dupes entirely to stage a series of encounters between competing tricksters: the "Mississippi operator" Charles Noble versus the cosmopolitan Frank Goodman; Goodman versus the hypocritical Transcendentalist Mark Winsome and his disciple Egbert; Goodman versus the boy huckster hawking fraudulent antifraud devices, and so on. As confidence men multiply, identification of *the* confidence man of the novel's title becomes impossible. "Our sentiments agree so, that were they written in a book, whose was whose, few but the nicest critics might determine," says Goodman to Noble at one point (158), and for once he speaks truthfully. Indeed, Melville's own dialogue drives home Goodman's observation when, some pages later, it mixes up the two men (208).[8] Despite the *Fidèle's* boisterous heterogeneity—what Melville calls its "Anarchis Cloots congress" of passengers (9)—as the novel draws to a close, it increasingly resembles a hall of mirrors.[9] By the penultimate scene, between Goodman and the ship's barber, the barber's disclosure that his name is Cream links him inexplicably to the "man in cream-colours" who opens the book— and linguistically, the entire premise of the confidence man conning the man who shaves him must have dizzied nineteenth-century readers, who would have recognized "shave" as a common slang term for "con," making the confidence man and the barber doubles for one another.

Most disconcertingly, several critics have noticed a strange doubling between the language of the confidence men and that of the narrator himself.[10] These repetitions tend to occur during the narrator's frequent digressions into literary analysis, making such moments seem less like interruptions in the novel's account of con artistry and more like continuations of it. In one excursus on characterization, for instance, Melville explains that a character who may seem inconsistent is "as much at variance with itself as the caterpillar is with the butterfly into which it changes"—that is, "not false but faithful to facts" (70). (It is worth noting how often Melville frames his discussions of literature in terms of authenticity and fraudulence; despite the "play of invention" presumably allowed literature, what interests Melville is the "requirement" of truth foisted upon it [69].) Later in the novel, however, the metaphor of the caterpillar and the butterfly gains a bewildering new significance when it reappears in the mouth of the oily Philosophical Intelligence Officer, who employs it to explain why an unpromising young servant may become a worthy man: "He may have been a caterpillar, but is now a butterfly" (124). Of course, the Philosophical Intelligence Officer uses this reasoning solely to persuade a suspicious customer to hire a servant through his employment agency, but this is the point—the claims that Melville makes on behalf of literature recur as the ruses of confidence men. As the same words pass between the author discussing his trade and the confidence men plying theirs, literature and fraud appear increasingly interchangeable.

Even the word "confidence" itself exemplifies this doubling, signifying both trust and the machinations that exploit such trust. As Wai Chee Dimock notes, "Alternatively a liability and a benefit, something to demand and something to resist, confidence generates two opposing syntaxes of meaning, the effect of which is to break down not so much its polarities as the substantive difference between the two."[11] The queasy joke on "confidence" comes to light quite literally when the quack herb doctor announces, "Take the wrapper from any of my vials and hold it to the light, you will see water-marked in capitals the word *confidence*, which is the countersign of the medicine, as I wish it was of the world" (83). Ostensibly soliciting the buyer's faith in patent medicine, the herb doctor's watermark inevitably also declares the article's true nature as a trick. Earlier I observed that the novel's galloping fraudulence outpaces the singularity that the title, with its definite article "the" and the specificity of "man," leads us to expect. But the particularity of the term "confidence man" itself increasingly wobbles over the course of the novel, as the word "confidence" becomes, to borrow the herb doctor's term, its own countersign.

"The Metaphysics of Indian-Hating" and the Difference Fraudulence Makes

Far from locating fraudulence in particular persons, as its title would suggest, *The Confidence-Man*, like antebellum readers, finds it everywhere at once. Yet the strangest and most involved instance of fraud's migrations in the novel, the story of the "Indian-hater" (140) that Charles Noble tells Frank Goodman, also recalls the responses to such diffuse fraudulence I have traced in this book, in that it nevertheless attempts to pin down fraudulence *somewhere*—specifically, somewhere else. The Indian-hater himself, Colonel John Moredock, occupies little of the story, most of which revolves around theorizing why Indian-hating has endured on the frontier even when Indians themselves, for the most part, have not. As Noble explains, Indian-hating constitutes a cultural inheritance of the backwoodsman, who from a young age "hears little . . . but histories of Indian lying, Indian theft, Indian double-dealing, Indian fraud and perfidy" (146) and accordingly commits himself to genocide. For years, critics have debated the earnestness of Melville's account of Native Americans' deceit and his seemingly sympathetic portrayal of the bloodthirsty backwoodsman. But in doing so, they have passed over one of the oddest elements of a thoroughly odd episode. At the end of Noble's discourse on "the metaphysics of Indian-hating," Goodman "gently interrupt[s]" him to make what is, given the context, a stunningly ironic request: "One moment," he says, "and let me refill my calumet" (151). The chapter ends with this line. That Goodman cuts short this account of Native American trickery to smoke a Native American pipe may simply signal the confidence man's own trickery, a trickery so devious it can only be compared with the racial disposition of Native Americans. But Native American vessels of one kind or another prove to be in general circulation on the *Fidèle*, for shortly afterward, when Goodman and Noble order a bottle of wine, it arrives in "a little bark basket, braided with porcupine quills, gaily tinted in the Indian fashion" (161), and when the two men follow the wine with cigars, these too "were brought in a pretty little bit of western pottery, representing some kind of Indian utensil" (168). Why does this succession of Indian artifacts—pipe, basket, bowl—accompany the metaphysics of Indian-hating?

The story of Colonel Moredock (which Melville borrowed from James Hall's 1835 *Sketches of History, Life, and Manners, in the West*) casts fraudulence as a racial trait that causes Native Americans to terrorize white settlers, much as blackface minstrelsy cast fraudulence as an African American trait and southwestern humor cast it as a backwoods trait. But the traffic in Native American artifacts on the *Fidèle* troubles the distinctions between Native American deceit and white American integrity the story works so hard to make. First, by equipping white Americans with Native American props, it blurs the racial difference between the two groups that the story produces and, more to the point, the moral difference that follows from it. The joke, in other words, is that the white Americans "play Indian" even as they excoriate the subjects of their pantomime. Second, it is telling that the Native American artifacts in circulation are all vessels, empty receptacles that the white passengers fill to their desire. While the "metaphysics of Indian-hating" assumes a knowledge of Native Americans' innate contents, these objects demonstrate that what white Americans really have at hand are Native American forms, whose contents they supply themselves. Finally, it is important that the passengers not only fill these forms, but that they do so in order to consume the contents. Their consumption suggests that white Americans do not relegate fraudulence to the cultural margins in order to leave it behind; they use and *enjoy* subaltern fraudulence, savoring the taste of its difference.

The ubiquity of Native American artifacts aboard the *Fidèle* jostles the embedded story of the "metaphysics of Indian-hating," so that its meaning can no longer be contained in the actions of Colonel Moredock alone but extends to its audience's patterns of consumption. In fact, Noble himself admits that his story tells us very little. As he explains, there are two kinds of Indian-haters, but what they have in common is that neither offers much insight into the practice of Indian-hating. The "Indian-hater *par excellence*" disappears into the "forest primeval" to pursue his quarry, so that this purest form of Indian-hating necessarily coincides with its disappearance from recorded knowledge (knowledge that, as the allusion to the famous first line of Longfellow's *Evangeline* suggests, is in any event always already framed by literature). "How evident that in strict speech there can be no biography of an Indian-hater *par excellence*, any more than one of a sword-fish or other deep sea denizen. . . . The career of the Indian-hater *par excellence* has the impenetrability of the fate of a lost steamer. Doubtless, events, terrible ones, have happened, must have happened, but the powers that be in nature have taken order that they shall never become news" (150). Still, there also exists "a species of diluted Indian-hater," who periodically returns home, longing for companionship. His very susceptibility to the "soft enticements of domestic life" (150) undermines his character *as* an Indian-hater, Noble observes regretfully, yet "this is the man who, by his very infirmity, enables us to form surmises, however inadequate, of what Indian-hating in its perfection is" (151). By definition, our knowledge of Indian-hating can only come from one who has abandoned its precepts, so it remains inevitably wanting, impaired by its own intelligibility. This epistemological cautionary tale, however, is exactly what we forget if we try to crack *The Confidence-Man* like a riddle, to sort its chaotic fakery and detect a pattern of organized deception beneath— some "little lower layer," as Elizabeth Foster says, quoting from *Moby-Dick* while seemingly forgetting that it is monomaniacal Ahab, surely not a model reader, who believes in the existence of such a thing.[12]

By contrast, the impenetrability of fraud in *The Confidence-Man* has delighted deconstructionist-minded readers, who see it as analogous to the doomed project of knowledge in *Moby-Dick*, which prohibits the "biography" of a "deep-sea denizen" (to borrow *The Confidence-Man*'s words) but leaves Ishmael buoyed up by emptiness.[13] (Actually, one could argue that such readings offer their own version of the riddle-and-answer model, in which the answer *The Confidence-Man* divulges is that language, knowledge, identity, and so on are meaningless.) In fact, *The Confidence-Man* revisits *Moby-Dick*'s famous ending in its own final pages, and I want to propose that this last instance of doubling instructively foregrounds a key difference between the two novels, one that calls for a more historicized reading than a strictly deconstructionist interpretation provides. While Ishmael survives the destruction of the Pequod in *Moby-Dick* by floating on the "life-buoy" of Queequeg's empty coffin, an even more unlikely life-preserver closes *The Confidence-Man*.[14] After the boy peddling "travelers' aids" fleeces his elderly customer, the man remembers he needs a life-preserver but doesn't know what one looks like. Goodman, however, obligingly finds him one:

> "They are something like this, sir, I believe," lifting a brown stool with a curved tin compartment underneath; "yes, this, I think, is a life-preserver, sir; and a very good one, I should say, though I

don't pretend to know much about such things, never using them
myself."

"Why, indeed, now! Who would have thought it? *that* a life preserver? That's the very stool I was sitting on, ain't it?"

"It is. And that shows that one's life is looked out for, when he
ain't looking out for it himself. In fact, any of these stools here will
float you, sir, should the boat hit a snag, and go down in the dark."
(251)

The old man's surprise is understandable, for as the footnotes to the Penguin edition of the novel delicately explain, the "brown stool" is "a kind of
chamber pot supplied for the use of passengers; the scatological allusion is
obvious."[15] According to the exuberant nihilism of *Moby-Dick*, a life-
preserver may be full of nothing, but in the duplicitous world of *The
Confidence-Man*, it is simply full of shit. While this trope is less conducive
to philosophizing, it powerfully evokes the antebellum world of humbug
that Melville knew so well.

Confidence in Print

The term "confidence man" was originally coined by the *New York Herald*
to describe an ingratiating gentleman named William Thompson who traveled around New York for several months in 1849, asking unsuspecting men
if they had the confidence to lend him their watches for a day. Trusting
Thompson's "genteel appearance," his victims would willingly hand over
their watches, but that was the last they would see of either Thompson
or the watches.[16] Thompson caused a stir among New Yorkers, inspiring
numerous newspaper commentaries and even a farce that Burton's Theatre
rushed to the stage two weeks after his arrest. But while modern readers of
The Confidence-Man have worked hard to trace its fraudulence to an individual culprit, Melville's contemporaries did exactly the opposite: they
insisted that Thompson could only be a small detail of a much bigger but
more elusive picture. An article in the *Merchant's Ledger*, subsequently
reprinted in Evert Duyckinck's *Literary World*, seized on the new term in
order to expand the definition beyond Thompson, sketching the generic
"confidence man of politics" and (with apparently unintentional irony) the
"confidence man of merchandise." Meanwhile, the *National Police Gazette*,

which reported on the case extensively, saw Thompson as evidence of
municipal corruption and asserted that he must be in league with the dis-
trict attorney.[17] Three days after the *Herald* triumphantly reported that
Thompson had been jailed, the newspaper ran an article titled "The Confidence Man on a Large Scale," wondering whether the problem had indeed
been solved:

> While lamenting the sudden withdrawal of this distinguished "oper-
> ator" from the active business of "the street," we cannot exclaim
> with the Moor—"Othello's occupation's gone!" As you saunter
> through some of those fashionable streets and squares which orna-
> ment the upper part of this magnificent city, you cannot fail to be
> struck by the splendor of some of the *palazzos* which meet the eye
> in all directions. . . . Those *palazzos*, with all their costly furniture.
> and all their splendid equipages, have been the product of the same
> genius in their proprietors, which has made the "Confidence Man"
> immortal and a prisoner at "the Tombs." His genius has been
> employed on a small scale in Broadway. Theirs has been employed
> in Wall Street. That's all the difference. He has obtained half a dozen
> watches. They have pocketed millions of dollars. He is a swindler.
> They are exemplars of honesty. He is a rogue. They are financiers.
> He is collared by the police. They are cherished by society. He eats
> the fare of a prison. They enjoy the luxuries of a palace. He is a
> mean, beggarly, timid, narrow-minded wretch, who has not a sou
> above a chronometer. They are respectable, princely, bold, high-
> soaring "operators," who are to be satisfied only with the plunder
> of a whole community.
>   How is it done? What is the secret? What is the machinery?[18]

The writer sardonically suggests that New Yorkers have once more been
duped. The stir over the petty "confidence man" Thompson was nothing
less than a shell game that deflected public attention away from the activities of the real confidence men, who continue to operate undetected in the
highest echelons of society, having defrauded not a handful of men but a
"whole community." As the *Herald* concludes, "the 'Confidence Man' who
battens and fattens on the plunder coming from the poor man and the man
of moderate means" is "the real 'Confidence Man'. . . . As for the 'Confidence Man' of the 'Tombs,' he is a cheat, a humbug, a delusion, a sham, a

mockery!"[19] In this article, the apparently straightforward designation of "confidence man" wobbles once more, this time under the pressure of its economic and political context. By focusing on Thompson's punishable attempts to separate wealthy gentlemen from their watches, the article asserts, New Yorkers ignore the legal fraud by which the "upper ten" exploit the "lower million" every day. Refusing the denomination of Thompson as "the Confidence Man"—indeed, insisting that any notion of *the* "Confidence Man" is itself fraudulent—the *Herald* urges readers to recognize the systemic "real 'Confidence Man'" instead.

The Confidence-Man rehearses this distinction between singularity and multiplicity within its own pages as the problem of "originality," a word it worries at from beginning to end. On the very first page, Melville introduces the "mysterious imposter" not in the flesh, but on a placard offering a reward for his capture, which portrays him as "quite an original." This designation would seem to support singular accounts of the confidence man and even his association with "original" sin until Melville adds, "though wherein his originality consisted was not clearly given" (3). These sorts of undercutting addendums will become the narrative signature of the novel, which has a confounding habit of making bold assertions only to chip away at them in the space of the same sentence.[20] Here Melville's qualifying statements suggest that the confidence man's originality is merely apparent, a suspicion that increases several chapters later when a cynical bystander who pronounces the quack herb doctor an "original genius" stands corrected: "as this age goes, not much originality about that" (91). Later, having ended one chapter with a description of the cosmopolitan's reputation as "QUITE AN ORIGINAL" (237), Melville opens the next by repeating the phrase and concluding it to be baseless. In yet another of the unexplained shifts from confidence games to literary criticism I described earlier, he asserts that those fictional characters often called original are actually "local, or of the age" (239). By associating the work of deception with the work of literature, this narrative intervention not only sets the book's own meaning on end but returns us with new eyes to the novel's opening scene and its introduction of the word "original." For there, too, "originality" is not a real human characteristic but a fiction of the placard—a spurious effect of print.

Indeed, in contrast to the conventional confidence man, who capitalizes on personal charisma, selling his ploy on the strength of his own charm, Melville's confidence men regularly mediate their tricks through print. Nor is this device surprising, for while the travelers on the *Fidèle* are actually fairly skeptical when it comes to personal claims, they are utterly credulous about the trustworthiness of writing and especially print. Thus, as I noted above, when the crowd assembled around Black Guinea begins to suspect that his "deformity [was] a sham, got up for financial purposes," their absurd response is to ask him "had he any documentary proof, any plain paper about him, attesting that his case was not a spurious one" (12, 13). But beginning with the dubious placard warning against the "mysterious imposter," *The Confidence-Man* abounds in the circulation of printed signs, business cards, account books, pamphlets, handbills, poems, labels, tracts, and circulars, which all abide by two rules: first, they are highly questionable, and second, they are believed nevertheless. So, for example, the land agent selling shares in New Jerusalem does not actively have to solicit his customer, who simply sees the "gilt inscription" stamped on his transfer-book, requests and receives "a small printed pamphlet" reporting on "the condition of [the] company," "turn[s] it over sagely," and announces, "I will invest" (48, 47, 49). Likewise, a "little dried-up man," "naturally numb in [his] sensibilities," is moved to feel "trustful and genial" by an anonymous ode to confidence distributed through the cabin "much in the manner of those railway book-peddlers who precede their proffers of sale by a distribution of puffs, direct or indirect, of the volumes to follow" (53). (In light of this book's first chapter, perhaps it is not irrelevant that the puff-like poem looked "as if fluttered down from a balloon" [53]). These texts inspire confidence by affecting to describe something real (New Jerusalem, the value of confidence), but the confidence they inspire guarantees that they need refer to nothing at all (the novel hints that New Jerusalem is merely "little dots" and "asterisks" on a map [50], and that the author of the ode has ulterior motives). By the time the novel's final dupe examines the "traveler's patent lock" he is being offered and exclaims, "This beats printing" (246), his yoking of scams and print hardly seems incongruous.

Critics of *The Confidence-Man* have traced its evident misgivings about literature to Melville's own disappointing book sales, to the bankruptcy of contemporary political discourse, and to the inherent emptiness of language itself.[21] As various as they are, these explanations share a common investment in the figure of Melville as an alienated visionary, whose gimlet eye sees through a world of pretense and sham that blinds his more gullible contemporaries. Certainly *The Confidence-Man* stands as one of the bleakest cultural critiques the mid-nineteenth-century United States produced. However, Melville himself suggests that its suspicions about print culture, at least, may be more symptomatic than idiosyncratic. When Charles Noble proposes reciting "a panegyric on the press," Frank Goodman eagerly accepts, having observed "of late" a worrisome "disposition to disparage the press." To Goodman's dismay, critics of the press insist "that it is proving with that great invention as with brandy or eau-de-vie, which, upon its first discovery, was believed by the doctors to be, as its French name implies, a panacea—a notion which experience, it may be thought, has not fully verified" (165). Disappointed that the press does not actually distribute justice and enlightenment, "these sour sages regard the press in the light of a Colt's revolver, pledged to no cause but his in whose chance hands it may be; deeming the one invention an improvement upon the pen, much akin to what the other is upon the pistol; involving along with the multiplication of the barrel, no consecration of the aim" (165). Goodman seems to take these insults rather personally.

> "For one," continued the cosmopolitan, grandly swelling his chest, "I hold the press to be neither the people's improvisatore, nor Jack Cade; neither their paid fool, nor conceited drudge. I think interest never prevails with it over duty. . . . Not only does the press advance knowledge, but righteousness. In the press, as in the sun, resides, my dear Charlie, a dedicated principle of beneficent force and light. . . . In a word, Charlie, what the sovereign of England is titularly, I hold the press to be actually—Defender of the Faith!—defender of the faith in the final triumph of truth over error, metaphysics over superstition, theory over falsehood, machinery over nature, and the good man over the bad. Such are my views, which, if stated at some length, you, Charlie, must pardon, for it is a theme upon which I cannot speak with cold brevity." (166)

Yet "Defender of the Faith" is an equivocal title at best aboard a ship as crammed with fraud as the *Fidèle*, whose ironic name, of course, means "faithful."

Goodman's praise of print has the opposite of the intended effect, for print emerges from his lucubrations looking fully as shady as the "sour sages" contend. When rival con artist Noble responds with his own "panegyric to the press," it confirms the press's capacity for trickery, for it turns out that the press he extols is "not Faust's, but Noah's"—the wine press, not the printing press. "You deceived me," objects Goodman plaintively; "you roguishly took advantage of my simplicity; you archly played upon my enthusiasm" (167). Noble's "deception" and the play on "press" that enables it offer a telling coda to Goodman's earlier enthusiasm, for it demonstrates quite literally the principle he had sought to refute: the press, indeed, is not what it claims to be. Instead, its ready adoption of a new identity marks it as yet another of the novel's confidence men. Although the joke of this scene lies in the difference it reveals between Goodman's and Noble's presses, the bigger (if more bitter) joke lies in their similarity. In the novel's signature move, Melville produces distinctions only to collapse them, as here the reassuring gap between the inebriating wine press and the sober printing press snaps shut when we recall Goodman's earlier comparison of the printing press to "brandy or eau-de-vie." We may yet cherish a notion of print advancing "the triumph of truth," but in its slippery puns, and still more in its entangled narratives of fraud and literary production, *The Confidence-Man* assures us otherwise. The printing press has intoxicated us all along, and never more so than in the service of "knowledge" and "righteousness."

Notes

Introduction

1. Poe, review of Lambert Wilmer, *The Quacks of Helicon, Graham's Magazine* 19 (August 1841), in *Essays and Reviews*, 1006.

2. Benjamin Franklin, *Public Advertiser*, 22 May 1765; quoted in Wonham, *Mark Twain and the Art of the Tall Tale*, 12.

3. See, for example, Harris, *Humbug*; Cook, *The Arts of Deception*.

4. See Kuhlmann, *Knave, Fool, and Genius*; Wadlington, *The Confidence Game in American Literature*; Lindberg, *The Confidence Man in American Literature*; Halttunen, *Confidence Men and Painted Women*; Lenz, *Fast Talk and Flush Times*; and Elmer, *Reading at the Social Limit*, chap. 4.

5. Christopher Caustic, M.D. [Thomas Green Fessenden], *Terrible Tractoration!! A Poetical Petition against Galvanizing Trumpery, and the Perkinistic Instiution, in Four Cantos* (London: Hurst, 1803); and *Terrible Tractoration, and Other Poems* (Boston: Russell, Shattuck and Co., 1836), vi.

6. Tompkins, *Sensational Designs*, 130.

7. Ibid., 125.

8. Volumes two and three of the American Antiquarian Society's five-volume *A History of the Book in America* offer the most thorough and up-to-date account of this transformation, but see also several important forebears: Lehmann-Haupt, Wroth, Silver, *The Book in America*; Tebbel, *A History of Book Publishing*, vol. 1; Mott, *A History of American Magazines*; and Charvat, *Literary Publishing in America*.

9. Tebbel, *A History of Book Publishing*, 257–262; Lehmann-Haupt, Wroth, and Silver, *The Book in America*, 72–90; Zboray, *A Fictive People*, chaps. 2 and 4; and Winship, "Manufacturing and Book Production."

10. Tebbel, *A History of Book Publishing*, 43; Winship, *American Literary Publishing in the Mid-Nineteenth Century*, 122; *List of Important and Attractive Books* (Boston: Phillips, Sampson, and Co., 1856). Some earlier publishers did offer books in cloth or leather bindings, but because binding by hand was expensive and time-consuming, they rarely bound entire editions. Instead, they sent the books to binders in batches to suit demand, and the books tended to lack the design elements—ornamentation, distinctive typefaces, blind and gold stamping—common to cased bindings. See Green, "The Rise of Book Publishing," 115–118.

11. Lehuu, *Carnival on the Page*, 64.

12. Johns, *The Nature of the Book*, 172.

13. McGill, *American Literature and the Culture of Reprinting*, 2.

14. For an example of this critical tendency in performance studies, see Diana Taylor's groundbreaking *The Archive and the Repertoire*, which pits the archive's "unchanging text," which "assures a stable signifier," against the "embodied," "ephemeral" performances that constitute a repertoire (19, 20). I discuss Taylor and the print/performance dichotomy further in Chapter 2. In new media studies, the tendency to reify print dates back to Marshall McLuhan's characterization of print as "uniform, continuous," and not "reacting" (*Understanding Media*, 172, 173), and it gained traction in the era of desktop publishing and, later, the internet. Thus Richard A. Lanham's influential essay "The Electronic Word: Literary Study and the Digital Revolution" (which first appeared in *New Literary History* in 1989) contrasts the "razzle dazzle" of desktop publishing with the "stable transparency" of the printed page, "clumsy, slow, unchangeable . . . and above all author-controlled" (rpt. in *The Electronic Word*, 5, 6); and Pierre Levy contends that the "static substrate" of the printed word encourages a "demand for a universal truth," while the "dynamic substrate" of hypertext allows for a multitude of possible readings (*Becoming Virtual*, 51). In the past decade, however, a growing number of new media scholars have complicated this division, arguing that forms of "new media" do not break with older ones but "remediate" them to stake their claims to newness; see Bolter and Grusin, *Remediation*; Manovich, *The Language of New Media*; and Gitelman, *Always Already New*. Their insights suggest that the digital media shift may be more phenomenological than technological, attuning us to the instability that has always existed in the printed word. As Jacques Derrida, once the leading proponent of the notion that the "idea of the book, which always refers to a natural totality, is profoundly alien to the sense of writing," put it in an interview thirty years later, "the adventures of technology grant us a sort of future anterior; they liberate our reading for a retrospective exploration of the past resources of paper, for its *previously* multimedia vectors" (*Of Grammatology*, 18; *Paper Machine*, 47). I thank Jeff Pruchnic for tutoring me in the role of print in new media studies.

15. The list of antebellum writers who had their works set to music is very long, but it includes Park Benjamin, William Cullen Bryant, James Fenimore Cooper, Augustine Joseph Hickey Duganne, Thomas Dunn English, Edward Everett, Sarah Josepha Hale, Fitz-Greene Halleck, Charles Fenno Hoffman, Lucy Larcom, Henry Wadsworth Longfellow, George Morris, Frances Sargent Osgood, Lydia Sigourney, Seba Smith, John Greenleaf Whittier, and Nathaniel Parker Willis. Cooper, who had thirteen of his novels adapted for the stage, set the record in this respect, but other dramatizations included Washington Irving's "Rip Van Winkle," Robert Montgomery Bird's *Nick of the Woods*, George Lippard's *The Quaker City* (which was cancelled before it opened for fear of riots), and, most famously, Harriet Beecher Stowe's *Uncle Tom's Cabin*, which spawned numerous stage versions. See Loney, "The Heyday of the Dramatized Novel."

16. Irmscher, *Longfellow Redux*, 11–12; Moyne, "Parodies of Longfellow's *Song of Hiawatha*," 94.

17. J[ulius]. A[ugustus]. Noble, letter to Otis, Broaders, and Company, 7 August 1840, Book Trades Collection, American Antiquarian Society, Worcester, Mass. Apparently, a previous, similar deal to repackage back issues of magazines had gone sour. Otis, Broaders, and Company offered Noble old volumes of the *Ladies Companion*, one of the magazines they distributed, promising to get the date altered to 1840, but Noble griped, "Those that you have attempted to alter to 1840 are done so bunglingly that there is not one single No of them but that the deception is plain as to be seen & which by the most stupid persons" (ibid.).

18. Thompson, *American Literary Annuals and Gift Books*, 13, 14. The other major bibliographer of gift books, Frederick Winthrop Faxon, agrees that the number of spurious gift books was "very large" (*Literary Annuals and Gift Books*, xvii).

19. Ordinary periodicals engaged in similar tricks. In 1845, for instance, the *American Lady's Wreath* warned readers that two of its agents had capitalized on the magazine's name and visual recognition by issuing a "spurious imitation," the *Lady's Album*. "Not content with imitating exactly the outward appearance of the Lady's Wreath," the upstart publishers had prefaced it with "the unblushing falsehood, that 'The Wreath has become the Album'" ("To Our Subscribers," *American Lady's Wreath* 6 [September 1845]: back cover). I thank Paul Erickson for bringing this to my attention.

20. Winship, "Manufacturing and Book Production"; Laurie, "Labor and Labor Organization." For an antebellum view of a print shop (though a self-interested one), see Jacob Abbott, *The Harper Establishment; or, How the Story Books Are Made* (New York: Harper and Brothers, 1855). Part of Harper and Brothers' "Story Books" series, a set of paperbacks "for the Instruction and Entertainment of the Young," this volume also made the Story Books its subject, putting on view their conditions of production.

21. Zboray, *A Fictive People*, chaps. 2 and 4.

22. See Charvat, *Literary Publishing in America*, chap. 1; and chap. 4 of *The Industrial Book*, "The National Book Trade System." *An Extensive Republic* and *The Industrial Book* do an excellent job of showcasing the diversity of local print cultures, as well as print cultures that did not explicitly fall under the rubric of the market.

23. Tebbel, *A History of Book Publishing*, 221.

24. Mott, *A History of American Magazines*, 1:341–342.

25. Pretzer, "The Quest for Autonomy and Discipline."

26. Among others, see Charvat, *The Profession of Authorship in America*; Kelley, *Private Woman, Public Stage*; Gilmore, *American Romanticism and the Marketplace*; Coultrap-McQuin, *Doing Literary Business*; Newbury, *Figuring Authorship in Antebellum America*; Whalen, *Edgar Allan Poe and the Masses*; and Zboray and Zboray, *Literary Dollars and Social Sense*. Leon Jackson's *The Business of Letters* breaks down the market-author opposition by applying Pierre Bourdieu's insight that capital circulates in symbolic and social currencies as well as financial ones.

27. For a trenchant critique of "the foreshortening effect of the author-concept," see McGill, *American Literature and the Culture of Reprinting*, who points out that the early literary marketplace's emphasis on exchange and reprinting actually worked against the idea of authorship (15–19, quotation on 16). I use the term "literary capitalism" in distinction from Benedict Anderson's "print-capitalism," although the two concepts overlap. But whereas Anderson's "print-capitalism" refers to the unity across space effected by the circulation of printed goods, I intend "literary capitalism" to emphasize the tensions between these words and evoke the conceptual dissonance within the system itself. See Anderson, *Imagined Communities*, especially chap. 2.

28. Jackson, *The Business of Letters*, 48, 40.

29. Ibid., 40, 3.

30. Stewart, *Crimes of Writing*, 36.

31. Wiley and Putnam borrowed the phrase from an approving review of the series in the *American Whig Review*, a journal they also published. The review itself may have been written by the series editor, Evert Duyckinck; such entangled reviewing practices are the subject of Chapter 1. See "Books Which Are Books," *American Whig Review* 1 (May 1845): 521; Greenspan, *George Palmer Putnam*, 169, 170, 187 n. 42.

32. "The Literature of the Present Day," *Graham's Monthly Magazine* 28 (September 1845): 100; Lippard, "Rumpus Grizzle," in *George Lippard, Prophet of Protest*, 247.

33. Parsons, "Epistle to Samuel Rogers," *Poems* (Boston: Ticknor and Fields, 1854), 19–20.

34. "Redding's Literary Depot," *Universal Yankee Nation*, 1 January 1842, 7. In fact, Pease's Hoarhound Candy capitalized on just this ambiguity: as P. T. Barnum noted approvingly in *The Humbugs of the World*, the company devised the clever strategy of disguising its advertisements as newspaper columns on "the most prominent topic of interest and general conversation. A column would "discourse eloquently upon that topic" for several paragraphs and "then glide off gradually into a panegyric of 'Pease's Hoarhound Candy'" (*The Humbugs of the World: An Account of Humbugs, Delusions, Impositions, Quackeries, Deceits and Deceivers Generally, in All Ages* [New York: Carleton, 1866], 58).

35. Stevenson, "Homes, Books, and Reading."

36. Warner, *Letters of the Republic*, esp. chaps. 2 and 3.

37. Fern, "A Breakfast-Table Reverie," in *Fresh Leaves* (New York: Mason Brothers, 1857), 294.

38. Barnum, *The Humbugs of the World*, 20.

39. Foucault, *Discipline and Punish*, 200.

40. Benjamin, "The Work of Art in the Age of Mechanical Reproduction," 221, 220.

41. Marx, *Capital*, 1:69.

42. Althusser, "Ideology and Ideological State Apparatuses," 165, 166.

43. Ibid., 168.

44. Wallerstein, *The Capitalist World-Economy*, 125.

45. "The Confidence Man on a Large Scale," *New-York Herald*, 11 July 1849, quoted in Bergmann, "The Original Confidence Man," 563–564.

46. Whereas Melville's first novel, *Typee*, garnered eighty-four reviews, and his second, *Omoo*, eighty-nine, *The Confidence-Man* mustered only forty-four, most just one or two paragraphs. The New York *Sun*'s review exemplifies critics' blandly dismissive stance: "To while away the dreary hours, take any of MELVILLE's works—you cannot go astray. He is a writer who never suffers his readers to get the blues or go to sleep. *The Confidence Man* is his last, but by no means the worst of his efforts" (8 April 1857; reprinted in Higgins and Parker, eds., *Herman Melville: The Contemporary Reviews*, 489).

Chapter 1. "One Vast Perambulating Humbug"

1. "The Booksellers' Dinner," *New-York American*, 3 April 1837, n.p.

2. Poe, review of *The Quacks of Helicon*, *Graham's Magazine* 19 (August 1841), in *Essays and Reviews*, 1006.

3. Dimock, "Planet and America, Set and Subset," 1. Dimock elaborates this argument in *Through Other Continents*. For a critique of Dimock's model, see Loughran, "Transcendental Islam."

4. Kaplan, *The Anarchy of Empire*, 16.

5. Anderson, *Imagined Communities*, 6.

6. Ibid., 36.

7. As Jonathan Culler emphasizes, Anderson's crucial literary claim is not about specific representations of nations in the novel, but about how the temporal-spatial organization of the novel offers "a structural condition of possibility" for imagining the nation, although many critics citing Anderson have confused these arguments—understandably so, since Anderson's own examples, which tend to be explicitly nationalist texts, often produce some slippage ("Anderson and the Novel," 37). For important critiques of Anderson, see Bhabha, "DissemiNation"; Chatterjee, *The Nation and Its Fragments*; and Cheah and Culler, eds., *Grounds of Comparison*, the special issue of *diacritics* (Winter 1999) devoted to Anderson's work.

8. Anderson, *Imagined Communities*, 36.

9. Loughran, *The Republic in Print*, 111, 304.

10. Pratt, *Archives of American Time*, 28.

11. Anderson, *Imagined Communities*, 6.

12. See Stewart, *Crimes of Writing*; and Lynch, *Deception and Detection in Eighteenth-Century Britain*. Given the difference in objectives (recovery project vs. wholesale national invention) and media (manuscript vs. print), it is no coincidence that while the British forgeries were the work of individuals, whose names remain attached to the texts in question, the sham that pervaded the antebellum United States was endemic, the product of a literary culture rather than certain miscreants.

13. The best and liveliest history of the literary nationalist movement, as well as the considerable resistance it faced, remains Perry Miller's *The Raven and the Whale*. Notwithstanding the efforts of the literary nationalists, the book trade remained strongly transatlantic into mid-century, and Britain continued to signify the gold standard for literary value, as the literary nationalists' proudest endorsements ("the American Dickens," "the American Hemans") inadvertently reveal. However, Elisa Tamarkin argues that American Anglophilia was not necessarily incompatible with nationalism; paradoxically, it helped constitute a national identity in which "Americans adore England as part of their national character" (*Anglophilia*, xxvii).

14. Emerson, "Literary Ethics," in *Collected Works*, 1:105–106. For a host of examples of literary nationalist grandstanding, see Spencer, *The Quest for Nationality*, chaps. 3 and 4.

15. L.M.P., "Necessity for a National Literature," *Knickerbocker* 25 (May 1845): 422.

16. "Introduction," *Democratic Review* 1 (October 1837): 15.

17. Brownson, "Address to the United Brothers Society of Brown University," reprinted in Rutland, *The Native Muse*, 282.

18. Lowell, "Introduction," *The Pioneer* 1 (January 1843): 1.

19. Lowell, *A Fable for Critics*, 72–73.

20. Lowell, "Our Contributors: Edgar Allan Poe," *Graham's Magazine* 27 (February 1845), reprinted in *Edgar Allan Poe: Critical Assessments*, 2:1.

21. McGill, *American Literature and the Culture of Reprinting*, 193. On the use of Native Americans in literary nationalist writing, see Jackson, "'Behold Our Literary Mohawk, Poe.'"

22. Fuller, "American Literature: Its Position in the Present Time, and Prospects for the Future," in *Papers on Literature and Art* (New York: Wiley and Putnam, 1846), 124.

23. "Schools in American Literature," *Literary World*, 19 October 1850, 307–308. The article's appearance in the *Literary World* checks the temptation to conflate attacks on sham literature with attacks on the Young America movement, since Evert Duyckinck, who edited the *Literary World*, was also literary editor of the *Democratic Review* and one of Young America's strongest proponents. Anxieties about American literary fakery, like the zeal for literary nationalism that generated them, extended across political divides, making them difficult to dismiss as simply another theater in the ongoing conflict between Whigs and Democrats. Lowell, the writer who offered perhaps the most sustained protest against literary nationalism, was a self-described radical and through his friendships with Duyckinck and William Jones, an affiliate of Young America, as was Margaret Fuller, despite her Boston address. The *Literary World* writer's fantastical imagery echoes Nathaniel Hawthorne's 1844 tale "A Select Party," which recounts a dinner hosted by "a Man of Fancy" at "one of his castles in the air." The most honored guest there is "the Master Genius, for whom our country is looking anxiously into the mist of time, as destined to fulfill the great mission of creating an American literature, hewing it, as it were, out of the unwrought granite of our intellectual quarries" (*Mosses from an Old Manse*, vol. 10 of *Works*, 57, 66).

24. "Literary Phenomena," *American Review* 4 (October 1846): 406.

25. Poe, "The Facts in the Case of M. Valdemar," in *Collected Works*, 3:1242.

26. "Literary Phenomena," 408, 406.

27. *New York Tribune*, 10 December 1845; *Popular Record of Modern Science*, 10 January 1846; both quoted in Thomas and Jackson, *The Poe Log*, 603, 617.

28. Tocqueville, *Democracy in America*, 488, 489.

29. "Puffing," *Baltimore Monument*, 12 May 1838, 252; "Mutual Puffing," *Old American Comic Almanac, 1841* (Boston: S. N. Dickinson, [1840]), 4. Although generally far from literary-minded, the *Old American Comic Almanac* seems to have been fond of deriding the editorial profession's pretensions to representation. An earlier issue includes an engraving of another rotund editor leaping out of his chair as he reads a letter saying, "Dear Sir You may be D—n'd. Put that in your paper. A *Real* Correspondent." Stoking such antipathies towards editors could backfire, however; in the American Antiquarian Society's copy of the same almanac that ran the item on "Mutual Puffing," a reader wrote over a particularly grotesque engraving of a cowering man with donkey ears, "Portrait of the Editor." See "The Editor," *Old American Comic Almanac, 1839* (Boston: S. N. Dickinson, [1838]), 19, and *Old American Comic Almanac, 1841*, 2.

30. Gould, "American Criticism on American Literature," *Eastern Magazine*, 15 March 1836, 277.

31. Poe, "Letter to the Editor," *Broadway Journal*, 8 March 1845, in *Essays and Reviews*, 1065.

32. Smith, review of *Statistical Annals of the United States of America*, *Edinburgh Review* 33 (January 1820): 80.

33. "Puffing," *American Annals of Education* 8 (October 1838): 470; Timothy Flint, "Obstacles to American Literature," *Knickerbocker* 2 (September 1833): 164.

34. Gould, "American Criticism on American Literature," 285.

35. Poe, "Letter to the Editor," in *Essays and Reviews*, 1065. Poe's scorn for literary nationalist puffery did not—and given his always precarious professional situation, perhaps could not—prevent him from participating in it himself. On Poe's puffs for the books in Evert Duyckinck's "Library of Choice Reading" series, which included his own *Tales*, see Claude Richard, "Poe and Young America." Meredith McGill inverts Richard's argument to contend that Poe did not align himself with Young America as a career move but that the literary nationalists forced the situation by claiming him as one of their own (189–204). J. Gerald Kennedy has argued that Poe's antipathies toward U.S. nationalism, literary and otherwise, shaped far more of his writing than we have recognized, and his analysis of Poe's 1844 burst of American-themed tales teases out indictments of slavery, Indian removal, and American exceptionalism ("'A Mania for Composition'"). Although I more readily see Poe as an opportunist than an anti-imperialist, capitalizing on these issues rather than denouncing them, I share Kennedy's belief that nationalism strongly influences Poe's writings, even when their settings are avowedly European.

36. Poe, review of Wilmer, in *Essays and Reviews*, 1010.

37. Lavante, *The Poets and Poetry of America* (1847; reprint, New York: Benjamin and Bell, 1887), 4.

38. See Espy, *The Philosophy of Storms* (Boston: C. C. Little and J. Brown, 1841).

39. Sellers, *The Market Revolution*.

40. Pessen, *Jacksonian America*, 142.

41. In 1862, the *New York Times* asserted that counterfeit bills comprised four-fifths of the paper money supply (Henkin, *City Reading*, 145).

42. Mihm, *A Nation of Counterfeiters*, 239.

43. The unflattering comparisons between literature and paper currency in the U.S. contrast markedly with the continuities between paper currency and imaginative writing Mary Poovey has identified in eighteenth- and nineteenth-century Britain, where she argues that these printed texts together ushered in a modern "credit economy." Comparisons between literature and paper currency function quite differently, however, if both of these credit economies profoundly lack credibility. Thus while Poovey contends that genres of fiction "became safe forms" for writers to explore the "problematic of representation," American writers, by contrast, found literary representations very risky indeed, as indicated by the frequency with which literary criticism was conducted in the idiom of exposing and debunking, and by the inescapable discourse of literary fraudulence more broadly (*Genres of the Credit Economy*, 6). Ian Baucom's breathtaking study *Specters of the Atlantic* proposes two further pillars of the credit economy: the slave trade, whose traffic in human beings helped usher in new risk-driven financial instruments, and historicism, whose speculative situations proceed from a notion of the "typical."

44. Emerson, "Nature," in *Collected Works*, 1:7. Subsequent citations will be given in the text.

45. Emerson, "The American Scholar," in *Collected Works*, 1:52.

46. For the sake of concision, my account greatly oversimplifies the essay's tortuous logic, which is actually far less coherent than I describe it here. Emerson begins by insisting on the constitutive power of nature, before which the "operations" of "Art . . . are so insignificant" that "they do not vary the result" (1:8). But he eventually suggests that nature has no meaning except that which *humans* invest in it. "Nature is thoroughly mediate," he insists. "It is made to serve" (1:25). Thus the ideal poet, guided by "the imperial muse," "possesses the power of subordinating nature for the purposes of expression," so that "all objects shrink and expand to serve the passion of the poet" (1:31, 32). As Christopher Newfield observes of the essay's endless contradictions and tautologies, Emerson "has the most impossible time trying to maintain any kind of dialectic between nature and the independent mind" (*The Emerson Effect*, 49.)

47. Dickens, *American Notes for General Circulation*, 64.

48. Dickens, *The Life and Adventures of Martin Chuzzlewit*, 151.

49. Ibid., 202.

50. Lippard, "The Spermaceti Papers," *The Citizen Soldier*, 5 July, 31 May, and 19 July 1843. Lippard's targets include Rumpus Grizzle (Rufus Griswold), the Grey Ham

(George R. Graham, publisher of *Graham's Magazine*), and Spermaceti Sam (Samuel Patterson, editor of the *United States Saturday Post*, a.k.a. the *Salt River Saturday Stick and Universal Lamp Post*).

51. Wilmer, *The Quacks of Helicon: A Satire* (Philadelphia: J. W. Macclefield, 1841), iv.

52. Adding insult to injury, Wilmer borrows this metaphor for American literature from a British source, Jonathan Swift's satire *A Tale of a Tub*. There Swift describes the "Learned *Aeolists*" (or Calvinists), who believe "the Original Cause of all Things to be *Wind*," "*Spiritus, Animus, Afflatus,* or *Anima*." Accordingly, their priests periodically gather together "in a circular Chain, with every Man a Pair of Bellows applied to his Neighbour's Breech, by which they blew up each other to the size and shape of a tun." Each priest then discharges his wind in a barrel, "where, having before duly prepared himself by the Methods already described, a secret Funnel is also convey'd from his Posteriors, to the Bottom of the barrel" to capture his eloquence for the benefit of his disciples (*A Tale of a Tub, Written for the Universal Improvement of Mankind* [London: John Nutt, 1704], 146, 149, 152).

53. Jones, "Home Criticism," in *Essays upon Authors and Books* (New York: Stanford and Swords, 1849), 28.

54. Harris, *Humbug*, 79.

55. Lowell, "Our Contributors: Edgar Allan Poe," 1.

56. [Mathews], "Nationality in Literature," *United States Magazine and Democratic Review* 20 (March 1847): 267. For a more specific inventory of American subjects, see L. M. P., "Necessity for a National Literature."

57. Longfellow, *Kavanagh*, 113.

58. "Introduction," *United States Magazine and Democratic Review* 1 (October 1837): 14.

59. "Literary Notices," *Boston Quarterly Review* 1 (January 1838): 125.

60. "Democracy and Literature," *United States Magazine and Democratic Review* 11 (August 1842): 196. For further examples of the literary nationalists' democratic rhetoric, see Spencer, *The Quest for Nationality*, 111–121.

61. Harris, *Humbug*, 73, 88; quoted in Harris, 77.

62. Baym, *Novels, Readers, and Reviewers*, 21.

63. "American Poets, and Their Critics," *Knickerbocker* 4 (July 1834): 13.

64. "Critics and Criticism of the Nineteenth Century," *United States Magazine and Democratic Review* 15 (August 1844): 162.

65. Warner's *The Letters of the Republic* remains the most influential, but see also Rice, *The Transformation of Authorship in America*. A spate of recent work has read Habermas against the grain in order to consider the affective dimensions of his "rational-critical" public sphere. Crucially, unlike rationalist models of the public sphere, affective models tend not to be grounded in any notion of authenticity. That is, while rationalist accounts of the public sphere hinge on its actual reason and discernment, affective interpretations do not require that emotions be sincerely felt, but instead

analyze their display. See, for example, Hendler, *Public Sentiments*; Dillon, *The Gender of Freedom*; and Warner, *Publics and Counterpublics*, where he advances a more skeptical paradigm of the public sphere than in his earlier work.

66. Henkin, *City Reading*, 12–13.

67. Ziff, *Literary Democracy*. F. O. Matthiessen's assertion that the authors he discusses "all wrote literature for democracy" (*American Renaissance*, xv) is an easy target, but see also Reynolds, *Beneath the American Renaissance*, and Powell, *Ruthless Democracy*. Assumptions about the democratizing effects of the nineteenth-century print explosion are not uniquely American; for a foundational account in this mode, see Altick, *The English Common Reader*, which tells "the story of how, though numberless tribulations, and against what sometimes appeared to be hopeless odds, there took root and eventually flourished in nineteenth-century England a revolutionary social concept: that of the democracy of print" (1). For a useful materialist corrective to these celebratory accounts, see Zboray, *A Fictive People*, especially chap. 1, where Zboray points out that the print explosion was not a natural efflorescence but a consequence of the capitalization of print.

68. Habermas, *The Structural Transformation of the Public Sphere*, 26, 27. Subsequent citations will be given in the text.

69. Jones, "Home Criticism," 30.

70. "Critics and Criticism of the Nineteenth Century," 161.

71. Lee, "Thoughts on Contemporaneous Criticism," *New-York Mirror*, 22 June 1839, 412.

72. [William Crafts], "Literary Sparring, No. IV," in Joseph T. Buckingham, ed., *Miscellanies Selected from the Public Journals*, vol. 1 (Boston: Joseph T. Buckingham, 1822), quoted in Jackson, *The Business of Letters*, 33–34.

73. In general, modern critics have preferred to see Poe as a dissenter to the literary status quo. Sidney Moss's study of Poe's critical skirmishes, for example, generously sums up Poe's career as "a fourteen-year attempt to extirpate practices injurious to American letters; a prolonged endeavor to get literary works judged by the canons of an honest and principled criticism; and a continual effort to develop and promulgate such canons" (*Poe's Literary Battles*, 36–37). But despite Poe's disgust at the "manufacture" of a "pseudo-public opinion," he participated avidly in the period's customary critical maneuvers, willingly puffing new books when he found it expedient, signing reviews for the *Broadway Journal* "††" and "Littelton Barry" in addition to his own name, and occasionally inflating interest in his own work by reviewing it himself. In June of 1846, smarting from an attack by Charles Frederick Briggs in the *Evening Mirror*, Poe combined the strategies of self-review and gift exchange, drafting a flattering biography of himself and asking his friend Joseph M. Field, the editor of the Saint Louis *Daily Reveille*, to print it "and influence one or two of your editorial friends to do the same." The requested puff appeared two weeks later. See Thomas and Jackson, *The Poe Log*, 645–646, 651.

74. Poe, review of Wilmer, in *Essays and Reviews*, 1010–1011, 1006.

75. Jackson, *The Business of Letters*, chap. 3.

76. W. S. Tryon reprints several specimens of puffs that Ticknor and Fields distributed for their books in *Parnassus Corner*, 184–186.

77. "Puffing System," *Southern Literary Journal* 2 (June 1836): 312. See also a contributor's follow-up article, "American Criticism and Critics" (July 1836): 393–400, and the editor's lengthy response (400–404).

78. Jackson, *The Business of Letters*, 89; Charvat, *The Profession of Authorship in America*, 174.

79. Poe, "The Literary Life of Thingum Bob, Esq.," in *Collected Works*, 3:1132, 1135. Subsequent citations will be given in the text.

80. Charvat, *The Profession of Authorship in America*, 176–177. Charvat unearths a number of incriminating paper trails behind Griswold's services, all of which confirm George Lippard's contemporary assessment that Griswold was "now Preacher, now Literary Pirate, at all times the Pink of Servility, the Cream of Humbug, the Skim milk of American Book Charlatanism" ("Rumpus Grizzle," in *George Lippard, Prophet of Protest*, 247). In his memoirs, the poet Charles Godfrey Leland even fingered the Cream of Humbug as the real author of the Prince of Humbug's 1855 autobiography, *The Life of P. T. Barnum* (Harris, *Humbug*, 208).

81. Tryon, *Parnassus Corner*, 189.

82. Melville, *Pierre*, 247, 245. Subsequent citations will be given in the text.

83. G[eoffrey] C[rayon] [Washington Irving], "Desultory Thoughts on Criticism," *Knickerbocker* 14 (August 1839): 176.

84. See Hindus, ed., *Walt Whitman*, 34–48.

85. [Mathews], "Nationality in Literature," 271. For attribution, see Rutland, *The Native Muse*, 302. Perry Miller reports that three years later, when Mathews published the novel *Chanticleer* anonymously, he couldn't resist also reviewing it anonymously in the *Literary World*, where he rhapsodized, "This is a delightful little book, true in its American conception, harmonized from real life to the poetical moral beauty of the era with which it is associated" ("An American Idyl," *Literary World*, 9 November 1850, 370). See *The Raven and the Whale*, 277.

86. "Puffing, a Fable," *Atkinson's Casket* 8 (August 1834): 384.

87. "American Poets, and Their Critics," 24. Original emphasis.

88. Ibid., 23. Original emphasis.

89. On fears surrounding anonymity and crowds, see Halttunen, *Confidence Men and Painted Women*, especially chap. 2.

90. "Literary Puffing," *Boston Weekly Magazine*, 19 December 1840, 110, 111.

91. Warner, *Letters of the Republic*, xiii.

92. Pollin, "*The Living Writers of America*: A Manuscript by Edgar Allan Poe," 165.

93. "Poets and Poetry of America," *New-York Mirror*, 8 March 1845, 347. Two years later, in a thinly disguised portrait of the New York literary scene, Poe's former co-editor at the *Broadway Journal*, Charles Frederick Briggs, turned the metaphor

around, describing Poe's own head as having "the appearance of a balloon" (Harry Franco [Charles Frederick Briggs], *The Trippings of Tom Pepper; or, the Results of Romancing* [New York: Burgess, Stringer, and Co., 1847], 160, quoted in Miller, *The Raven and the Whale*, 183).

94. Longfellow, "Defense of Poetry," *North American Review* 34 (January 1832): 75. Specifically, Longfellow warns American poets to reject the examples of Shelley ("To a Skylark") and Keats ("Ode to a Nightingale"). Benjamin T. Spencer reports that during the 1830s admonitions against "the skylark and the nightingale" escalated into a "full-scale campaign"; see *The Quest for Nationality*, 86–87.

95. Poe, "Mellonta Tauta," in *Collected Works of Edgar Allan Poe*, 3:1303.

96. Gettman, *A Victorian Publisher*, 73. See also Sutherland, "Henry Colbourn, Publisher." At the time of "The Balloon Hoax," Ainsworth also edited *The New Monthly Magazine*, which Colbourn owned.

97. Poe, review of William Harrison Ainsworth, *Guy Fawkes, Graham's Magazine* 19 (November 1841) in *Essays and Reviews*, 101.

98. Thomas Mabbott has located the story's original in the Philadelphia *Public Ledger* of June 5, 1844. See "Origins of 'The Angel of the Odd,'" 8. Claude Richard has also read the story as a literary satire, specifically a parody of the Transcendentalists. See "Arrant Bubbles: Poe's 'The Angel of the Odd,'" 66–72.

99. Both the title of the tale and the spelling of its protagonist's name continued to change as it was reprinted. For convenience, I use the title and spelling in Pollin's edition, which reflects Poe's final revision. In an article that reads "Hans Pfaall" and Locke's moon hoax as "capitalizing on the contingency" of systems of scientific and literary valuation "largely set in print," Marcy J. Dinius argues that Poe only conceived of "Hans Pfaall" as a hoax after the fact, in an attempt to capitalize on the success of Locke's hoax, which had appeared two months later ("Poe's Moon Shot," 2). As Dinius points out, when the *Southern Literary Messenger* first published "Hans Pfaall," it was titled "Hans Phaall—A Tale." Poe's efforts to reclassify the tale as a hoax seem to have enjoyed some success, however; three months later, it was reprinted in the *New York Transcript* under the much more scientific title, "Lunar Discoveries, Extraordinary Aerial Voyage of Baron Hans Phall" (2–5 September 1835).

100. Poe, "The Unparalleled Adventure of One Hans Pfaall," in *The Imaginary Voyages*, 396, 388. Subsequent citations will be given in the text. Pollin points out that pemmican "is a strange food to be found in Rotterdam" in his notes to the story (469). Poe discusses pemmican at length in *The Journal of Julius Rodman*; see *The Imaginary Voyages*, 534–535.

101. The image probably alludes to Washington Irving's *Diedrich Knickerbocker's History of New York*, which Pollin also gives as a source for Poe's description of the pipe-smoking Dutchmen. Knickerbocker recounts there, "The pipe, in fact, was the great organ of reflection and deliberation of the New Netherlander. . . . His pipe was never out of his mouth" (quoted in *The Imaginary Voyages*, 459). If Poe, here as elsewhere, made the *Knickerbocker* a satirical target, he may have put it to practical

use, as well: Pollin suggests that the tale draws on an article about ballooning, "Leaves from an Aeronaut," that appeared in the magazine a few months before the publication of "Hans Pfaall" (370).

102. Quoted in Miller, *The Raven and the Whale*, 260. Poe, who clashed frequently with Clark, lampooned him in "The Literary Life of Thingum Bob, Esq.," where Bob learns his outrageous critical style from, among other sources, "Lewis G. Clarke on Tongue" (1141).

103. Poe to Harrison Hall, 2 September 1836, quoted in *Collected Works*, 2:202. Although "Tales of the Folio Club" never appeared in book form, many of the tales were published individually in various magazines.

104. Poe, review of Wilmer, in *Essays and Reviews*, 1011.

105. Lowell, *A Fable for Critics*, 4.

106. Edmund Reiss points out the etymology and analyzes its significance to the story in "The Comic Setting of 'Hans Pfaall.'"

Chapter 2. Backwoods and Blackface

1. Poe, review of Joseph Rodman Drake, *The Culprit Fay, and Other Poems*, and Fitz Greene Halleck, *Alnwick Castle, with Other Poems*, *Southern Literary Messenger* 2 (April 1836), in *Essays and Reviews*, 506.

2. Poe, "Critical Notices," *Southern Literary Messenger* 2 (April 1836): 340.

3. Poe, review of Theodore S. Fay, *Norman Leslie*, *Southern Literary Messenger* 2 (December 1835), in *Essays and Reviews*, 540.

4. [Kennard], "Who Are Our National Poets?" *Knickerbocker* 26 (October 1845), reprinted in *Inside the Minstrel Mask*, 52.

5. See Smith-Rosenberg, *Disorderly Conduct*; Saxton, *The Rise and Fall of the White Republic*; and Lott, *Love and Theft*.

6. Taylor, *The Archive and the Repertoire*, 19.

7. Ibid., 27, 28.

8. Dillon, "Print, Manuscript, and Performance," 366.

9. The first autobiography, *The Life and Adventures of Colonel David Crockett, of West Tennessee* (1833), republished as *Sketches and Eccentricities of Col. David Crockett, of West Tennessee* (1833), was actually the work of Mathew St. Clair Clarke. But Crockett and Clarke were friends, and Crockett may have fed Clarke some of his material. Many regard the second autobiography, *A Narrative of the Life of David Crockett, of the State of Tennessee* (1834), as self-penned. However, Crockett enlisted a fellow congressman, Thomas Chilton, to help him craft this, his campaign autobiography, and it remains impossible to say for certain which man was responsible for which parts—and in any event, the entire volume borrows heavily from *The Life and Adventures. An Account of Col. Crockett's Tour to the North and Down East* (1835) was a piece of Whig party propaganda capitalizing on Crockett's name. Finally, immediately following Crockett's death at the Alamo, a fourth autobiography appeared, *Col. Crockett's Exploits and Adventures in Texas* (1836), written by Philadelphia playwright

Richard Penn Smith. For an exhaustive account of the autobiographies' authorship, see Shackford, *David Crockett*, 184–186, 258–264, 264–273, 273–281.

10. This subtitle appears on the 1839 almanac (Nashville: Ben Harding, [1838]). Other years have similar titles (e.g., *Davy Crockett's Almanack, 1844: Life and Manners in the Backwoods; Terrible Battles and Adventures of Border Life; With Rows, Sprees, and Scrapes in the West*). Lofaro's facsimile edition of the 1839–1841 almanacs, *The Tall Tales of Davy Crockett*, invaluably shows the Crockett tales in their original contexts. Three other collections, Dorson, ed., *Davy Crockett: American Comic Legend*; Meine, ed., *The Crockett Almanacks*; and Lofaro, ed., *Davy Crockett's Riproarious Shemales and Sentimental Sisters*, contain helpful material but extract the tales from the almanacs' meteorological tables, squibs, and illustrations.

11. "Go Ahead Reader," *Davy Crockett's Almanack of Wild Sports in the West, Life in the Backwoods, Sketches of Texas, and Rows on the Mississippi* (Nashville: Published by the heirs of Col. Crockett, [1838]), 2.

12. "Introduction—by Ben Harding," *The Crockett Almanac, 1839, Containing Adventures, Exploits, Sprees and Scrapes in the West, and Life and Manners in the Backwoods* (Nashville: Ben Harding, [1838]), 2.

13. "Adventure with a Tar," *The Crockett Almanac, 1839*, 24. Crockett's own "spirited" drawings, the almanacs explain, circumvent pen and paper as well; despite being in the publishing business, he "drew on birch bark with a burnt stick" ("Explanatory Preface," *Davy Crockett's Almanack, of Wild Sports in the West, Life in the Backwoods, Sketches of Texas, and Rows on the Mississippi*, 2).

14. "Introduction—by Ben Harding," *The Crockett Almanac, 1839*, 2; "Preface—by Ben Harding," *The Crockett Almanac, 1840, Containing Adventures, Exploits, Sprees and Scrapes in the West, and Life and Manners in the Backwoods* (Nashville: Ben Harding, [1839]), 2.

15. Dorson, *American Folklore*, 203. For a more recent but faithful recapitulation of this position, see David Reynolds's claim that the almanacs demonstrate "a presurrealistic style surging from the hot heart of democratic humor" (*Beneath the American Renaissance*, 453). A notable exception is Carroll Smith-Rosenberg's chapter on Crockett, which I discuss later in this chapter.

16. "Conspiracy Documents," *Yale Literary Magazine* 2 (June 1837): 252; "Fashions in Dress," *New-Yorker*, 30 March 1839, 20. Occasionally the almanacs seem to have addressed themselves to their bourgeois readers directly. *Fisher's Crockett Almanac* for 1843, for instance, intersperses the customary backwoods yarns with "Valuable Recipes" for cleaning silver, carpets, "table baizes," mahogany furniture, etc.

17. Emerson, "Europe and European Books," in *Essays and Lectures*, 1250.

18. Seelye, "A Well-Wrought Crockett."

19. "Ben Harding and the Pirates," *The Crockett Almanac, 1839*, 25.

20. On southwestern humor's "hopeless longing" to forge bonds between these middle-class urban white men, see Pratt, *Archives of American Time*, chap. 3 (quotation on 130).

21. Smith-Rosenberg, *Disorderly Conduct*, 93, 103.

22. Ibid., 108.

23. Gramsci, *Selections from Cultural Writings*, 208; see also 199–212. My distinction between popular and populist draws on the work of Stuart Hall, especially his essays "Notes on Deconstructing 'the Popular,'" "Popular-Democratic vs. Authoritarian Populism: Two Ways of 'Taking Democracy Seriously,'" and "Popular Culture and the State."

24. "Davy Crockett," *Crockett's Yaller Flower Almanac, for '36* (Snagsville, Salt-River: Boon Crockett and Squire Downing, [1835]), 19–20.

25. Gramsci, *Selections from Cultural Writings*, 202.

26. "Explanatory Preface," *Davy Crockett's Almanack of Wild Sports in the West, Life in the Backwoods, Sketches of Texas, and Rows on the Mississippi*, 3; "Introduction—by Ben Harding," *The Crockett Almanac, 1838*, 2; "Introduction" and "Latest from the Mines," *The Crockett Almanac, 1841, Containing Adventures, Exploits, Sprees and Scrapes in the West, and Life and Manners in the Backwoods* (Nashville: Ben Harding, [1840]), 2, 4; and "Preface," *Ben Hardin's* [sic] *Crockett Almanac, 1842* (New York: Turner and Fisher, [1841]), 3. One 1848 almanac, torn between eulogy and fantasy, reports both Crockett's death at the Alamo *and* his survival there. See "Death of Crockett" and "Crockett at the Alamo," *Crockett's 1848 Almanac* (Detroit: Luther Beecher, [1847]), 23, 32–34.

27. "Tussle with a Bear," *The Crockett Almanac, 1841*, 9–10.

28. "Introduction—by Ben Harding," *The Crockett Almanac, 1839*, 2.

29. "Adventure with a Tar," *The Crockett Almanac, 1839*, 23. To be accurate, Harding has not actually read the almanac, for in keeping with the almanac's anti-print culture stance, he attests he is illiterate: "I got my larning under the lee of the long boat, and swear my prayers at a lee earing in a gale o' wind," he brags, but "our boson . . . used to read your allmynack to us on the forecastle . . . and I could spell out your crocodile's tails from their heads when I see 'em drawed out in your book" (ibid.).

30. Bartlett, *Dictionary of Americanisms: A Glossary of Words and Phrases, Usually Regarded as Peculiar to the United States* (New York: Bartlett and Welford, 1848), v, iv. All subsequent citations will appear in the text.

31. Shackford, *David Crockett*, 184–186.

32. Trumpener, *Bardic Nationalism*. Susan Stewart analyzes the antiquarian longing for—and sometimes invention of—oral tradition in *Crimes of Writing*; see especially chaps. 3 and 4.

33. Lott, *Love and Theft*, 18,16.

34. *White's New Ethiopian Song Book* (New York: H. Long and Brother, 1850), 59; "Jim Crow," in *Crockett's Free-and-Easy Song Book* (Philadelphia: James Kay, Jr., and Brother, 1839), 36.

35. "Jim Crow" (Boston: Leonard Deming, n.d. [1837–40]); "Songs of the Virginia Serenaders" (Boston: Keith's Music Publishing House, 1844).

36. Lott, *Love and Theft*, 97.

37. Lhamon, introduction to *Jump Jim Crow*, 1.

38. Quoted in Toll, *Blacking Up*, v. On nationalist uses of blackface, see Rogin, "The Two Declarations of American Independence," 13–30.

39. [Kennard], "Who Are Our National Poets?" 50, 51, 52. I discuss Kennard's article, whose praise of minstrelsy begins ironically and unexpectedly turns serious, at greater length later in this chapter.

40. Scrapbook [1830–1834?], Manuscripts Department, American Antiquarian Society, Worcester, Mass.

41. The phrase "counterfeit presentments" comes from the third act of *Hamlet*. Furious with his mother for marrying his dead father's brother and murderer, Hamlet holds their portraits up to her and demands that she compare them: "Look upon this picture, and on this, / The counterfeit presentment of two brothers" (III.iv.53–54). By "counterfeit presentment," Hamlet simply means the portraits themselves, as artistic representations. Yet the phrase also plays on the more negative meaning of "counterfeit," for Claudius's devotion to "our late dear brother" (I.ii.19) is, of course, entirely false. Shakespeare's phrase thus holds depiction and deception in suspension, rendering them nearly indistinguishable. The phrase's ambiguous straddling of representation and misrepresentation earned it wide popularity in the nineteenth-century United States, especially in discussions of literature. If today the phrase seems an awkward fit with American literature, for some writers at the time, this irony was exactly what made it so appropriate. Thus *Parnassus in Pillory*, a mid-century satire of American literature by the pseudonymous "Motley Manners" (actually poet and future dime novelist Augustine Joseph Hickey Duganne), pictures the popular poet Henry Beck Hirst reenacting the scene from *Hamlet* with a key difference: looking upon a portrait of Shakespeare, he pronounces himself the bard's own "counterfeit presentment" (*Parnassus in Pillory: A Satire* [New York: Adriance, Sherman, and Co., 1851], 28). Hirst's presumptuousness highlights the gap between the early mimetic sense of "counterfeit" and its increasingly negative suggestions of fraudulence.

42. [Kennard], "Who Are Our National Poets?" 52, 53–54. T. D. Rice's British reception offers an instructive contrast: when he toured England in the 1830s, promotional broadsides archly advertised the arrival of "Jim Crow, the American Mountebank."

43. [Nathanson], "Negro Minstrelsy, Ancient and Modern," *Putnam's Monthly* 5 (January 1855): 72. The article is reprinted with attribution in *The Negro and His Folklore in Nineteenth-Century Periodicals* (Austin: University of Texas Press, 1967), 36–50.

44. Nevin, "Stephen C. Foster and Negro Minstrelsy," 608.

45. See Lott, *Love and Theft*; Saxton, *The Rise and Fall of the White Republic*; and Roediger, *The Wages of Whiteness*.

46. [Nathanson], "Negro Minstrelsy," 72.

47. Bagg, *Four Years at Yale*, 268.

48. Toll, *Blacking Up*, 31.

49. "Gossip with Readers and Correspondents," *Knickerbocker* 38 (November 1851): 564.

50. Buckley, "Paratheatricals and Popular Stage Entertainment," 466.

51. A remarkable artifact at the American Antiquarian Society suggests the appeal of identifying with Jim Crow. On the first and last pages of John G. Stearns's anti-masonic pamphlet *Plain Truth: Containing Remarks on Various Subjects Relative to the Institution of Speculative Freemasonry* (Cazenovia, [N.Y.]: J. F. Fairchild, 1828), some-one has stamped "JIM CROW." The stamp appears to be a hand stamp in which the owner could set a line of type. (The "M" is upside-down in the first impression and has been corrected in the second.) Readers commonly used such stamps to identify their books, but this particular reader seems to have used the stamp as an occasion to test out a new identity for himself.

52. Poe, "The Facts in the Case of M. Valdemar," in *Collected Works*, 3:1242.

53. [Nathanson], "Negro Minstrelsy," 38, 42–43.

54. "Virginia Mummy," in Lhamon, ed., *Jump Jim Crow*, 176. Subsequent cita-tions will be given in the text.

55. I borrow the phrase "power of blackness" from a long history in American literary criticism, which begins with Melville's compliment to Hawthorne on his "great power of blackness" ("Hawthorne and His Mosses, By a Virginian Spending July in Vermont," *Literary World*, 17 August 1850, 126), was canonized in Harry Levin's New Critical study *The Power of Blackness*, and has been revisited by Toni Morrison and others for its racial connotations (see Morrison, *Playing in the Dark*, 37).

56. Rourke, *American Humor*, 91.

57. Rourke's own shifting periodization may account for some of the confusion. At some points she pictures minstrelsy and southwestern humor as contemporary phenomena, writing, "The Negro minstrel joined with the Yankee and the backwoods-man to make a comic trio, appearing in the same era, with the same timely intensity" (98). Elsewhere, however, she constructs a cause and effect relationship in which "Negro minstrelsy ar[ose] from the southwest" (90).

58. One exception here is Michael Rogin, who notes these figures' coincidence: "Yankee, backwoodsman, and blackface minstrel, emerging simultaneously in asser-tions of American nationalism, were the first voices of the American vernacular against aristocratic Europe. Each proclaiming a regional identity—Northeast, West, and South—each also came to signify the new nation as a whole" ("The Two Declarations of American Independence," 17).

59. "Jim Crow" (Boston: Leonard Deming, n.d. [1837–1840]).

60. "Go Ahead Reader," *Davy Crockett's Almanack of Wild Sports in the West, Life in the Backwoods, Sketches of Texas, and Rows on the Mississippi*, 2. Crockett's line about the wildcats is ubiquitous, but see, for example, *Sketches and Eccentricities of Col. David Crockett*, 164, and *Davy Crockett's Almanack of Wild Sports in the West, Life in the Backwoods, Sketches of Texas, and Rows on the Mississippi*, 32. The phrase seems to have appeared for the first time in James Kirke Paulding's 1831 play *The Lion of the*

West (itself partially based on the historical David Crockett), and subsequently joined the literary Davy Crockett's repertoire. For another version of "Jump Jim Crow" using this line, see *Crockett's Free-and-Easy Song Book*, 20. The book groups "Jim Crow," "Gumbo Chaff," "Jim Brown," and other minstrel songs with songs about Crockett.

61. On the motif of Crockett's grin, see Hauck, *Davy Crockett*, 129–130.

62. "Zip Coon, A Popular Negro Song, as Sung by Mr. Geo. W. Dixon" (New York: Firth and Hall, n.d. [mid-1830s]); "Gumbo Chaff, A Negro Song, Sung with Great Applause at the Theatres" (New York: Firth and Hall, [1830s–1840s?]); Meine cites this version of "Jump Jim Crow," which Rice performed at the Warren Theater in Boston, in his introduction to *The Crockett Almanacks: Nashville Series, 1835–1838*, ix–x.

63. *Davy Crockett's Almanack of Wild Sports of the West, and Life in the Backwoods* (Nashville: Snag and Sawyer, 1834), 37; *Crockett's Yaller Flower Almanac, for '36*, 29; *De Darkie's Comic All-Me-Nig, 1846* (Boston: James Turner; Philadelphia: Colon and Adriance; Baltimore: J. B. Keller, [1845]); *Bone Squash's Black Joke Al-Ma-Nig, For de Year Arter Last, 1852* (Philadelphia: Fisher and Brother, [1851]). *De Darkie's Comic All-Me-Nig* reuses at least one of the plates that Turner and Fisher used in their *Crockett Awl-Man-Axe for 1839*, an illustration of a black servant thumbing his nose at a black gentleman.

64. "Introduction—by Ben Harding," *The Crockett Almanac, 1839*, 2.

65. Crockett, *The Life and Adventures of Colonel David Crockett, of West Tennessee*, 135, 136.

66. Crockett, *An Account of Col. Crockett's Tour to the North and Down East*, 32.

67. *The Life of Jim Crow, Showing How He Got His Inspiration as a Poet* (Philadelphia: James M'Minn, 1835), 4. All subsequent citations will appear in the text. A second edition appeared in 1837, as did *The Origin of Jim Crow, Being an Authentic Account of the Life and Adventures of that Comic American Nigger, Jim Crow* (London, J. S. Hodgson, 1837). Three years later, another autobiography, "A Faithful Account of the Life of Jim Crow, the American Negro Poet," rounded out the songbook *Jim Crow's Vagaries, or, Black Flights of Fancy: Containing a Choice Collection of Nigger Melodies* (London: Orlando Hodgson, 1840). Lhamon reprints the 1835 *Life* and "A Faithful Account" in *Jump Jim Crow*, 386–398, 399–404.

68. Wolfe, "Davy Crockett Songs," 167, 170.

69. *The Negro Singer's Own Book; Containing Every Negro Song that Has Ever Been Sung or Printed* (Philadelphia: Turner and Fisher, 1846), quoted in Wolfe, "Davy Crockett Songs," 163–164.

70. Wolfe, "Davy Crockett Songs," 166.

71. See, for example, "A Street Fight," *The Crockett Almanac, 1841* (Boston: J. Fisher, [1840]), n.p.; "Crockett Stopping a Duel Among His Brother Congressmen" and "Colonel Crockett Delivering His Celebrated Speech to Congress," *Davy Crockett's Almanac, 1844, Life and Manners in the Backwoods: Terrible Battles and Adventures of Border Life: With Rows, Sprees, and Scrapes in the West* (Boston: James Fisher, [1843]), n.p. The latter is especially interesting for Crockett's deflationary imagery; he declares, "Mr. Speaker! The broken fenced state o' the nation, the broken banks, broken hearts,

and broken pledges o' my brother congressmen here around me, has rize the boiler o' my indignation, clar up to the high pressure pinte, an therefore I have riz to let off the steam of my hull hog patriotism, without roundaboutation, an without the trimmins."

72. "Zip Coon," in *Series of Old American Songs, Reproduced in Facsimile From Original or Early Editions in the Harris Collection of American Poetry and Plays, Brown University*, ed. S. Damon Foster (Providence: Brown University Library, 1936), quoted in Lewis, "Daddy Blue," 268.

73. Berlant, *The Queen of America Goes to Washington City*, 25, 27.

74. Ibid., 36.

75. For an explicit statement of this belief, see Margaret Fuller's review of Frederick Douglass's 1845 slave narrative, which admiringly lists among the characteristics of the "African Race" "a ready skill at imitation and adaptation" (*New York Tribune*, 10 June 1845, 2).

76. Frances A. Kemble, *Journal of a Residence on a Georgian Plantation in 1838–1839* (New York: Harper and Brothers, 1864), 127, 128.

77. Lott, *Love and Theft*, 99.

78. [Kennard], "Who Are Our National Poets?" 52, 56.

79. Ibid., 57, 59.

80. Thomas Chandler Haliburton, ed., *Traits of American Humour, by Native Authors* (London: Colburn and Co., 1852), 1:xii. Bartlett takes a similar view in his *Dictionary of Americanisms*, where he savors the "exaggerated and metaphorical language peculiar to the people of that region"—despite, of course, his admission that he has never spoken with any of those people, but simply read about them in books and newspapers (vi).

81. Quoted in Jordan, "Humor of the Backwoods, 1820–1840," 27.

82. This statement, headed "To the Editorial Fraternity," appears on the back cover of a wrapper that binds together two other Dickinson publications, *The Old American Comic Almanac, 1841* and *The People's Almanac, 1841* (Boston: S. N. Dickinson, [1840]). I thank Jackie Penny at the American Antiquarian Society for alerting me to a cache of letters between former director of the AAS Clarence Brigham and Crockett scholar Franklin Meine, in which they discuss the Crockett almanacs and this statement in particular.

83. "Preface to the Crockett Almanac," *Crockett Almanac, 1842; Improved Edition, Containing Real Stories* (Boston: S. N. Dickinson, [1841]), 2.

84. "The Panther's Leap," "How to Capture a Bear," *Crockett Almanac, 1842; Improved Edition*, 13, 20.

85. Hooper, *Adventures of Captain Simon Suggs*, 12.

Chapter 3. "Slavery Never Can Be Represented"

1. Douglass, *My Bondage and My Freedom*, 207, 208.

2. The title page of *Autobiography of a Female Slave* is printed with an 1857 publication date, but as Joe Lockard explains, this was a ploy by publisher J. S. Redfield "to keep the book fresher" (afterword to Griffith, *Autobiography of a Female Slave*, 408).

3. Sekora, "Black Message/White Envelope," 497. Sekora concludes of the slave narrative categorically, "It is not an Afro-American genre" (509).

4. Douglass, *Narrative of the Life of Frederick Douglass*, 6.

5. McBride, *Impossible Witnesses*, 5.

6. Jacobs, *Incidents in the Life of a Slave Girl*, 1.

7. Andrews, *To Tell a Free Story*, 26.

8. Douglass, *Narrative of the Life of Frederick Douglass*, 56.

9. "Stop the Swindler," *Emancipator*, 20 April 1843, 197. Pro-slavery advocates were quick to return the compliment. David Meredith Reese included the American Anti-Slavery Society in his treatise *Humbugs of New-York: Being a Remonstrance against Popular Delusion; Whether in Science, Philosophy, or Religion* (New York: J. S. Taylor, 1838), calling it "the most gigantic imposture which ever afflicted either the church or the state" (209). Abolitionist David Ruggles responded by pronouncing Reese "of all the humbugs yet imposed upon the good citizens of Gotham, the greatest 'beyond compare'" (*An Antidote for a Poisonous Combination Recently Prepared by a "Citizen of New-York,"* Alias *Dr. Reese, Entitled, "An Appeal to the Reason and Religion of American Christians," &c. Also, David Meredith Reese's "Humbugs" Dissected* [New York: William Stuart, 1838], 32).

10. William Lloyd Garrison, "The American Union," *Liberator*, 10 January 1845, quoted in Castiglia, *Interior States*, 127.

11. On Equiano, see Acholonu, *The Igbo Roots of Olaudah Equiano*; Carretta, *Equiano*; and Bugg, "The Other Interesting Narrative."

12. Brown, "A Lecture Delivered Before the Female Anti-Slavery Society of Salem," 108.

13. See Andrews's chronological bibliography of slave narratives at http://docsou th.unc.edu/neh/chron.html.

14. Hartman, *Scenes of Subjection*, chap. 1.

15. Parker, "The American Scholar," 37.

16. Ephraim Peabody, "Narratives of Fugitive Slaves," *Christian Examiner* 47 (July 1849): 62.

17. "Black Letters; Or Uncle Tom-Foolery in Literature," *Graham's Magazine* 42 (February 1853): 209. As the title of the article suggests, the article is intended as a review of *Uncle Tom's Cabin*. However, the writer considers Stowe's novel to be just the most prominent example of the literary monopoly currently enjoyed by books about slavery.

18. Ibid.

19. Howe, *The Refugees from Slavery in Canada West* (Boston: Wright and Potter, 1864), quoted in Andrews, *To Tell a Free Story*, 2.

20. Frederickson, *The Black Image in the White Mind*, 55.

21. *New York Tribune*, 25 January 1858, 2.

22. "An Impudent Imposter," *Liberator*, 25 December 1857, 206.

23. *New York Tribune*, 25 January 1858, 2.

24. Space does not permit a full reading of *The Slave* or *Autobiography of a Female Slave* here, but on the former see Samuels, "The Identity of Slavery," 167–168; and Bentley, "White Slaves," especially 202–207. On the latter see Joe Lockard's afterword, 403–418.

25. William Andrews maintains a list of fictionalized slave narratives on the University of North Carolina's "Documenting the American South" website: http://doc south.unc.edu/neh/alphafiction.html.

26. Elizabeth Peabody, letter to Francis Adeline Seward, 22 May 1857, in *Letters of Elizabeth Palmer Peabody*, 284.

27. Nichols, "Who Read the Slave Narratives?"; Rohrbach, *Truth Stranger than Fiction*, chap. 2.

28. Elizabeth Peabody, letter to Francis Adeline Seward, 22 May 1857, in *Letters of Elizabeth Palmer Peabody*, 284.

29. Emerson, *Richard Hildreth*, 51, 52.

30. Castiglia, *Interior States*, 130.

31. [Hildreth], *The Slave, or Memoirs of Archy Moore* (Boston: John H. Eastburn, 1836), 1:9–10. The title of Hildreth's text underwent numerous changes, perhaps as Hildreth angled for different points of entry into the literary market. Although it remained *The Slave* through six editions, in 1852, Hildreth added another 150 pages and retitled it *The White Slave; or, Memoirs of a Fugitive* (Boston: Tappan and Whittemore, 1852), and in 1856 he renamed it *Archy Moore, The White Slave; or, Memoirs of a Fugitive* (New York: Miller, Orton, and Mulligan, 1856). However, from the beginning it was best known as *Archy Moore*, a title that downplayed allegorical possibilities in favor of verisimilitude. The *Liberator* referred to it as such in a review on January 14, 1837, and the publishers of Hildreth's subsequent book, *Despotism in America; or An Inquiry into the Nature and Results of the Slave-Holding System in the United States* (Boston: Whipple and Damrell, 1840), advertise on its title page, "By the Author of 'Archy Moore.' " Perhaps these writers were following the advice of "an accomplished lady in Worcester County," who told the *Liberator*, "I cannot but hope, that when another edition of 'The Slave' shall be published, the title will be changed to simple 'Archy Moore.' . . . If the character of this work were not so conspicuous in its title, it seems to be just what is wanted, to find its way and carry conviction, among those who are so willfully blind they cannot see, and so pertinaciously deaf they will not hear. Many a modern sentimentalist who would readily purchase 'Archy Moore,' would scorn to read 'The Slave' " ("Archy Moore," *Liberator*, 31 March 1837, 55).

32. Griffith, *Autobiography of a Female Slave*, 10. In addition, the narrator's skin color may be calculated to enlist the sympathies of a white readership put off by physical difference; it also plays on contemporary anxieties about white slavery.

33. Ibid., 84, 129–130.

34. [Hildreth], *The Slave*, 1:3.

35. Hildreth reprints both reviews in his introduction to the 1856 edition of *Archy Moore* (x, xi).

Notes to Pages 111–117

36. "The Slave: or Memoirs of Archy Moore," *Emancipator*, 8 March 1838, 174.

37. Griffith, *Autobiography of a Female Slave*, 86.

38. "New Publications," *Liberator*, 28 November 1856, 190; "New Anti-Slavery Novel," *Boston Evening Transcript*, 3 December 1856, n.p.

39. *Christian Inquirer* review reprinted in "A Remarkable Work," *Liberator*, 9 January 1858, 8; "Literary Intelligence," *Christian Examiner* 62 (1857): 152; *Louisville Journal* review reprinted in "Autobiography of a Female Slave," *Liberator*, 23 January 1857, 13.

40. Quoted in "New Anti-Slavery Novel," n. p.

41. "Literary Intelligence," 152; "A Remarkable Work," 8.

42. Williams, *Narrative of James Williams, an American Slave, Who Was for Several Years a Driver on a Cotton Plantation in Alabama* (New York: American Anti-Slavery Society, 1838), 29. Subsequent citations will be given in the text.

43. Minutes of the Executive Committee of the American Anti-Slavery Society, 4 January 1838, quoted in Fabian, *The Unvarnished Truth*, 79.

44. "James Williams—The Fugitive Slave," *Emancipator*, 25 January 1838, 151.

45. "Narrative of James Williams," *Liberator*, 9 March 1838, 39; "From *Human Rights*. Narrative of James Williams," *Herald of Freedom*, 17 March 1838, 9; "Narrative of James Williams. By J. G. Whittier," *Pennsylvania Freeman*, 1 March 1838, 99. The Boston edition of the narrative was titled *Authentic Narrative of James Williams, An American Slave* (Boston: Isaac Knapp, 1838).

46. Advertisement in the *Liberator*, 30 March 1838, 51. The advertisement ran periodically until October 19 of that year.

47. [Untitled letter to the editor], *Pennsylvania Freeman*, 24 May 1838, n.p.; "Narrative of James Williams," *Liberator*, 9 March 1838, 39.

48. [Untitled letter to the editor], *Herald of Freedom*, 7 July 1838, 74–75.

49. "Suggested by Reading the Narrative of James Williams," *Herald of Freedom*, 23 June 1838, 66–67.

50. "James Williams in Every Family," *Liberator*, 12 April 1838, 194; [Untitled letter to the editor], *Pennsylvania Freeman*, 24 May 1838, n.p.

51. Quoted in the *Liberator*, 14 September 1838, 148.

52. "James Williams in Every Family," 194.

53. *Anti-Slavery Examiner* 6 (1838); *Narrative of James Williams, An American Slave* (Boston: Abolitionist's Library, 1838). Both eight-page editions were printed on a single sheet, which was then folded into quarters. For a full bibliography of the *Narrative of James Williams*, see Currier, *A Bibliography of John Greenleaf Whittier*, 32–39.

54. "Alabama Beacon versus James Williams," *Emancipator*, 30 August 1838, 71.

55. Quoted in "Alabama Beacon versus James Williams," 71.

56. Ibid.

57. See Gara, "The Professional Fugitive in the Abolition Movement."

58. "Alabama Beacon versus James Williams," 71.

59. "Tricks of Abolitionism," *New-York Commercial Advertiser*, 19 September 1838, n.p.

60. "Narrative of James Williams," *Pennsylvania Freeman*, 13 September 1838, n.p.

61. Lewis Tappan, diary entry, 25 August 1838, Lewis Tappan Papers, 1809–1903, microfilm (Washington, D.C.: Library of Congress, 1975).

62. "Alabama Beacon versus James Williams," 71.

63. "'Narrative of James Williams.' Statement Authorized by Executive Committee," *Emancipator*, 25 October 1838, 104; *Liberator*, 2 November 1838, n.p. Within seven months, however, Williams's narrative discreetly rejoined the American Anti-Slavery Society's publications lists, prompting the *African Repository and Colonial Journal*, the official organ of the American Colonization Society, to fume, "As the Abolitionists are thus active in circulating what they have, in the most formal and solemn manner, repudiated as false and libellous [*sic*], we deem it due to truth and justice to copy the official statement referred to" (that is, the Executive Committee's official retraction) ("Narrative of James Williams," *African Repository and Colonial Journal* 15 [June 1839]): 161.

64. Osofsky, *Puttin' on Ole Massa*, 12; Blassingame, *Slave Testimony*, 23. Vernon Loggins's 1931 study of African American writing gives a more complete account but sounds most of the same notes. He calls this "forgery of a singular type" "the most interesting deceptive narrative of the period [1790–1840]" but less on its own merits than for the controversy it occasioned. Williams's narrative, he writes, enjoyed the admiration of the abolitionist community and a wide circulation until "the evidence from the South proved without a doubt that it was false," in "the sensation of the year in the anti-slavery press" (*The Negro Author*, 101).

65. Andrews, *To Tell a Free Story*, 88; Fabian, *The Unvarnished Truth*, 84; Browder, *Slippery Characters*, 22. Williams certainly existed, as Lewis Tappan's diary entries attest. At the height of the controversy, Tappan recorded his impressions of hearing his former visitor's story: "Mr. Birney & myself publish in Emancipator, dated 30th, a long statement respecting 'The Narrative of Jas. Williams'—chiefly written by Mr. B. I have no doubt whatever of its authenticity. No one who conversed with him at the length I did could question it" (diary entry, 29 August 1838).

66. "From the *Delaware Republican*. Falsehood Refuted," *Liberator*, 12 December 1845, 197.

67. "Letter from Frederick Douglass," *Liberator*, 12 February 1846, 35. Eyewitness testimony also verified the narrative of Solomon Northup, whose *Twelve Years a Slave* drew attention to the traffic in freemen kidnapped in the North and transported to the South to be sold as slaves. When the narrative appeared in 1853, Northup's description of his captors caught the eye of Thaddeus St. John, a judge in Fonda, New York. St. John recalled a trip he took in the spring of 1841, during which he encountered two old friends—first in Baltimore, where they were traveling with an unknown black man, and several weeks later, in Washington, where they were alone and dressed considerably more expensively. Northup's account of his kidnapping and his sale in Washington, St. John realized, matched his recollections, and he contacted Northup to arrange a visit. The two men immediately recognized each other, and St. John, along

with Northup's friend and rescuer Henry B. Northup, set out to capture and prosecute the now-identified kidnappers. The case became increasingly tangled up in the legal system and was eventually dismissed, but not before witnesses, including two additional slave traders and Northup's purchaser, had confirmed Northup's account (even as they denied any knowledge that he was sold illegally). See Sue Eakin and Joseph Logsdon's introduction to Northup, *Twelve Years a Slave*, xvii–xxiii.

68. For the Virginians' genealogies, I consulted various family trees in the University of Virginia library. Much of this information is also available online through amateur genealogy websites. I used the 1830 census for the Virginia names and the 1840 census for the Alabama names because most of the planters in Greene County seem to be recent arrivals in 1833. When Williams reaches the neighborhood he observes, "The clearings were all new, and the houses were rudely constructed of logs" (39).

69. "'Narrative of James Williams.' Statement Authorized by the Executive Committee," 104.

70. Yellin reproduces the advertisement on page 237 of her edition of *Incidents in the Life of a Slave Girl*.

71. These include the *Alabama Reporter*, the *Alexandria Gazette*, the *Arkansas State Gazette*, the *Arkansas Times and Advocate*, the *Baltimore Sun*, the *Columbus Democrat*, the *New Orleans Commercial Bulletin*, the *New Orleans Courier*, the *Frankfort Argus*, the *Georgia Messenger*, the *Maryland Advocate*, the *Mississippian*, the *Mobile Commercial Register*, the *Nashville Union*, the *New Orleans Bee*, the *North Alabamian*, the *New Orleans Picayune*, the *Richmond Enquirer*, the *Richmond Whig*, the *Savannah Republican*, the *Southern Banner*, the *Southern Herald*, the *Telegraph and Texas Register*, and the *Natchez Weekly Courier and Journal*.

72. Stewart, *Crimes of Writing*, 145, 146, 147.

73. Douglass, *Narrative of the Life of Frederick Douglass*, 13.

74. [Untitled item], *Emancipator*, 8 February 1838, 158.

75. "Alabama Beacon versus James Williams," 71. Coincidentally, that same year Sturge published a narrative by another fugitive named James Williams, who had been a slave on a West Indian sugar plantation. This James Williams's narrative also came under attack, but the dispute over its authenticity ended quite differently than that of the other Williams. The British government convened a commission of inquiry, headed by the governor of Jamaica, to investigate the story, and Williams testified before a committee of the House of Commons. In the end, the committee determined his story to be true. See James Williams, *A Narrative of Events Since the 1st of August, 1834* (London: For the Central Negro Emancipation Committee, 1838); Fladeland, *Men and Brothers*, 249.

76. Lydia Maria Child, letter to Angelina Weld, 26 December 1838, in Barnes and Dumond, eds., *Letters of Theodore Weld, Angelina Grimké Weld, and Sarah Grimké*, 732.

77. "Alabama Beacon versus James Williams," 71.

78. Roper, *A Narrative of the Adventures and Escape of Moses Roper, from American Slavery*, 3rd ed. (London: Harvey and Darton, 1839), 91. Subsequent citations will be given in the text.

79. Fabian, *Unvarnished Truth*, 84.

80. Andrews, *To Tell a Free Story*, 63. Compare Williams's convincing transparency with the convincing opacity of Theodore Dwight Weld's white informants in *American Slavery as It Is*, who constitute "a *cloud* of witnesses who speak what they know and testify what they have seen, and all these *impregnably fortified* by proofs innumerable" (*American Slavery As It Is: Testimony of a Thousand Witnesses* [New York: American Anti-Slavery Society, 1839], 10, emphasis mine).

81. My analysis here draws on Michelle Burnham's reading of Harriet Jacobs's "loophole of retreat," as Jacobs called the garret where she hid for seven years. Burnham argues that the phrase, which Jacobs borrows from poet William Cowper, aptly describes Jacobs's tactic of hiding in plain sight, or finding freedom in confinement, for a loophole by definition "so resembles that which it opposes" that "it evades the conceptual opposition between oppression and resistance" (*Captivity and Sentiment*, 159). One might likewise consider imposture to form a loophole in abolitionist discourse.

82. Sánchez-Eppler, *Touching Liberty*, 31, 136. The distinction in general between slave narratives and anti-slavery fiction is often not so stable as Sánchez-Eppler's formulation would indicate. In fact, the frequency with which slave narratives enlist the conventions of sentimental fiction suggests that this genre itself may be the best example of anti-slavery literature's tendency to translate its subject into its audience's terms.

83. Reprinted in "James Williams in Every Family," *Emancipator*, 12 April 1838, 194.

84. "From *Human Rights*. Narrative of James Williams," *Herald of Freedom*, 17 March 1838, 9.

85. "Alabama Beacon versus James Williams," 71.

86. "New Publication," *Pennsylvania Freeman*, 5 April 1838, n. p.

87. Foucault, "What Is an Author?" 123, 137–138.

88. Morrison, *Playing in the Dark*, 6.

89. Andrews, *To Tell a Free Story*, 89.

90. Stepto, "Distrust of the Reader in Afro-American Narratives," 303, 309.

91. duCille, "Where in the World Is William Wells Brown?" 458. A narrative titled *The Light and the Truth of Slavery* (Springfield, Mass.: n.p., 1845), whose author is given only as Aaron, tested the abolitionist movement's patience for non-autobiographical writing by former slaves. Although Aaron is a former slave and the text generally follows the form of a narrative, the book cannot be called a slave narrative, as Aaron never describes his days as a slave. Instead, the book shifts the focus from the author to the white men and women he encounters in his travels through the northern United States. Moreover, even this narrative only accounts for part of the book; Bible verses, poems, sermons, and letters from sources ranging from English poet Thomas Campbell to Toussaint L'Ouverture break up the narrative throughout. Indeed, the book

seems to have originated as a commonplace book, in which Aaron's various hosts transcribed his words and, at times, added some of their own. *The Light and the Truth of Slavery* even troubles the confessional mode syntactically, as the narrative constantly moves from first to third person ("When Aaron struck into Litchfield again, I went to a tavern" [13]). The *Emancipator* warned readers away from the book: "A colored man, calling himself Aaron, is going about, selling what purports to be a memoir of himself, in the character of a fugitive from slavery. We have not seen him, but from what we are told, we do not think his labors are calculated to be of any benefit to the cause of humanity. Of the credibility of his story, our readers can judge as well as we. Intelligent people of color think him no credit to their class" ("Aaron," *Emancipator*, 26 April 1845, 2). Whether it was as dubious as the *Emancipator* suggests is unclear; Aaron's excoriation of white abolitionists' hypocrisy and racism may have sharpened the newspaper's suspicions.

92. Winks, "The Making of a Fugitive Slave Narrative," 115. Moreover, Henson's fabrications, unlike Williams's, were readily apparent. Any reader who took the time to compare the narratives would find that, as Winks writes, "He could exaggerate, transmuting the mundane into the dramatic (his broken shoulders became more crippling with each edition), and he could move with the times, as he did when he excised the more obsequious passages from the original version of his life for later editions, when he struck entirely a passing reference to being arrested for debt, or when he added a chapter in 1858 on his exploits in returning to the South to help other fugitives to escape, a phase of his activities unaccountably forgotten in 1849. He incorporated a pious refusal to participate in the Nat Turner rebellion into his local lectures, although the rebellion actually took place after he had reached Canada West. He claimed that he personally had written his books although in 1849, as we have seen, he recorded that he learned to read 'a little' and one of his abolitionist supporters noted that he could 'barely write and cannot read.' In the first post–Civil War edition of the autobiography he said he was a captain in the Second Essex Company of Colored Volunteers—which he was not—and that his company captured the *Anne*, which he misspelled" (125).

93. Ibid., 125; Henson, *Truth Is Stranger than Fiction: An Autobiography of the Rev. Josiah Henson* (Boston: B. B. Russell and Co., 1879), viii.

94. "Alabama Beacon versus James Williams," 71. In its refusal to entertain the possibility that Williams was capable of fictionalizing the narrative, the American Anti-Slavery Society finally found common ground with the *Alabama Beacon*. Although J. B. Rittenhouse excoriated the narrative as false, he attributed it to Whittier, whom he accused of committing an "abandoned forgery" (quoted in "Alabama Beacon versus James Williams," 71).

95. "Narrative of James Williams," *Liberator*, 9 March 1838, 39.

96. "Narrative of James Williams," *Liberator*, 28 September 1838, 153.

97. *Fifth Annual Report of the Executive Committee of the American Anti-Slavery Society* (New York: William S. Dorr, 1838); "Narrative of James Williams" (undated

clipping pasted in Lewis Tappan's diary, probably from the *Liberator*), Lewis Tappan Papers, 1809–1903, microfilm (Washington, D.C.: Library of Congress, 1975).

98. [Untitled item], *Pennsylvania Freeman*, 23 August 1838, n.p.

Chapter 4. Mediums of Exchange

1. Griswold, *The Female Poets of America* (Philadelphia: Carey and Hart, 1849), 8. Griswold's competitors were Caroline May, ed., *The American Female Poets* (Philadelphia: Lindsay and Blakiston, 1848), and another collection titled *The Female Poets of America*, edited by Thomas Buchanan Read (Philadelphia: E. H. Butler & Co., 1849).

2. Ibid., 7. In *The Madwoman in the Attic*, Sandra Gilbert and Susan Gubar quote this passage as evidence that male writers have historically preserved creativity as a trait proper to themselves. Griswold does not dismiss the possibility of women's "literary power," Gilbert and Gubar observe, but he implies that "when such creative energy appears in a woman it may be anomalous, freakish, because as a 'male' characteristic it is essentially 'unfeminine'" (10).

3. Douglas, *The Feminization of American Culture*, 186.

4. "Cicely," "Interesting to Ladies. From *The Musical World*," *Pittsfield Sun*, 22 September 1853, 1. A headnote indicates the article's original publication in the *Buffalo Daily Republic*.

5. Marx, *Capital*, 1:52–53.

6. Kelley, *Private Woman, Public Stage*, 152.

7. Brodhead, *Cultures of Letters*, 53.

8. That Fern is one of only two mid-nineteenth-century bestselling female authors to be the subject of a scholarly biography, Warren's *Fanny Fern*, suggests the extent of critics' investment in her privacy, her "rare 'life,'" as Brodhead puts it (*Cultures of Letters*, 63).

9. See, for example, Harris, *Nineteenth-Century American Women's Novels*, 20 and passim; and Coultrap-McQuin, *Doing Literary Business*, 2–26.

10. Gallagher, "George Eliot and *Daniel Deronda*," 40, 39.

11. Ibid., 39.

12. On the transformation of the literary marketplace into a mass market, see Mott, *Golden Multitudes*.

13. Huyssen, *After the Great Divide*; Radway, "On the Gender of the Middlebrow Consumer"; Geary, "The Domestic Novel as a Commercial Commodity," 368.

14. Baym, *Novels, Readers, and Reviewers*, 255.

15. J.F.C., "Literary Lion Hunting, No. II: Coteries and Petti-Coteries," *United States Review* 36 (August 1855): 142, 143, emphasis added. The author's initials may be a reference to that most masculine of American authors, James Fenimore Cooper, who had died four years before.

16. *New York Ledger*, 16 June 1855; quoted in Warren, "Uncommon Discourse," 55–57.

17. Fern, "Celebrity," *New York Ledger*, 10 December 1864, 4. When the steamboat "Fanny Fern" met an unfortunate end in 1858, a New York bookstore capitalized on the ensuing confusion by placing an advertisement in *Harper's Weekly* headed "Fanny Fern Blown Up But No Bones Broken": "People start in great amaze, / From their eyes they wildly gaze, / Crying as they hurry past, / 'Fanny Fern is gone at last!' / Keep cool, people—'tis not so—/ Fanny Fern is still the go. / 'Twas a Fanny Fern afloat, / Name bestowed upon a boat. / Read the choicest works of Fanny / Get a book and gift from Ranney." (Quoted in McGinnis, "Fanny Fern, American Novelist," 20.)

18. *Life and Beauties of Fanny Fern* (New York: H. Long and Brother, 1855), 42. Moulton was quick to exploit the association between Fern's commodification and prostitution, cracking, "Fanny's price—we mean the price of her articles—was two dollars a column" (41). Karen Halttunen has suggested that mid-nineteenth-century concerns about "painted ladies" tell us more about "respectable" society than about these women themselves. Ubiquitous images of "painted ladies," she explains, "expressed the deep concern of status-conscious social climbers that they themselves and those around them were 'passing' for something they were not" (*Confidence Men and Painted Women*, xv). Fern's perceived artifice may well have been amplified by the liminal class status of the newspapers she wrote for, especially the *New York Ledger*. Michael Denning convincingly argues in *Mechanic Accents* that the *Ledger* "achieved its wide circulation by uniquely straddling the boundary between the two worlds of genteel and sensational culture. It was the most respectable story paper, the least respectable magazine" (218 n. 3). I suspect that the *Ledger*'s position at the troublesome lower-middle-class boundary also plays a role in Fern's commodification. While high literature ostensibly transcends its physical form, mass literature is burdened by a stubborn materiality; price defines the dime novel, but *Middlemarch* is priceless.

19. Marx, *Capital*, 1:52.

20. My phrasing pays tribute to Catherine Gallagher's important study *Nobody's Story: The Vanishing Acts of Women Writers in the Marketplace, 1670–1820*, and my understanding of Fern is indebted to Gallagher's triangulation of women, authorship, and the marketplace. However, whereas the women authors Gallagher discusses deliberately perform the "vanishing acts" of her title, I focus on disembodiment as a symptom of women authors' circulation within the marketplace. Furthermore, for Gallagher, such vanishing acts "delineated crucial features of 'the author' for the period in general," making women "magnifying glasses" for broader historical "metamorphoses of authorship" (xiii, xv), but I am interested in vanishing as a gender-specific effect of authorship.

21. Fern, *Fern Leaves from Fanny's Portfolio* (Auburn, N.Y.: Derby and Miller, 1853), v.

22. Topsy was an important intertext for Fern's generation of women authors. J. C. Derby, Fern's publisher, noted of one of her contemporaries in his reminiscences, "Mrs. [Mary J.] Holmes thinks that she was born to be a writer of romance; or, like Topsy, she *growed* to be one" (*Fifty Years among Authors, Books and Publishers* [New

York: G. W. Carleton and Co., 1884], 573). Stowe herself famously—although perhaps apocryphally—attested that God wrote *Uncle Tom's Cabin*.

23. Stowe, *Uncle Tom's Cabin*, 356.

24. The *Oxford English Dictionary* dates the first usage of this sense of "stereotype" to 1850.

25. In "The Still Small Voice," Fern writes, "He had gazed at that stereotyped street panorama, till his eyes were drooping with weariness," and in "The Widow's Trials," "All the usual phrases of stereotyped condolence had fallen upon her ear" (*Fern Leaves*, 11, 17).

26. Hart, *The Female Prose Writers of America: With Portraits, Biographical Notices, and Specimens of Their Writings*, rev. and enl. ed. (Philadelphia: E. H. Butler & Co., 1855), 471, 472.

27. [Cooke], "The Memorial of A. B., or Matilda Muffin," *Atlantic Monthly* 5 (February 1860): 186. Subsequent citations will be given in the text.

28. Matilda Muffin's writing process recalls Edgar Allan Poe's caricature of female magazine writers, Psyche Zenobia, the heroine of "How to Write a Blackwood Article" and its sequel, "A Predicament," whose *pièce de résistance* is an account of her own beheading. However, Eliza Richards has shown that despite Poe's apparent distaste for women's writing, his own literary production relied heavily on interactions with a community of female "poetesses"; see Richards, *Gender and the Poetics of Reception*.

29. E. A. B., "To Fanny Fern," *Olive Branch*, 10 April 1852, n.p.

30. I thank Jana Argersinger for pointing out the citation to me.

31. Barthes, "The Death of the Author," 142.

32. Jameson, *Postmodernism*, xvi. Jameson, to be fair, is careful to state, "In periodizing a phenomenon of this kind, we have to complicate the model with all kinds of supplementary epicycles" (xix). Yet his recognition of the nonsynchronicity of "the dawning collective consciousness of a new system" and "the coming into being of fresh cultural forms of expression," assumes a collective experience of this system in the first place, overlooking the discontinuities of its dynamics.

33. Ibid., 6.

34. See Admari, "Bonner and 'The Ledger.'"

35. Claire Pettengill discusses the porousness of genre distinctions in Fern's work in "Against Novels." Fern's identity was still not widely known by the time she published *Ruth Hall*, but a novel about a pseudonymous female newspaper writer who becomes wildly famous and publishes a bestselling book of her sketches, by a pseudonymous female newspaper writer who had become wildly famous and published a bestselling book of her sketches, certainly suggested a connection between author and heroine. Readers were only able to link the two with the person Sara Payson Willis, however, when William Moulton published a tell-all article titled "'Who Is Fanny Fern?' A Plain Statement of the Facts" in the December 30, 1854 issue of the *True Flag*.

36. Fern, *Ruth Hall: A Domestic Tale of the Present Time* (New York: Mason Brothers, 1855), 330. All subsequent citations will be given in the text.

37. Warren, introduction to Fern, *Ruth Hall and Other Writings*, xxx; and Harris, *Nineteenth-Century American Women's Novels*, 127.

38. Otter, *Melville's Anatomies*, 231.

39. "Ruth Hall," *Southern Quarterly Review* 11 (April 1855): 448.

40. Brown, *Domestic Individualism*, 140.

41. See Warren, *Fanny Fern*; Walker, *Fanny Fern*; and, in the last category, Kelley, *Private Woman, Public Stage*; Coultrap-McQuin, *Doing Literary Business*; and Tonkovich, *Domesticity with a Difference*, in addition to the works I discuss below.

42. Wood [Douglas], "The 'Scribbling Women' and Fanny Fern"; Walker, *Fanny Fern*; and Harris, *Nineteenth-Century American Women's Novels*, 127. Douglas and Walker describe a neater transition than *Ruth Hall* will support; its tone is more uneven than they allow, and it ends on a strong sentimental note. (Wood became better known under the name Ann Douglas; for the sake of recognizability I refer to her by that name in the text.)

43. Laffrado, "'I Thought From the Way You *Writ*, That You Were a Great Six-Footer of a Woman,'" 84, 95.

44. Homestead, *American Women Authors and Literary Property*, 151, 153.

45. Fern, "Borrowed Light," *True Flag*, 9 April 1853, n.p.

46. Fern, *A New Story Book for Children* (New York: Mason Brothers, 1864), 8.

47. Wood [Douglas], "The 'Scribbling Women' and Fanny Fern," 18.

48. Warren, *Fanny Fern*, 103.

49. Walker, *The Nightingale's Burden*, 45.

50. Larcom, "Fern-Life," in *American Women Poets of the Nineteenth Century*, 231–232.

51. Herman Melville similarly links together women, writing, and unproductivity in "The Paradise of Bachelors and the Tartarus of Maids," where the narrator, a professional "seedsman," visits a New England paper mill from which he intends to order envelopes for his seeds. In contrast to the prolific seedsman, whose business is "so extensively . . . broadcast, indeed, that at length [his] seeds were distributed through all the Eastern and Northern States, and even fell into the far soil of Missouri and the Carolinas," the mill operatives are all "pale virgin[s]" who manufacture nothing but blank writing paper. See *The Piazza Tales*, 324, 334.

52. Fern, *Fern Leaves*, 16.

53. Fern, *Fresh Leaves* (New York: Mason Brothers, 1857), 9, 20.

54. Ibid., v.

55. Fern, [Untitled item], *Musical World and Times*, 13 August 1853, 230.

56. [Untitled letter to the editor], *Olive Branch*, 24 April 1852, n.p.

57. Fern, "To Jack Plane," *Olive Branch*, 13 March 1852, n.p. Fern would later revisit the theme of the public's knowledge of herself, and her private lack of it, in a column addressing France's Empress Eugenia: "My name is Fanny Fern, your Highness; and any further information you require, you can procure of anybody in the United States, for they all know more about my own affairs that I do myself!" (*Fern Leaves*, 388).

58. Fern, "A Pen and Ink Sketch," reprinted in [Moulton], *Life and Beauties of Fanny Fern*, 280.

59. [Untitled letter to the editor], *Olive Branch*, 3 July 1852, n.p.

60. Berlant, "The Female Woman," 445, 449.

61. Ibid., 432. In his discussion of Fern in *Melville's Anatomies*, Samuel Otter makes a similar observation about the narrative conventions of sentimentality. He writes, "For Fern, convention is not the inert, vacant container that many modern critics would describe, with their preference for irony and subversion. Instead it is a set of forms saturated with affect and rife with possibilities" (235). Although Otter focuses on Fern's use of specific affective conventions, rather than her broader engagement with conventionality, his observations have been very suggestive for my own thinking on her work.

62. Doane, *The Desire to Desire*, 180, 181. Doane builds on Luce Irigaray's notion of mimicry, in which women "assume the feminine role deliberately" in order "to make 'visible,' by an effect of playful repetition, what was supposed to remain invisible: the cover-up of a possible operation of the feminine in language" (Irigaray, *This Sex Which Is Not One*, 76).

63. Butler, *Gender Trouble*, 145, 146.

64. Ibid., 146.

65. Stowe, *Uncle Tom's Cabin*, 368.

66. After completing this chapter, I was excited to discover Kevin Floyd's book *The Reification of Desire: Toward a Queer Marxism*, which likewise reads reification against the grain, although at a very different historical moment. Floyd proposes that Herbert Marcuse's early work offers a model for understanding "reification as liberation" at a moment when both psychoanalysis and capitalism were emphatically reifying sexual desire and gender difference. He quotes Marcuse's surprising embrace of reification in "The Affirmative Character of Culture": "When the body has completely become an object, a beautiful thing, it can foreshadow a new happiness. In suffering the most extreme reification man triumphs over reification" (quoted in Floyd, 124). Marcuse ultimately reneges on the revolutionary potential of reified bodies in his own writing, eventually abandoning it entirely, but Floyd argues that the gay liberation movement took up the ideas that Marcuse could not fully develop.

67. [Untitled letter to the editor], *Olive Branch*, 28 August 1852, n.p.

68. Hawthorne, "Mrs. Hutchinson," in *Miscellaneous Prose and Verse*, 67.

69. Ibid., 19.

70. Hawthorne, letter to William Ticknor, 19 January 1855, in *The Letters, 1853–1856*, 304.

71. Hawthorne, letter to William Ticknor, 2 February 1855, in *The Letters: 1853–1856*, 307–308.

72. [Moulton], *Life and Beauties of Fanny Fern*, 32–33.

73. Ibid., 14, 145.

74. "Ruth Hall," 443, 440, 441, 443, 439, 449.

75. Fern, "A Word to Editors," *New York Ledger*, 5 May 1868, 8. See also "Have We Any Men Among Us?" *Musical World and Times*, 24 September 1853, reprinted in *Ruth Hall and Other Writings*, 262; "Facts for Unjust Critics," *New York Ledger*, 13 June 1857, 4; and "My Critics," *New York Ledger*, 26 November 1864, 4.

76. [Untitled letters to the editor], *Olive Branch*, 31 January 1852 and 6 March 1852, n.p. It is impossible to know if Fern really received these letters or invented them. But in either scenario, her writing promotes a distinction between the demands of male facticity and the possibilities of female fictionality.

77. [Untitled letters to the editor], *Olive Branch*, 1 May 1852 and 15 May 1852, n.p.

78. [Untitled letters to the editor], *Olive Branch*, 10 January 1852, 17 January 1852, and 24 January 1852, n.p.

79. See Fisher, "Queer Money."

Conclusion

1. For a history of satanic and divine interpretations of *The Confidence-Man*, see Bellis, "Melville's *The Confidence-Man*," 549–550. The most recent edition of the novel, Hershel Parker and Mark Niemeyer's 2006 Norton Critical Edition, continues to read it as a "theological allegory"; see footnotes throughout and Parker's essay for the edition, "The Confidence Man's Masquerade" (293–303).

2. Trimpi, *Melville's Confidence Men and American Politics in the 1850s*. Trimpi takes her cue from other scholars' identifications of Emerson, Thoreau, Poe, and Abbott Lawrence, asking, "If four of the characters demonstrably allude to men in Melville's historical context, why may we not hypothesize that all of them possibly may?" (4).

3. *Literary Gazette* [London], 11 April 1857, reprinted in Higgins and Parker, eds., *Herman Melville: The Contemporary Reviews*, 493.

4. Melville, *The Confidence-Man: His Masquerade*, 98. Subsequent citations will be given in the text. All citations are to the Northwestern-Newberry edition unless otherwise indicated.

5. Rogin, *Subversive Genealogy*, 242.

6. Ngai, *Ugly Feelings*, 70.

7. Halttunen, *Confidence Men and Painted Women*, 33.

8. Leon Howard first detected the mistake; see *Herman Melville*, 232. Rachel Cole, who counters the novel's long history of "I spy"-style criticism by positing that the defining feature of the Confidence-Man is his ability to "avoid . . . substantive identity," points out that Goodman and Noble's fond fellowship dissolves the "characteristic styles that initially inflect their voices (the cosmopolitan curtails the excessively whimsical eloquence we see in his speech on the misanthrope; Charlie indulges less frequently in the crude colloquialisms that initially litter his talk)" ("At the Limits of Identity," 387).

9. Characters' tendencies to double each other correspond to a tendency to self-divide. As Peggy Kamuf has noted, the appearance of the first confidence man is

attended by a temporal hiccup in which he seems to do two things at once: "At sunrise on a first of April, there appeared, suddenly as Manco Capac at the lake Titicaca, a man in cream-colors, at the water-side in the city of St. Louis. . . . In the same moment with his advent, he stepped aboard the favorite steamer *Fidèle*" (3). Kamuf observes that this "same moment" contains "an advent, without precedent, that advances a step as it comes into view," or the man's simultaneous appearance in space and movement forward in space (*The Division of Literature*, 202).

10. See Tichi, "Melville's Craft and Theme of Language Debased in *The Confidence-Man*"; and Dimock, *Empire for Liberty*, 206–210. Both Tichi and Dimock relate this slippage to the novel's peculiar treatment of storytelling, in which five different characters set out to tell stories but are unable to do so in their own words; either the narrator relieves the storyteller of that responsibility ("we shall venture to tell it in other words than his" [59]) or the storyteller finds himself "tyrannized over" (207) by the person from whom he first heard the story and can only repeat him "word for word" (142). Dimock mentions the repetition of the caterpillar-butterfly metaphor on 207.

11. Dimock, *Empire for Liberty*, 190.

12. Foster, introduction to Melville, *The Confidence-Man*, ed. Elizabeth S. Foster, xlviii.

13. See, for example, Kamuf, *The Division of Literature*; Gaudino, "The Riddle of *The Confidence-Man*"; and Renker, "'A ———!': Unreadability in *The Confidence Man*."

14. Melville, *Moby-Dick*, 573.

15. Melville, *The Confidence-Man*, ed. Stephen Matterson, 340, n. 297.

16. "Arrest of the Confidence Man," *New York Herald*, 8 July 1849, n.p.

17. Bergmann, "The Original Confidence Man," 566, 569.

18. "The Confidence Man on a Large Scale," *New York Herald* 11 July 1849, quoted in Bergmann, "The Original Confidence Man," 563–564.

19. Ibid., 565.

20. Numerous critics have commented on this stylistic eccentricity, but Jean-Christophe Agnew puts it best: "Melville so encumbers his prose with ambiguous codicils and self-canceling clauses that, from a contractualist point of view, the narrative seems entirely written in small print" (*Worlds Apart*, 198–199).

21. See, respectively, Baym, "Melville's Quarrel with Fiction"; Tichi, "Melville's Craft and Theme of Language Debased in *The Confidence-Man*"; Gaudino, "The Riddle of *The Confidence-Man*"; and Renker, "'A———!': Unreadability in *The Confidence Man*."

Works Cited

[Aaron]. *The Light and the Truth of Slavery*. Springfield: n.p., 1845.

"Aaron." *Emancipator*, 26 April 1845, 2.

Abbott, Jacob. *The Harper Establishment; or, How the Story Books Are Made*. New York: Harper and Brothers, 1855.

Acholonu, Catherine Obianuju. *The Igbo Roots of Olaudah Equiano*. Owerri, Nigeria: Afa Publications, 1989.

Admari, Ralph. "Bonner and 'The Ledger.'" *American Book Collector* 6 (1935): 176–193.

Agnew, Jean-Christophe. *Worlds Apart: The Market and the Theater in Anglo-American Thought, 1550–1750*. New York: Cambridge University Press, 1986.

"Alabama Beacon Versus James Williams." *Emancipator*, 30 August 1838, 71.

Althusser, Louis. "Ideology and Ideological State Apparatuses (Notes Towards an Investigation)." In *Lenin and Philosophy and Other Essays*, trans. Ben Brewster, 127–186. New York: Monthly Review Press, 1971.

Altick, Richard D. *The English Common Reader: A Social History of the Mass Reading Public, 1800–1900*. Chicago: University of Chicago Press, 1957.

"American Criticism and Critics." *Southern Literary Journal* 2 (July 1836): 393–400.

"American Poetry." *Democratic Review* 8 (November 1840): 399–430.

"American Poets, and Their Critics." *Knickerbocker* 4 (July 1834): 11–24.

Anderson, Benedict. *Imagined Communities: Reflections on the Origin and Spread of Nationalism*. Rev. ed. London: Verso, 1991.

Andrews, William L. *To Tell a Free Story: The First Century of Afro-American Autobiography, 1769–1865*. Urbana: University of Illinois Press, 1986.

"Archy Moore." *Liberator*, 31 March 18 37, 55.

"Arrest of the Confidence Man." *New-York Herald*, 8 July 1849, n.p.

"Autobiography of a Female Slave." *Liberator*, 23 January 1857, 13.

Bagg, Lyman Hotchkiss. *Four Years at Yale*. New Haven: C. C. Chatfield and Co., 1871.

Barnes, Gilbert H., and Dwight L. Dumond, eds. *Letters of Theodore Dwight Weld, Angelina Grimké Weld, and Sarah Grimké, 1822–1844*. 2 vols. New York: D. Appleton-Century, 1934.

Barnum, P. T. *The Humbugs of the World: An Account of Humbugs, Delusions, Impositions, Quackeries, Deceits and Deceivers Generally, in All Ages*. New York: Carleton, 1866.

Barthes, Roland. "The Death of the Author." In *Image-Music-Text*, trans. Stephen Heath, 142–148. New York: Hill and Wang, 1977.

Bartlett, John Russell. *Dictionary of Americanisms: A Glossary of Words and Phrases, Usually Regarded as Peculiar to the United States*. New York: Bartlett and Welford, 1848.

Baucom, Ian. *Specters of the Atlantic: Finance Capital, Slavery, and the Philosophy of History*. Durham: Duke University Press, 2005.

Baym, Nina. "Melville's Quarrel with Fiction." *PMLA* 94 (1979): 909–923.

———. *Novels, Readers, and Reviewers: Responses to Fiction in Antebellum America*. Ithaca: Cornell University Press, 1984.

Bellis, Peter J. "Melville's *The Confidence-Man*: An Uncharitable Interpretation." *American Literature* 59 (December 1987): 548–569.

Ben Hardin's Crockett Almanac, 1842. New York: Turner and Fisher, [1841].

Benjamin, Walter. "The Work of Art in the Age of Mechanical Reproduction." In *Illuminations*, ed. Hannah Arendt, trans. Harry Zohn, 217–251. New York: Schocken Books, 1968.

Bentley, Nancy. "White Slaves: The Mulatto Hero in Antebellum Fiction." In *Subjects and Citizens: Nation, Race, and Gender from* Oroonoko *to* Anita Hill, ed. Michael Moon and Cathy N. Davidson, 195–216. Durham: Duke University Press, 1995.

Bergmann, Johannes Dietrich. "The Original Confidence Man." *American Quarterly* 21 (Autumn 1969): 560–577.

Berlant, Lauren. "The Female Woman: Fanny Fern and the Form of Sentiment." *American Literary History* 3 (1991): 429–454.

———. *The Queen of America Goes to Washington City: Essays on Sex and Citizenship*. Durham: Duke University Press, 1997.

Bhabha, Homi K. "DissemiNation: Time, Narrative, and the Margins of the Modern Nation." In *Nation and Narration*, ed. Homi K. Bhabha, 291–322. London: Routledge, 1990.

"Black Letters; Or Uncle Tom-Foolery in Literature." *Graham's Magazine* 42 (February 1853): 209–215.

Blassingame, John. *Slave Testimony: Two Centuries of Letters, Speeches, Interviews, and Autobiographies*. Baton Rouge: Louisiana State University Press, 1977.

Bolter, Jay David, and Richard Grusin. *Remediation: Understanding New Media*. Cambridge: MIT Press, 2000.

Bone Squash's Black Joke Al-Ma-Nig, For de Year Arter Last, 1852. Philadelphia: Fisher and Brother, [1851].

"Books Which Are Books." *American Whig Review* 1 (May 1845): 521–525.

"The Booksellers' Dinner." *New-York American*, 3 April 1837, n.p.

Brodhead, Richard. *Cultures of Letters: Scenes of Reading and Writing in Nineteenth-Century America*. Chicago: University of Chicago Press, 1993.

Browder, Laura. *Slippery Characters: Ethnic Impersonators and American Identities*. Chapel Hill: University of North Carolina Press, 2000.

Brown, Gillian. *Domestic Individualism: Imagining Self in Nineteenth-Century America.* Berkeley: University of California Press, 1990.

Brown, William Wells. "A Lecture Delivered Before the Female Anti-Slavery Society of Salem." 1847. In *Williams Wells Brown: A Reader*, ed. Ezra Greenspan, 107–129. Athens: University of Georgia Press, 2008.

Brownson, Orestes. "Address to the United Brothers Society of Brown University." 1839. In *The Native Muse: Theories of American Literature from Bradford to Whitman*, ed. Richard Rutland, 277–290. New York: E. P. Dutton, 1972.

Buckley, Peter G. "Paratheatricals and Popular Stage Entertainment." In *The Cambridge History of American Theatre*, vol. 1, ed. Don B. Wilmeth and Christopher Bigby, 424–481. Cambridge: Cambridge University Press, 1998.

Bugg, John. "The Other Interesting Narrative: Olaudah Equiano's Public Book Tour." *PMLA* 121 (October 2006): 1424–1442.

Burnham, Michelle. *Captivity and Sentiment: Cultural Exchange in American Literature, 1682–1861.* Hanover, N. H.: University Press of New England, 1997.

Butler, Judith. *Gender Trouble: Feminism and the Subversion of Identity.* New York: Routledge, 1990.

Carretta, Vincent. *Equiano, the African: Biography of a Self-Made Man.* Athens: University of Georgia Press, 2005.

Castiglia, Christopher. *Interior States: Institutional Consciousness and the Inner Life of Democracy in the Antebellum United States.* Durham: Duke University Press, 2008.

Caustic, Christopher, M. D. [Thomas Green Fessenden]. *Terrible Tractoration!! A Poetical Petition Against Galvanizing Trumpery, and the Perkinistic Institution, in Four Cantos.* London: Hurst, 1803.

———. *Terrible Tractoration, and Other Poems.* Boston: Russell, Shattuck and Co., 1836.

Charvat, William. *Literary Publishing in America, 1790–1850.* Amherst: University of Massachusetts Press, 1959.

———. *The Profession of Authorship in America, 1800–1879.* Ed. Matthew J. Bruccolli. Columbus: Ohio State University Press, 1968.

Chatterjee, Partha. *The Nation and Its Fragments: Colonial and Postcolonial Histories.* Princeton: Princeton University Press, 1993.

Cheah, Pheng, and Jonathan Culler, eds. *Grounds of Comparison: Around the Work of Benedict Anderson.* Special issue of *diacritics* 29 (Winter 1999).

"Cicely." "Interesting to Ladies. From *The Musical World*." *Pittsfield Sun*, 22 September 1853, n.p.

Cole, Rachel. "At the Limits of Identity: Realism and American Personhood in Melville's *Confidence Man*." *Novel* 39 (Summer 2006): 384–401.

"Conspiracy Documents." *Yale Literary Magazine* 2 (June 1837): 251–260.

Cook, James W. *The Arts of Deception: Playing with Fraud in the Age of Barnum.* Cambridge: Harvard University Press, 2001.

[Cooke, Rose Terry]. "The Memorial of A. B., or Matilda Muffin." *Atlantic Monthly* 5 (February 1860): 186–191.

Coultrap-McQuin, Susan. *Doing Literary Business: American Women Writers in the Nineteenth Century*. Chapel Hill: University of North Carolina Press, 1990.

C[rayon], G[eoffrey] [Washington Irving]. "Desultory Thoughts on Criticism." *Knickerbocker* 14 (August 1839): 175–178.

"Critics and Criticism of the Nineteenth Century." *United States Magazine and Democratic Review* 15 (August 1844): 153–162.

The Crockett Almanac, 1839, Containing Adventures, Exploits, Sprees and Scrapes in the West, and Life and Manners in the Backwoods. Nashville: Ben Harding, [1838].

The Crockett Almanac, 1840, Containing Adventures, Exploits, Sprees and Scrapes in the West, and Life and Manners in the Backwoods. Nashville: Ben Harding, [1839].

The Crockett Almanac, 1841. Boston: J. Fisher, [1840].

The Crockett Almanac, 1841, Containing Adventures, Exploits, Sprees and Scrapes in the West, and Life and Manners in the Backwoods. Nashville: Ben Harding, [1840].

Crockett Almanac, 1842; Improved Edition, Containing Real Stories. Boston: S. N. Dickinson, [1841].

Crockett Comic Almanack. Gotham: Doleful Serious, 1842.

Crockett, David. *An Account of Col. Crockett's Tour to the North and Down East*. Philadelphia: Carey and Hart, 1835.

———. *Col. Crockett's Exploits and Adventures in Texas*. Philadelphia: T. K. and P. G. Collins, 1836.

———. *The Life and Adventures of Colonel David Crockett, of West Tennessee*. Cincinnati: Published for the Proprietor, 1833.

———. *A Narrative of the Life of David Crockett, of the State of Tennessee*. Philadelphia: Carey and Hart, 1834.

———. *Sketches and Eccentricities of Col. David Crockett, of West Tennessee*. New York: J. J. Harper, 1833.

Crockett's 1848 Almanac. Detroit: Luther Beecher, [1847].

Crockett's Free-and-Easy Song Book: A New Collection of the Most Popular Stage Songs, as Given by the Best Vocalists of the Present Day. Philadelphia: James Kay, Jr. and Brother, 1839.

Crockett's Yaller Flower Almanac, for '36. Snagsville, Salt-River: Boon Crockett and Squire Downing, [1835].

Culler, Jonathan. "Anderson and the Novel." *diacritics* 29 (1999): 20–39.

Currier, Thomas Franklin. *A Bibliography of John Greenleaf Whittier*. Cambridge: Harvard University Press, 1937.

Davy Crockett's Almanac, 1844: Life and Manners in the Backwoods, Terrible Battles and Adventures of Border Life; With Rows, Sprees, and Scrapes in the West. Boston: James Fisher, [1843].

Davy Crockett's Almanack of Wild Sports of the West, and Life in the Backwoods. Nashville: Snag and Sawyer, 1834.

Davy Crockett's Almanack of Wild Sports in the West, Life in the Backwoods, Sketches of Texas, and Rows on the Mississippi. Nashville: Published by the heirs of Col. Crockett, 1838.

De Darkie's Comic All-Me-Nig, 1846. Boston: James Turner; Philadelphia: Colon and Adriance; Baltimore: J. B. Keller, [1845].

"Democracy and Literature." *United States Magazine and Democratic Review* 11 (August 1842): 196–200.

Denning, Michael. *Mechanic Accents: Dime Novels and Working-Class Culture in America.* Rev. ed. London: Verso, 1998.

Derby, J. C. *Fifty Years among Authors, Books and Publishers.* New York: G. W. Carleton and Co., 1884.

Derrida, Jacques. *Of Grammatology.* Trans. Gayatri Chakravorty Spivak. Baltimore: Johns Hopkins University Press, 1976.

———. *Paper Machine.* Trans. Rachel Bowlby. Stanford: Stanford University Press, 2005.

Dickens, Charles. *American Notes for General Circulation.* New York: Harper and Brothers, 1842.

———. *The Life and Adventures of Martin Chuzzlewit.* Philadelphia: Lea and Blanchard, 1844.

Dillon, Elizabeth Maddock. *The Gender of Freedom: Fictions of Liberalism and the Literary Public Sphere.* Stanford: Stanford University Press, 2004.

———. "Print, Manuscript, and Performance: Prospects for Early American Studies." *Early American Literature* 41 (2006): 365–369.

Dimock, Wai Chee. *Empire for Liberty: Melville and the Poetics of Individualism.* Princeton: Princeton University Press, 1989.

———. "Planet and America, Set and Subset." Introduction to *Shades of the Planet: American Literature as World Literature,* ed. Wai Chee Dimock and Lawrence Buell, 1–16. Princeton: Princeton University Press, 2007.

———. *Through Other Continents: American Literature Across Deep Time.* Princeton: Princeton University Press, 2006.

Dinius, Marcy J. "Poe's Moon Shot: 'Hans Phaall' and the Art and Science of Antebellum Print Culture." *Poe Studies/Dark Romanticism* 37 (2004): 1–10.

Doane, Mary Ann. *The Desire to Desire: The Woman's Film of the 1940s.* Bloomington: Indiana University Press, 1987.

Dorson, Richard M. *American Folklore.* Chicago: University of Chicago Press, 1959.

———, ed. *Davy Crockett: American Comic Legend.* New York: Rockland Editions, 1939.

Douglas, Ann. *The Feminization of American Culture.* New York: Anchor Books, 1977.

Douglass, Frederick. *My Bondage and My Freedom. The Frederick Douglass Papers,* series 2, vol. 2 , ed. John W. Blassingame, John R. McKivigan, and Peter P. Hinks. New Haven: Yale University Press, 2003.

———. *Narrative of the Life of Frederick Douglass, an American Slave, Written by Himself. The Frederick Douglass Papers,* series 2, vol. 1, ed. John W. Blassingame, John R. McKivigan, and Peter P. Hinks. New Haven: Yale University Press, 1999.

duCille, Ann. "Where in the World Is William Wells Brown? Thomas Jefferson, Sally

Hemings, and the DNA of African American Literary History." *American Literary History* 12 (Autumn 2000): 443–462.

Dumond, Dwight L., ed. *Letters of James Gillespie Birney, 1831–1857*. 2 vols. New York: D. Appleton-Century Co., 1938.

E. A. B. "To Fanny Fern." *Olive Branch*, 10 April 1852, n.p.

Elmer, Jonathan. *Reading at the Social Limit: Affect, Mass Culture, and Edgar Allan Poe*. Stanford: Stanford University Press, 1995.

Emerson, Donald E. *Richard Hildreth*. Baltimore: Johns Hopkins University Press, 1946.

Emerson, Ralph Waldo. *The Collected Works of Ralph Waldo Emerson*, vol. 1, ed. Alfred R. Ferguson. Cambridge: Harvard University Press, 1971.

———. *Essays and Lectures*. Ed. Joel Porte. New York: Library of America, 1983.

Espy, James Pollard. *The Philosophy of Storms*. Boston: C. C. Little and J. Brown, 1841.

Fabian, Ann. *The Unvarnished Truth: Personal Narratives in Nineteenth-Century America*. Berkeley: University of California Press, 2000.

"Fashions in Dress." *The New-Yorker*, 30 March 1839, 19–20.

Faxon, Frederick Winthrop. *Literary Annuals and Gift Books*. Boston: Boston Book Co., 1912.

Fern, Fanny. "Borrowed Light." *True Flag*, 9 April 1853, n.p.

———. "Celebrity." *New York Ledger*, 10 December 1864, 4.

———. "Facts for Unjust Critics." *New York Ledger*, 13 June 1857, 4.

———. *Fern Leaves from Fanny's Portfolio*. Auburn, N.Y.: Derby and Miller, 1853.

———. *Fresh Leaves*. New York: Mason Brothers, 1857.

———. "My Critics." *New York Ledger*, 26 November 1864, 4.

———. *A New Story Book for Children*. New York: Mason Brothers, 1864.

———. *Ruth Hall: A Domestic Tale of the Present Time*. New York: Mason Brothers, 1855.

———. *Ruth Hall and Other Writings*. Ed. Joyce W. Warren. New Brunswick: Rutgers University Press, 1986.

———. "To Jack Plane." *Olive Branch*, 13 March 1852, n.p.

———. [Untitled item]. *Musical World and Times*, 13 August 1853, 230.

———. "A Word to Editors." *New York Ledger*, 5 May 1868, n.p.

Fifth Annual Report of the Executive Committee of the American Anti-Slavery Society. New York: William S. Dorr, 1838.

Fisher, Will. "Queer Money." *ELH* 66 (Spring 1999): 1–23.

Fisher's Crockett Almanac, 1843. New York: Turner and Fisher, 1842.

Fladeland, Betty. *Men and Brothers: Anglo-American Antislavery Cooperation*. Urbana: University of Illinois Press, 1972.

Flint, Timothy. "Obstacles to American Literature." *Knickerbocker* 2 (September 1833): 161–170.

Floyd, Kevin. *The Reification of Desire: Toward a Queer Marxism*. Minneapolis: University of Minnesota Press, 2009.

Foucault, Michel. *Discipline and Punish: The Birth of the Prison.* Trans. Alan Sheridan. New York: Vintage, 1995.

———. "What Is an Author?" In *Language, Counter-Memory, Practice: Selected Essays and Interviews,* ed. Donald F. Bouchard, trans. Donald F. Bouchard and Sherry Simon, 113–138. Ithaca: Cornell University Press, 1977.

Frederickson, George M. *The Black Image in the White Mind.* New York: Harper and Row, 1971.

"From *Human Rights.* Narrative of James Williams." *Herald of Freedom,* 17 March 1838, 9.

"From the *Delaware Republican.* Falsehood Refuted." *Liberator,* 12 December 1845, 197.

Fuller, S. Margaret. "American Literature: Its Position in the Present Time, and Prospects for the Future." In *Papers on Literature and Art.* New York: Wiley and Putnam, 1846.

———. Review of Frederick Douglass, *Narrative of the Life of Frederick Douglass, An American Slave, Written by Himself. New York Tribune,* 10 June 1845, 2.

Gallagher, Catherine. "George Eliot and *Daniel Deronda*: The Prostitute and the Jewish Question." In *Sex, Politics, and Science in the Nineteenth-Century Novel: Selected Papers from the English Institute, 1983–84,* ed. Ruth Yeazell, 39–62. Baltimore: Johns Hopkins University Press, 1986.

———. *Nobody's Story: The Vanishing Acts of Women Writers in the Marketplace, 1670–1820.* Berkeley: University of California Press, 1994.

Gara, Larry. "The Professional Fugitive in the Abolition Movement." *Wisconsin Magazine of History* 48 (1965): 196–204.

Gaudino, Rebecca J. Kruger. "The Riddle of *The Confidence-Man.*" *Journal of Narrative Technique* 14 (Spring 1984): 124–141.

Geary, Susan. "The Domestic Novel as a Commercial Commodity: Making a Best Seller in the 1850s." *Papers of the Bibliographical Society of America* 70 (1976): 365–393.

Gettman, Royal A. *A Victorian Publisher: A Study of the Bentley Papers.* Cambridge: Cambridge University Press, 1960.

Gilbert, Sandra, and Susan Gubar. *The Madwoman in the Attic: Studies in the Nineteenth-Century Literary Imagination.* New Haven: Yale University Press, 1979.

Gilmore, Michael T. *American Romanticism and the Marketplace.* Chicago: University of Chicago Press, 1985.

Gitelman, Lisa. *Always Already New: Media, History, and the Data of Culture.* Cambridge: MIT Press, 2006.

"Gossip with Readers and Correspondents." *Knickerbocker* 38 (November 1851): 552–570.

Gould, Edward S. "American Criticism on American Literature." *Eastern Magazine,* 15 March 1836, 276–287.

Gramsci, Antonio. *Selections from Cultural Writings.* Ed. David Forgacs and Geoffrey Nowell-Smith, trans. William Boelhower. Cambridge: Harvard University Press, 1985.

Green, James N. "The Rise of Book Publishing." In *An Extensive Republic: Print, Culture, and Society in the New Nation 1790–1840*, ed. Robert A. Gross and Mary Kelley, 75–127. Vol. 2 of *A History of the Book in America*. Chapel Hill: University of North Carolina Press, 2010.

Greenspan, Ezra. *George Palmer Putnam: Representative American Publisher.* University Park: Pennsylvania State University Press, 2000.

[Griffith, Mattie.] *Autobiography of a Female Slave.* New York: J. S. Redfield, 1857. Reprint, with an afterword by Joe Lockard, Jackson: University Press of Mississippi, 1998.

Griswold, Rufus Wilmot. *The Female Poets of America.* Philadelphia: Carey and Hart, 1849.

"Gumbo Chaff, A Negro Song, Sung with Great Applause at the Theatres." New York: Firth and Hall, n.d. [1830s–40s?].

Habermas, Jürgen. *The Structural Transformation of the Public Sphere: An Inquiry into a Category of Bourgeois Society.* Trans. Thomas Burger with the assistance of Frederick Lawrence. Cambridge: MIT Press, 1991.

Haliburton, Thomas Chandler, ed. *Traits of American Humour, by Native Authors.* 3 vols. London: Colburn and Co., 1852.

Hall, Stuart. "Notes on Deconstructing 'the Popular.'" In *People's History and Socialist Theory*, ed. Raphael Samuel, 227–239. London: Routledge and Kegan Paul, 1981.

———. "Popular Culture and the State." In *Popular Culture and Social Relations*, ed. Tony Bennet, Colin Mercer, and Janet Woollacott, 22–49. Milton Keynes, England: Open University Press, 1986.

———. "Popular-Democratic vs. Authoritarian Populism: Two Ways of 'Taking Democracy Seriously.'" In *Marxism and Democracy*, ed. Alan Hunt, 157–185. London: Lawrence and Wishart, 1980.

Halttunen, Karen. *Confidence Men and Painted Women: A Study of Middle-Class Culture in America, 1830–1870.* New Haven: Yale University Press, 1982.

Harris, Neil. *Humbug: The Art of P. T. Barnum.* Boston: Little, Brown, 1973.

Harris, Susan K. *Nineteenth-Century American Women's Novels: Interpretive Strategies.* Cambridge: Cambridge University Press, 1990.

Hart, John S. *The Female Prose Writers of America: With Portraits, Biographical Notices, and Specimens of Their Writings.* Rev. and enl. ed. Philadelphia: E. H. Butler and Co., 1855.

Hartman, Saidiya V. *Scenes of Subjection: Terror, Slavery, and Self-Making in Nineteenth-Century America.* New York: Oxford University Press, 1997.

Hauck, Richard Boyd. *Davy Crockett: A Handbook.* Lincoln: University of Nebraska Press, 1982.

Hawthorne, Nathaniel. *The Letters, 1853–1856.* Vol. 17 of *The Centenary Edition of the Works of Nathaniel Hawthorne*, ed. Thomas Woodson, James A. Rubino, L. Neal Smith, and Norman Holmes Pearson. Columbus: Ohio State University Press, 1987.

————. *Miscellaneous Prose and Verse.* Vol. 23 of *The Centenary Edition of the Works of Nathaniel Hawthorne*, ed. Thomas Woodson, Claude M. Simpson, and L. Neal Smith. Columbus: Ohio State University Press, 1994.

————. *Mosses from an Old Manse.* Vol. 10 of *The Centenary Edition of the Works of Nathaniel Hawthorne*, ed. William Charvat et al. Columbus: Ohio State University Press, 1974.

Hendler, Glenn. *Public Sentiments: Structures of Feeling in Nineteenth-Century American Literature.* Chapel Hill: University of North Carolina Press, 2001.

Henkin, David M. *City Reading: Written Words and Public Spaces in Antebellum New York.* New York: Columbia University Press, 1998.

Henson, Josiah. *Truth Is Stranger than Fiction: An Autobiography of the Rev. Josiah Henson.* Boston: B. B. Russell and Co., 1879.

Higgins, Brian, and Hershel Parker, eds., *Herman Melville: The Contemporary Reviews.* Cambridge: Cambridge University Press, 1995.

[Hildreth, Richard.] *The Slave: or Memoirs of Archy Moore.* 2 vols. Boston: John H. Eastburn, 1836.

————. *The White Slave; or, Memoirs of a Fugitive.* Boston: Tappan and Whittemore, 1852.

————. *Archy Moore, The White Slave; or, Memoirs of a Fugitive.* New York: Miller, Orton, and Mulligan, 1856.

Hindus, Milton, ed. *Walt Whitman: The Critical Heritage.* London: Routledge and Kegan Paul, 1971.

Homestead, Melissa J. *American Women Authors and Literary Property, 1822–1869.* Cambridge: Cambridge University Press, 2005.

Hooper, Johnson Jones. *Adventures of Captain Simon Suggs, Late of the Tallapoosa Volunteers; Together with "Taking the Census" and Other Alabama Sketches.* Philadelphia: T. B. Peterson and Brothers, 1845. Reprint, with an introduction by Johanna Nicol Shields, Tuscaloosa: University of Alabama Press, 1993.

Howard, Leon. *Herman Melville: A Biography.* Berkeley: University of California Press, 1951.

Huyssen, Andreas. *After the Great Divide: Modernism, Mass Culture, Postmodernism.* Bloomington: Indiana University Press, 1986.

"An Impudent Imposter." *Liberator*, 25 December 1857, 206.

"Introduction." *Democratic Review* 1 (October 1837): 1–15.

Irigary, Luce. *This Sex Which Is Not One.* Trans. Catherine Porter with Carolyn Burke. Ithaca: Cornell University Press, 1985.

Irmscher, Christoph. *Longfellow Redux.* Urbana: University of Illinois Press, 2006.

J. F. C. "Literary Lion Hunting, No. II." *United States Review* (August 1855): 133–146.

Jackson, Leon. "'Behold Our Literary Mohawk, Poe': Literary Nationalism and the 'Indianation' of Antebellum American Culture." *ESQ* 48 (2002): 97–133.

————. *The Business of Letters: Authorial Economies in Antebellum America.* Stanford: Stanford University Press, 2008.

Jacobs, Harriet. *Incidents in the Life of a Slave Girl, Written by Herself.* Ed. Jean Fagan Yellin. Cambridge: Harvard University Press, 1987.

"James Williams in Every Family." *Liberator*, 12 April 1838, 194.

"James Williams—The Fugitive Slave." *Emancipator*, 25 January 1838, 151.

Jameson, Fredric. *Postmodernism, or, the Cultural Logic of Late Capitalism.* Durham: Duke University Press, 1991.

———. "Reification and Utopia in Mass Culture." In *Signatures of the Visible*. New York: Routledge, 1992: 9–34.

"Jim Crow." Boston: Leonard Deming, n.d. [1837–40].

Jim Crow's Vagaries, or, Black Flights of Fancy: Containing a Choice Collection of Nigger Melodies. London: Orlando Hodgson, 1840.

Johns, Adrian. *The Nature of the Book: Print and Knowledge in the Making.* Chicago: University of Chicago Press, 1998.

Jones, William Alfred. "Home Criticism." 1847. *Essays upon Authors and Books.* New York: Stanford and Swords, 1849.

Jordan, Philip D. "Humor of the Backwoods, 1820–1840." *Mississippi Valley Historical Review* 25 (June 1938): 25–38.

Kamuf, Peggy. *The Division of Literature, or the University in Deconstruction.* Chicago: University of Chicago Press, 1997.

Kaplan, Amy. *The Anarchy of Empire in the Making of U.S. Culture.* Cambridge: Harvard University Press, 2005.

Kelley, Mary. *Private Woman, Public Stage: Literary Domesticity in Nineteenth-Century America.* New York: Oxford University Press, 1984.

Kemble, Frances A. *Journal of a Residence on a Georgian Plantation in 1838–1839.* New York: Harper and Brothers, 1864.

[Kennard, James K., Jr.] "Who Are Our National Poets?" *Knickerbocker* 26 (October 1845). Reprinted in *Inside the Minstrel Mask: Readings in Nineteenth-Century Black-face Minstrelsy*, ed. Annemarie Bean, James V. Hatch, and Brooks McNamara, 50–63. Hanover, N.H.: Wesleyan University Press, 1996.

Kennedy, J. Gerald. "'A Mania for Composition': Poe's Annus Mirabilis and the Violence of Nation-Building." *American Literary History* 17 (Spring 2005): 1–35.

Kuhlmann, Susan. *Knave, Fool, and Genius: The Confidence Man as He Appears in Nineteenth-Century American Fiction.* Chapel Hill: University of North Carolina Press, 1973.

L. M. P. "Necessity for a National Literature." *Knickerbocker* 25 (May 1845): 415–423.

Laffrado, Laura. "'I Thought From the Way You *Writ*, That You Were a Great Six-Footer of a Woman': Gender and the Public Voice in Fanny Fern's Newspaper Essays." In *In Her Own Voice: Nineteenth-Century American Women Essayists*, ed. Sherry Lee Linkon, 81–96. New York: Garland, 1997.

Lanham, Richard A. *The Electronic Word: Democracy, Technology, and the Arts.* Chicago: University of Chicago Press, 1993.

Larcom, Lucy. "Fern-Life." In *American Women Poets of the Nineteenth Century: An Anthology*, ed. Cheryl Walker, 231–232. New Brunswick: Rutgers University Press, 1992.

Laurie, Bruce. "Labor and Labor Organization." In *The Industrial Book, 1840–1880*, ed. Scott E. Casper, Jeffrey D. Groves, Stephen W. Nissenbaum, and Michael Winship, 70–89. Vol. 3 of *A History of the Book in America*. Chapel Hill: University of North Carolina Press, 2007.

"Lavante." *The Poets and Poetry of America, A Satire.* 1847. New York: Benjamin and Bell, 1887.

Lee, Henry Stanhope. "Thoughts on Contemporaneous Criticism." *New-York Mirror*, 22 June 1839, 412.

Lehmann-Haupt, Hellmut, in collaboration with Lawrence C. Wroth and Rollo G. Silver. *The Book in America: A History of the Making and Selling of Books in the United States.* New York: R. R. Bowker Company, 1951.

Lehuu, Isabelle. *Carnival on the Page: Popular Print Media in Antebellum America.* Chapel Hill: University of North Carolina Press, 2000.

Lenz, William E. *Fast Talk and Flush Times: The Confidence Man as a Literary Convention.* Columbia: University of Missouri Press, 1985.

"Letter from Frederick Douglass." *Liberator*, 12 February 1846, 35.

Levin, Harry. *The Power of Blackness: Hawthorne, Poe, Melville.* New York: Knopf, 1958.

Levy, Pierre. *Becoming Virtual: Reality in the Digital Age.* Trans. Robert Bononno. New York: Plenum, 1998.

Lewis, Barbara. "Daddy Blue: The Evolution of the Dark Dandy." In *Inside the Minstrel Mask: Readings in Nineteenth-Century Blackface Minstrelsy*, ed. Annemarie Bean, James V. Hatch, and Brooks McNamara, 257–272. Hanover, N.H.: Wesleyan University Press, 1996.

Lhamon, W. T., Jr., ed. *Jump Jim Crow: Lost Plays, Lyrics, and Street Prose of the First Atlantic Popular Culture.* Cambridge: Harvard University Press, 2003.

The Life of Jim Crow, Showing How He Got His Inspiration as a Poet. Philadelphia: James M'Minn, 1835.

Lindberg, Gary. *The Confidence Man in American Literature.* New York: Oxford University Press, 1982.

Lippard, George. "Rumpus Grizzle." In *George Lippard, Prophet of Protest*, ed. David S. Reynolds, 246–249. New York: Peter Lang, 1986.

———. "The Spermaceti Papers." *The Citizen Soldier*, 31 May–16 August 1843.

List of Important and Attractive Books. Boston: Phillips, Sampson, and Co., 1856.

"The Literature of the Present Day." *Graham's Monthly Magazine* 28 (September 1845): 97–102.

"Literary Intelligence." *Christian Examiner* 62 (1857): 152.

"Literary Notices." *Boston Quarterly Review* 1 (January 1838): 125–126.

"Literary Phenomena." *American Review* 4 (October 1846): 405–408.

"Literary Puffing." *Boston Weekly Magazine*, 19 December 1840, 46–47.

Lofaro, Michael A., ed. *Davy Crockett's Riproarious Shemales and Sentimental Sisters: Women's Tall Tales from the Crockett Almanacs, 1835–1856*. Mechanicsburg, Pa.: Stackpole Books, 2001.

———. *The Tall Tales of Davy Crockett: The Second Nashville Series of Crockett Almanacs, 1839–1841*. Knoxville: University of Tennessee Press, 1987.

Loggins, Vernon. *The Negro Author: His Development in America*. New York: Columbia University Press, 1931.

Loney, Glenn. "The Heyday of the Dramatized Novel." *Educational Theatre Journal* 9 (October 1957): 194–200.

Longfellow, Henry Wadsworth. "Defense of Poetry." *North American Review* 34 (January 1832): 56–79.

———. *Kavanagh*. Boston: Ticknor, Reed, and Fields, 1849.

Lott, Eric. *Love and Theft: Blackface Minstrelsy and the American Working Class*. New York: Oxford University Press, 1993.

Loughran, Trish. *The Republic in Print: Print Culture in the Age of U.S. Nation Building, 1770–1870*. New York: Columbia University Press, 2007.

———. "Transcendental Islam: The Worlding of Our America: A Response to Wai Chee Dimock." *American Literary History* 21 (Spring 2009): 53–66.

Lowell, James Russell. *A Fable for Critics; or Better, A Glance at a Few of Our Literary Progenies from the Tub of Diogenes; That Is, a Series of Jokes, by a Wonderful Quiz*. New York: G. P. Putnam, 1848.

———. "Introduction." *The Pioneer* 1 (January 1843): 1–3.

———. "Our Contributors: Edgar Allan Poe." *Graham's Magazine* 27 (February 1845). Reprinted in *Edgar Allan Poe: Critical Assessments*, vol. 2, ed. Graham Clarke, 1–10. Mountfield, East Sussex, England: Helm Information, 1991.

Lynch, Jack. *Deception and Detection in Eighteenth-Century Britain*. Aldershot, England: Ashgate, 2008.

Mabbott, Thomas. "Origins of 'The Angel of the Odd.'" *Notes and Queries* 160 (1931): 8.

"Manners, Motley" [Augustine Joseph Hickey Duganne]. *Parnassus in Pillory: A Satire*. New York: Adriance, Sherman, and Co., 1851.

Manovich, Lev. *The Language of New Media*. Cambridge: MIT Press, 2001.

Marx, Karl. *Capital: A Critique of Political Economy*. 3 vols. Trans. Samuel Moore and Edward Aveling, ed. Frederick Engels. New York: International Publishers, 1967.

[Mathews, Cornelius.] "An American Idyl." *Literary World*, 9 November 1850, 370–371.

———. "Nationality in Literature." *United States Magazine and Democratic Review* 20 (March 1847): 264–272.

Matthiessen, F. O. *The American Renaissance: Art and Expression in the Age of Emerson and Whitman*. New York: Oxford University Press, 1941.

McBride, Dwight. *Impossible Witnesses: Truth, Abolitionism, and Slave Testimony*. New York: New York University Press, 2001.

McGill, Meredith. *American Literature and the Culture of Reprinting, 1834–1853*. Philadelphia: University of Pennsylvania Press, 2003.

McGinnis, Patricia I. "Fanny Fern, American Novelist." *Biblion: The University Library Journal* (1969): 2–37.

McLuhan, Marshall. *Understanding Media: The Extensions of Man*. New York: McGraw-Hill, 1964.

Meine, Franklin J., ed. *The Crockett Almanacks: Nashville Series, 1835–1838*. Chicago: Caxton Club, 1955.

Melville, Herman. *The Confidence-Man: His Masquerade*. Ed. Elizabeth S. Foster. New York: Hendricks House, 1954.

———. *The Confidence-Man: His Masquerade*. Vol. 10 of *The Writings of Herman Melville*, ed. Harrison Hayford, Hershel Parker, and G. Thomas Tanselle. Evanston and Chicago: Northwestern University Press and the Newberry Library, 1984.

———. *The Confidence-Man: His Masquerade*. Ed. Stephen Matterson. London: Penguin, 1990.

———. *The Confidence-Man: His Masquerade*. Ed. Hershel Parker and Mark Niemeyer. New York: W. W. Norton, 2006.

———. *Moby-Dick; or, The Whale*. Vol. 6 of *The Writings of Herman Melville*, ed. Harrison Hayford, Hershel Parker, and G. Thomas Tanselle. Evanston and Chicago: Northwestern University Press and the Newberry Library, 1988.

———. *The Piazza Tales, and Other Prose Pieces, 1839–1860*. Vol. 9 of *The Writings of Herman Melville*, ed. Harrison Hayford, Hershel Parker, and G. Thomas Tanselle. Evanston and Chicago: Northwestern University Press and the Newberry Library, 1987.

———. *Pierre; or, the Ambiguities*. Vol. 7 of *The Writings of Herman Melville*, ed. Harrison Hayford, Hershel Parker, and G. Thomas Tanselle. Evanston and Chicago: Northwestern University Press and the Newberry Library, 1972.

[Melville, Herman.] "Hawthorne and His Mosses, By a Virginian Spending July in Vermont." *Literary World*, 17 August 1850, 125–127.

Mihm, Stephen. *A Nation of Counterfeiters: Capitalists, Con Men, and the Making of the United States*. Cambridge: Harvard University Press, 2007.

Miller, Perry. *The Raven and the Whale: The War of Words and Wits in the Era of Poe and Melville*. New York: Harcourt, Brace and Company, 1956.

Morrison, Toni. *Playing in the Dark: Whiteness and the Literary Imagination*. New York: Vintage, 1992.

Moss, Sidney P. *Poe's Literary Battles: The Critic in the Context of His Literary Milieu*. Durham: Duke University Press, 1963.

Mott, Frank Luther. *Golden Multitudes: The Story of Best Sellers in the United States*. New York: Macmillan, 1947.

———. *A History of American Magazines, 1741–1930*. 5 vols. Cambridge: Belknap Press, 1958–1968.

[Moulton, William.] *The Life and Beauties of Fanny Fern*. New York: H. Long and Brother, 1855.

Moyne, Ernest H. "Parodies of Longfellow's *Song of Hiawatha.*" *Delaware Notes* 30 (1957): 93–108.

"Narrative of James Williams." *African Repository and Colonial Journal* 15 (June 1839): 161.

"Narrative of James Williams." *Liberator*, 9 March 1838, 39.

"Narrative of James Williams." *Pennsylvania Freeman*, 13 September 1838, n.p.

"Narrative of James Williams. By J. G. Whittier." *Pennsylvania Freeman*, 1 March 1838, 99.

"'Narrative of James Williams.' Statement Authorized by Executive Committee." *Emancipator*, 25 October 1838, 104.

[Nathanson, Y. S.] "Negro Minstrelsy, Ancient and Modern." *Putnam's Monthly* 5 (January 1855): 72–79.

The Negro Singer's Own Book; Containing Every Negro Song that Has Ever Been Sung or Printed. Philadelphia: Turner and Fisher, 1846.

Nevin, Robert P. "Stephen C. Foster and Negro Minstrelsy." *Atlantic Monthly* 20 (November 1867): 608–616.

"New Anti-Slavery Novel." *Boston Evening Transcript*, 3 December 1856, n.p.

"New Publication." *Pennsylvania Freeman*, 5 April 1838, n.p.

"New Publications." *Liberator*, 28 November 1856, 190.

Newbury, Michael. *Figuring Authorship in Antebellum America.* Stanford: Stanford University Press, 1997.

Newfield, Christopher. *The Emerson Effect: Individualism and Submission in America.* Chicago: University of Chicago Press, 1996.

Ngai, Sianne. *Ugly Feelings.* Cambridge: Harvard University Press, 2005.

Nichols, Charles H. "Who Read the Slave Narratives?" *Phylon Quarterly* 20 (1959): 149–162.

Noble, J[ulius]. A[ugustus]. Letter to Otis, Broaders, and Company, 7 August 1840. Book Trades Collection, American Antiquarian Society, Worcester, Mass.

Northup, Solomon. *Twelve Years a Slave.* Ed. Sue Eakin and Joseph Logsdon. Baton Rouge: Louisiana State University Press, 1968.

Old American Comic Almanac, 1839. Boston: S. N. Dickinson, 1838.

Old American Comic Almanac, 1841. Boston: S. N. Dickinson, 1840.

The Origin of Jim Crow, Being an Authentic Account of the Life and Adventures of that Comic American Nigger, Jim Crow. London: J. S. Hodgson, 1837.

Osofsky, Gilbert. *Puttin' on Ole Massa: The Slave Narratives of Henry Bibb, William Wells Brown, and Solomon Northup.* New York: Harper and Row, 1969.

Otter, Samuel. *Melville's Anatomies.* Berkeley: University of California Press, 1999.

Parker, Theodore. "The American Scholar." 1849. In *The American Scholar*, ed. George Willis Cooke, 1–53. Boston: American Unitarian Association, 1907.

Parsons, Thomas William. *Poems.* Boston: Ticknor and Fields, 1854.

Peabody, Elizabeth Palmer. *Letters of Elizabeth Palmer Peabody: American Renaissance Woman.* Ed. Bruce A. Ronda. Middletown, Conn.: Wesleyan University Press, 1984.

Peabody, Ephraim. "Narratives of Fugitive Slaves." *Christian Examiner* 47 (July 1849): 61–93.

Pessen, Edward. *Jacksonian America: Society, Personality, and Politics.* Homewood, Ill.: Dorsey Press, 1969.

Pettengill, Claire C. "Against Novels: Fanny Fern's Newspaper Fictions and the Reform of Print Culture." *American Periodicals* 6 (1996): 61–91.

Poe, Edgar Allan. *Collected Works.* 3 vols. Ed. Thomas Ollive Mabbott. Cambridge: Belknap Press, 1969–1978.

———. "Critical Notices." *Southern Literary Messenger* 2 (April 1836): 326–340.

———. *Essays and Reviews.* Ed. G. R. Thompson. New York: Library of America, 1984.

———. *The Imaginary Voyages:* The Narrative of Arthur Gordon Pym, *"The Unparalleled Adventure of One Hans Pfaall," "The Journal of Julius Rodman."* Ed. Burton R. Pollin. Boston: Twayne, 1981.

"Poets and Poetry of America." *New-York Mirror,* 8 March 1845, 347.

Pollin, Burton R. "*The Living Writers of America*: A Manuscript by Edgar Allan Poe." *Studies in the American Renaissance* (1991): 151–211.

Poovey, Mary. *Genres of the Credit Economy: Mediating Value in Eighteenth- and Nineteenth-Century Britain.* Chicago: University of Chicago Press, 2008.

Powell, Timothy B. *Ruthless Democracy: A Multicultural Interpretation of the American Renaissance.* Princeton: Princeton University Press, 2000.

Pratt, Lloyd. *Archives of American Time: Literature and Modernity in the Nineteenth Century.* Philadelphia: University of Pennsylvania Press, 2010.

Pretzer, William S. "The Quest for Autonomy and Discipline: Labor and Technology in the Book Trades." In *Needs and Opportunities in the History of the Book: America, 1639–1876,* ed. David D. Hall and John B. Hench, 13–59. Worcester: American Antiquarian Society, 1987.

"Puffing." *American Annals of Education* 8 (October 1838): 470.

"Puffing." *Baltimore Monument,* 12 May 1838, 252.

"Puffing." *New-York Mirror,* 27 June 1835, 414.

"Puffing: A Fable." *Atkinson's Casket* 8 (August 1834): 384.

"Puffing System." *Southern Literary Journal* 2 (June 1836): 312–315.

Radway, Janice. "On the Gender of the Middlebrow Consumer and the Threat of the Culturally Fraudulent Female." *South Atlantic Quarterly* 93 (Fall 1994): 871–893.

"Redding's Literary Depot." *Universal Yankee Nation,* 1 January 1842, 7.

Reese, David Meredith. *Humbugs of New-York: Being a Remonstrance Against Popular Delusion; Whether in Science, Philosophy, or Religion.* New York: J. S. Taylor, 1838.

Reiss, Edmund. "The Comic Setting of 'Hans Pfaall.'" *American Literature* 29 (1957): 306–309.

"A Remarkable Work." *Liberator,* 9 January 1858, 8.

Renker, Elizabeth. "'A ———!': Unreadability in *The Confidence Man.*" In *The Cambridge Companion to Herman Melville,* ed. Robert S. Levine, 114–134. Cambridge: Cambridge University Press, 1998.

Reynolds, David S. *Beneath the American Renaissance: The Subversive Imagination in the Age of Emerson and Melville.* New York: Knopf, 1988.

Rice, Grantland S. *The Transformation of Authorship in America.* Chicago: University of Chicago Press, 1997.

Richard, Claude. "Arrant Bubbles: Poe's 'The Angel of the Odd.'" In *The Naiad Voice: Essays on Poe's Satiric Hoaxing,* ed. Dennis W. Eddings, 66–72. Port Washington, N.Y.: Associated Faculty Press, 1983.

———. "Poe and Young America." *Studies in Bibliography* 21 (1968): 25–58.

Richards, Eliza. *Gender and the Poetics of Reception in Poe's Circle.* Cambridge: Cambridge University Press, 2004.

Roediger, David. *The Wages of Whiteness: Race and the Making of the American Working Class.* London: Verso, 1991.

Rogin, Michael Paul. *Subversive Genealogy: The Politics and Art of Herman Melville.* New York: Knopf, 1983.

———. "The Two Declarations of American Independence." *Representations* 55 (Summer 1996): 13–30.

Rohrbach, Augusta. *Truth Stranger than Fiction: Race, Realism and the U.S. Literary Marketplace.* New York: Palgrave, 2002.

Roper, Moses. *A Narrative of the Adventures and Escape of Moses Roper, from American Slavery.* 3rd ed. London: Harvey and Darton, 1839.

Rourke, Constance. *American Humor: A Study of the National Character.* New York: Harcourt, Brace, and Company, 1931.

Ruggles, David. *An Antidote for a Poisonous Combination Recently Prepared by a "Citizen of New-York," Alias Dr. Reese, Entitled, "An Appeal to the Reason and Religion of American Christians," &c. Also, David Meredith Reese's "Humbugs" Dissected.* New York: William Stuart, 1838.

"Ruth Hall." *Southern Quarterly Review* 11 (April 1855): 438–450.

Rutland, Richard, ed. *The Native Muse: Theories of American Literature from Bradford to Whitman.* New York: Dutton, 1972.

Samuels, Shirley. "The Identity of Slavery." In *The Culture of Sentiment: Race, Gender, and Sentimentality in Nineteenth-Century America,* ed. Shirley Samuels, 157–171. New York: Oxford University Press, 1992.

Sánchez-Eppler, Karen. *Touching Liberty: Abolition, Feminism, and the Politics of the Body.* Berkeley: University of California Press, 1993.

Saxton, Alexander. *The Rise and Fall of the White Republic: Class Politics and Mass Culture in Nineteenth-Century America.* London: Verso, 1990.

"Schools in American Literature." *Literary World,* 19 October 1850, 307–309.

Scrapbook [1830–1834?]. Manuscripts Department, American Antiquarian Society, Worcester, Mass.

Seelye, John. "A Well-Wrought Crockett: Or, How the Fakelorists Passed Through the Credibility Gap and Discovered Kentucky." In *Davy Crockett: The Man, The Legend, The Legacy, 1786–1986,* ed. Michael A. Lofaro, 34–43. Knoxville: University of Tennessee Press, 1985.

Sekora, John. "Black Message/White Envelope: Genre, Authenticity, and Authority in the Antebellum Slave Narrative." *Callaloo* 10 (1987): 482–515.

Sellers, Charles. *The Market Revolution: Jacksonian America, 1815–1846.* New York: Oxford University Press, 1991.

Shackford, James Atkins. *David Crockett: The Man and the Legend.* Chapel Hill: University of North Carolina Press, 1956.

"The Slave: or Memoirs of Archy Moore." *Emancipator*, 8 March 1838, 174.

Smith, Sydney. Review of Adam Seybert's *Statistical Annals of the United States of America. Edinburgh Review* 33 (January 1820): 69–80.

Smith-Rosenberg, Carroll. *Disorderly Conduct: Visions of Gender in Victorian America.* New York: Oxford University Press, 1985.

"Songs of the Virginia Serenaders." Boston: Keith's Music Publishing House, 1844.

Spencer, Benjamin. *The Quest for Nationality: An American Literary Campaign.* Syracuse: Syracuse University Press, 1957.

Stepto, Robert B. "Distrust of the Reader in Afro-American Narratives." In *Reconstructing American Literary History*, ed. Sacvan Bercovitch, 300–322. Cambridge: Harvard University Press, 1986.

Stevenson, Louise. "Homes, Books, and Reading." In *The Industrial Book, 1840–1880*, ed. Scott E. Casper, Jeffrey D. Groves, Stephen W. Nissenbaum, and Michael Winship, 319–331. Vol. 3 of *A History of the Book in America.* Chapel Hill: University of North Carolina Press, 2007.

Stewart, Susan. *Crimes of Writing: Problems in the Containment of Representation.* Durham: Duke University Press, 1994.

"Stop the Swindler." *Emancipator*, 20 April 1843, 197.

Stowe, Harriet Beecher. *Uncle Tom's Cabin.* New York: Penguin, 1981.

"Suggested by Reading the Narrative of James Williams." *Herald of Freedom*, 23 June 1838, 66–67.

Sutherland, John. "Henry Colbourn, Publisher." *Publishing History* 19 (1986): 59–84.

Swift, Jonathan. *A Tale of a Tub, Written for the Universal Improvement of Mankind.* London: John Nutt, 1704.

Tamarkin, Elisa. *Anglophilia: Deference, Devotion, and Antebellum America.* Chicago: University of Chicago Press, 2008.

Tappan, Lewis. Papers, 1809–1903. Microfilm. Washington, D.C.: Library of Congress, 1975.

Taylor, Bayard. *Eldorado, or, Adventures in the Path of Empire.* New York: G. P. Putnam, 1850.

Taylor, Diana. *The Archive and the Repertoire: Performing Cultural Memory in the Americas.* Durham: Duke University Press, 2003.

Tebbel, John. *A History of Book Publishing in the United States.* Vol. 1. New York: R. R. Bowker, 1972.

Thomas, Dwight, and David K. Jackson. *The Poe Log: A Documentary Life of Edgar Allan Poe, 1809–1849.* Boston: G. K. Hall, 1987.

Thompson, Ralph. *American Literary Annuals and Gift Books, 1825–1865.* New York: H. W. Wilson Co., 1936.

Tichi, Cecelia. "Melville's Craft and Theme of Language Debased in *The Confidence-Man.*" *ELH* 39 (December 1972): 639–658.

"To Our Subscribers." *American Lady's Wreath* 6 (September 1845): back cover.

"To the Editorial Fraternity." Wrapper binding *The Old American Comic Almanac, 1841* and *The People's Almanac, 1841.* Boston: S. N. Dickinson, [1840].

Tocqueville, Alexis de. *Democracy in America.* Trans. George Lawrence, ed. J. P. Mayer. New York: Harper and Row, 1988.

Toll, Robert C. *Blacking Up: The Minstrel Show in Nineteenth-Century America.* New York: Oxford University Press, 1974.

Tompkins, Jane. *Sensational Designs: The Cultural Work of American Fiction, 1790–1860.* New York: Oxford University Press, 1986.

Tonkovich, Nicole. *Domesticity with a Difference: The Nonfiction of Catharine Beecher, Sarah J. Hale, Fanny Fern, and Margaret Fuller.* Jackson: University Press of Mississippi, 1997.

"Tricks of Abolitionism." *New-York Commercial Advertiser,* 19 September 1838, n.p.

Trimpi, Helen P. *Melville's Confidence Men and American Politics in the 1850s.* Hamden, Conn.: Archon Books, 1987.

Trumpener, Katie. *Bardic Nationalism: The Romantic Novel and the British Empire.* Princeton: Princeton University Press, 1997.

Tryon, W. S. *Parnassus Corner: A Life of James T. Fields, Publisher to the Victorians.* Boston: Houghton Mifflin, 1963.

[Untitled item]. *Emancipator,* 8 February 1838, 158.

[Untitled item]. *Liberator,* 14 September 1838, 148.

[Untitled item]. *New York Tribune,* 25 January 1858, 2.

[Untitled item], *Pennsylvania Freeman,* 23 August 1838, n.p.

[Untitled letter to the editor]. *Herald of Freedom,* 7 July 1838, 74–75.

[Untitled letter to the editor]. *Pennsylvania Freeman,* 24 May 1838, n.p.

[Untitled letters to the editor]. *Olive Branch,* January–August 1852, n.p.

Wadlington, Warwick. *The Confidence Game in American Literature.* Princeton: Princeton University Press, 1975.

Waldstreicher, David. "Reading the Runaways: Self-Fashioning, Print Culture, and Confidence in Slavery in the Eighteenth-Century Mid-Atlantic." *William and Mary Quarterly* 56 (April 1999): 243–272.

Walker, Cheryl. *The Nightingale's Burden: Women Poets and American Culture Before 1900.* Bloomington: Indiana University Press, 1982.

Walker, Nancy A. *Fanny Fern.* New York: Twayne, 1993.

Wallerstein, Immanuel. *The Capitalist World-Economy.* Cambridge: Cambridge University Press, 1979.

Warner, Michael. *Letters of the Republic: Publication and the Public Sphere in Eighteenth-Century America.* Cambridge: Harvard University Press, 1990.

―――. *Publics and Counterpublics*. New York: Zone Books, 2002.

Warren, Joyce W. *Fanny Fern: An Independent Woman*. New Brunswick: Rutgers University Press, 1992.

―――. "Uncommon Discourse: Fanny Fern and the New York Ledger." In *Periodical Literature in Nineteenth-Century America*, ed. Kenneth M. Price and Susan Belasco Smith, 51–68. Charlottesville: University of Virginia Press, 1995.

Weld, Theodore Dwight. *American Slavery As It Is: Testimony of a Thousand Witnesses*. New York: American Anti-Slavery Society, 1839.

Whalen, Terence. *Edgar Allan Poe and the Masses: The Political Economy of Literature in Antebellum America*. Princeton: Princeton University Press, 1999.

White's New Ethiopian Song Book. New York: H. Long and Brother, 1850.

"'Who Is Fanny Fern?' A Plain Statement of the Facts." *True Flag*, 30 December 1854, n.p.

Williams, James. *A Narrative of Events Since the 1st of August, 1834*. London: For the Central Negro Emancipation Committee, 1838.

Williams, James. *Authentic Narrative of James Williams, An American Slave*. Boston: Isaac Knapp, 1838.

―――. *Narrative of James Williams, An American Slave*. Boston: Abolitionist's Library, 1838.

―――. *Narrative of James Williams, An American Slave*. Special edition of the *Anti-Slavery Examiner* 6 (1838).

―――. *Narrative of James Williams, an American Slave, Who Was for Several Years a Driver on a Cotton Plantation in Alabama*. New York: American Anti-Slavery Society, 1838.

Wilmer, Lambert A. *The Quacks of Helicon: A Satire*. Philadelphia: J. W. Macclefield, 1841.

Winks, Robin W. "The Making of a Fugitive Slave Narrative: Josiah Henson and Uncle Tom—A Case Study." In *The Slave's Narrative*, ed. Charles T. Davis and Henry Louis Gates, Jr., 112–146. Oxford: Oxford University Press, 1985.

Winship, Michael. *American Literary Publishing in the Mid-Nineteenth Century: The Business of Ticknor and Fields*. Cambridge: Cambridge University Press, 1995.

―――. "Manufacturing and Book Production." In *The Industrial Book, 1840–1880*, ed. Scott E. Casper, Jeffrey D. Groves, Stephen W. Nissenbaum, and Michael Winship, 40–69. Vol. 3 of *A History of the Book in America*. Chapel Hill: University of North Carolina Press, 2007.

Wolfe, Charles K. "Davy Crockett Songs: Minstrels to Disney." In *Davy Crockett: The Man, the Legend, the Legacy, 1786–1986*, ed. Michael A. Lofaro, 159–190. Knoxville: University of Tennessee Press, 1985.

Wonham, Henry B. *Mark Twain and the Art of the Tall Tale*. New York: Oxford University Press, 1993.

Wood, Ann D[ouglas]. "The 'Scribbling Women' and Fanny Fern: Why Women Wrote." *American Quarterly* 23 (1971): 3–24.

Zboray, Ronald J. *A Fictive People: Antebellum Economic Development and the American Reading Public.* Oxford: Oxford University Press, 1993.

Zboray, Ronald J., and Mary Saracino Zboray. *Literary Dollars and Social Sense: A People's History of the Mass Market Book.* New York: Routledge, 2005.

Ziff, Larzer. *Literary Democracy: The Declaration of Cultural Independence in America.* New York: Viking Press, 1981.

"Zip Coon, A Popular Negro Song, as Sung by Mr. Geo. W. Dixon." New York: Firth and Hall, n.d. [mid-1830s].

Index

Page numbers in italics indicate illustrations.

Acknowledgments

I owe a great deal to the teachers, colleagues, friends, and institutions generous enough to believe in a book about fraudulence. Fellowships from the Beinecke Rare Book and Manuscript Library, the American Antiquarian Society, and the Library Company of Philadelphia supported my archival research. I thank the staff at each library for their assistance and, in many situations, their considerable detective work. In particular, I am indebted to Paul Erickson, Vincent Golden, Lauren Hewes, Jackie Penny, Elizabeth Pope, and David Whitesell at the American Antiquarian Society, and to Jim Green, Connie King, and Phil Lapsansky at the Library Company of Philadelphia, who generously shared their enormous stores of knowledge about U.S. print culture. At Yale University, a fellowship from the Mrs. Giles Whiting Foundation supported early research and writing; at Wayne State University, sabbatical leave, a University Research Grant, and a Josephine Nevins Keal fellowship supported the final stages. A publication subvention grant from Wayne State's College of Liberal Arts and Sciences and matching funds from the Department of English paid for indexing and illustrations.

Earlier versions of Chapters 1 and 4 appeared, respectively, as "Democratic Representations: Puffery and the Antebellum Print Explosion" in *American Literature* 79 (December 2007), and "Mediums of Exchange: Fanny Fern's Unoriginality" in *ESQ* 55, no. 1 (2009). I thank the editors for permission to reprint the material here.

Over the years I have been lucky to learn from some wonderful teachers. Elizabeth Maddock Dillon glimpsed the contours of this project before I ever did, and her continuing guidance and friendship have been sustaining. Wai Chee Dimock encouraged me to think about the backstage of literary nationalism, and Michael Denning saw me through the middle innings. I first began to think through nineteenth-century ideas about fraudulence with Tom Otten, and our conversations sparked many of the questions that came to structure this book. Trish Loughran taught my first college English class and remains one of my most important mentors and closest friends; I am proud to share her company in the bummer school of American literature. Many official and unofficial colleagues have read portions of this book and discussed its ideas with me over the past ten years. Rebecca Berne, Kimberly Juanita Brown, Rachel Buurma, Paul Erickson, Hsuan Hsu, Sarah Kareem, Eric Lott, Trish Loughran, Justine Murison, Don Pease, Lloyd Pratt, Amy Reading, Martha Schoolman, Caleb Smith, Hilary Strang, and Lisa Ze Winters all provided vital criticism. Jordan Stein probably read every page of the manuscript, and his insights have brought more to it than I can enumerate—but I hope he knows, anyway. A number of other communities have sustained this project: the Americanist Reading Group, the Marxist Reading Group, and the Photo-Memory Workshop at Yale; several incarnations of the Futures of American Studies Institute; the Americanist Dissertation Seminar at Columbia, which kindly welcomed an outsider; and the Marxist Reading Group at Wayne State. My fellow fellows at the American Antiquarian Society, especially Sari Edelstein and Derrick Spires, asked key questions and shared important materials. The final manuscript would never have been completed without the camaraderie of my writing log companions, Kidada Williams and Lisa Ze Winters.

Living in Detroit has taught me more than I ever imagined about the ways something can be made and unmade at the same time. I thank Richard Grusin for bringing me here, as well as for his advocacy as department chair. Jonathan Flatley makes Detroit an exceptionally generative place to think, and Kathryne Lindberg made it both a warm and an exacting one. Sarika Chandra, Robert Diaz, and Lisa Ze Winters light up the Americanist corner of the Maccabees building, and I'm grateful for their solidarity every day.

Many thanks to all at Penn Press who made this book a material reality. Jerry Singerman's interest in the project was invigorating. His editorial acumen sharpened its arguments, and his wry humor made business correspondence a pleasure. Caroline Winschel and Noreen O'Connor-Abel deftly steered the manuscript through the publication process, and Gail Kienitz helped me say what I meant. I am especially grateful to my anonymous reader, whose wonderful intuition and incisive suggestions improved the book immeasurably.

Several other people deserve particular mention. John Pat Leary is my most constant, crucial interlocutor. His conversation animates my thinking at every turn, making this book more interesting to write as well as drawing me back to the world outside of it. Most of all, I thank my father, Alan Cohen, and my mother, Michele Langer, who exemplify intellectual curiosity themselves, who so wholeheartedly encouraged my own, and who never let a dinner go by without sending me to look up something in the dictionary. This book is yours.